INDUSTRIAL RELATIONS IN THE PRIVATISED COAL INDUSTRY

For Billy

Industrial Relations in the Privatised Coal Industry

Continuity, change and contradictions

EMMA WALLIS
Employment Research Institute
Napier University, Edinburgh

Ashgate

Aldershot • Burlington USA • Singapore • Sydney

Published by
Ashgate Publishing Ltd
Gower House
Croft Road
Aldershot
Hants GU11 3HR
England

Ashgate Publishing Company
131 Main Street
Burlington
Vermont 05401
USA

Ashgate website: http://www.ashgate.com

British Library Cataloguing in Publication Data
Wallis, Emma
    Industrial relations in the privatised coal industry :
    continuity, change and contradictions
    1. Industrial relations - Great Britain - Case studies
    2. Coal trade - Deregulation - Great Britain - Case studies
    3. Coal mines and mining - Government ownership - Great
    Britain
    I. Title
    331'.0422334'0941

Library of Congress Catalog Card Number: 00-132587

ISBN 0 7546 1275 9

Printed and bound by Athenaeum Press, Ltd.,
Gateshead, Tyne & Wear.

Contents

List of Figures

List of Tables

Please note: tables containing fieldwork data which appear in chapters five to seven are not listed here.

Acknowledgements

The mining communities of South Yorkshire provided the inspiration for this book. Their struggle against industrial contraction was, of course, unsuccessful, and having witnessed the closure of all but one of the pits in my hometown, I had some vague notion of wanting to document the final days of coal. I hope I have done this sympathetically.

I was fortunate to have attended Northern College in Barnsley, and more fortunate still to have been taught by Ruth Winterton. Ruth gave me invaluable advice at this time, and perhaps more importantly helped me to believe that I was capable of more than working in a factory.

I must also express my gratitude to Jonathan Winterton, who supervised the thesis on which this book is based. In addition to sharing his expertise, assisting with access and commenting on countless drafts of each chapter, he also supported me through the inevitable periods of self doubt, and managed to remain my friend in spite of this.

Huw Beynon was the external examiner for my PhD thesis. His comments and suggestions were invaluable, and undoubtedly lead to improvements both to the thesis, and to the book also.

This book could not have been possible without the love and support of my partner, Billy. Having worked at Manvers Main, and Maltby collieries for a total of twenty-seven years, he was able to advise on technical matters, and provide a flavour of coal industry industrial relations back in the good old days. Billy gave me his unreserved encouragement throughout my education, and during the production of this book, and although I will never be able to repay him, I thank him for everything from the bottom of my heart.

Finally, in their own way, Ivy, Harry, Christine, Graham, Eileen, Denis, Raymond, Barbara, my Mother and my Auntie Sarah also made this book possible.

List of Abbreviations

ACAS	Advisory Conciliation and Arbitration Service
AEEU	Amalgamated Electrical and Engineering Union
AUEW	Amalgamated Union of Engineering Workers
BACM	British Association of Colliery Management
BC	British Coal
DTI	Department of Trade and Industry
EETPU	Electrical Electronic Telecommunication and Plumbing Union
ESI	Electricity Supply Industry
FIDO	Face Information Digested On-line
IDS	Incomes Data Services
IEA	International Energy Agency
ILO	International Labour Office
IMPACT	In-built Machine Performance And Condition Testing
IRRR	Industrial Relations Review and Report
JNNC	Joint National Negotiating Committee
MFGB	Miners' Federation of Great Britain
MIDAS	Machine Information Display and Automation System
MINOS	Mine Operating System
NACODS	National Association of Colliery Overmen Deputies and Shotfirers
NCB	National Coal Board
NEC	National Executive Committee (NUM)
NPLA	National Power Loading Agreement
NRT	National Reference Tribunal
NUM	National Union of Mineworkers
OECD	Organisation for Economic Co-operation and Development
REC	Regional Electricity Company
TNC	Trans-National Corporation
TUPE	Transfer of Undertakings (Protection of Employment) Regulations
UDM	Union of Democratic Mineworkers

1 Introduction

Because coal is the most abundant indigenous energy source in the UK, and was the engine of the first industrial revolution, the mining industry has been of tremendous strategic and symbolic importance. Numerous literary works have drawn upon the powerful imagery associated with coal mining (e.g. Lawrence, 1994, Zola, 1954), and as mining has always involved arduous physical work in dangerous conditions, the coal miner has been viewed as the 'archetypal proletarian' (Harrison, 1978). Because of this, the industry, which has been characterised by periodic crises and conflicts (Raynes, 1928), has often been regarded as a 'special case' (Samuel, 1925; Hughes and Moore, 1972).

When the coal industry was taken into public ownership in 1947, the National Coal Board (NCB) became the focus of study as the epitome of the post war nationalisation programme (Haynes, 1953; Baldwin, 1955). Industrial relations within the industry prior to nationalisation had been characterised by bitter conflict, and because of this, much of the academic interest in the public sector coal industry was concerned with the labour relations implications of public ownership.

The end of the nationalised era is of equal significance however, this being illustrated by the description of the proposed de-nationalisation of coal as the 'ultimate privatisation'. Resistance to the restructuring programme which preceded privatisation led to the 1984-85 strike. This was the last major industrial dispute to take place in the industry before it was returned to the private sector, which generated a vast literature, comprising analyses of the dispute (e.g. Beynon, 1985; Winterton and Winterton, 1989), explorations of the role of coalfield women in the strike (e.g. Miller, 1986; Seddon, 1986; Stead, 1987), and examinations of the civil liberties issues arising from the policing of the dispute (e.g. Fine and Millar, 1985). Journalistic accounts of the dispute were also produced (e.g. Wilsher, Macintyre and Jones, 1985; Adeney and Lloyd, 1986), as were personal accounts of the strike by key participants (e.g. Ottey, 1985;

Macgregor, 1986; Smith, 1997). Literature of equal importance also emerged from within the mining communities themselves (e.g. Barnsley Women Against Pit Closures, 1984; 1985; Worsborough Community Group, 1985; People of Thurcroft, 1986; Douglass, 1986; Dolby, 1987; Sheffield Women Against Pit Closures, 1987), which encompassed poetry (e.g. Gittins, 1986), and photographic art (e.g. Pattison and Beynon, 1984).

Following the defeat of the 1984-85 strike, this attention was redirected towards the transition of the coal industry from public corporation to private enterprise (Gibbon and Bromley, 1990; Pendleton and Winterton, 1993), the social consequences of the associated restructuring (e.g. Wright, 1985; Wade, 1985; Beynon, Hudson and Sadler, 1986; Edwards, 1993), and the implications for the coal industry of privatising the electricity supply industry (e.g. Gladstone and Dewhirst, 1988; Fothergill and Guy, 1993; Green, 1994). More recently, however, academics have begun to explore the changes apparent within the coal industry since privatisation, and as was the case when the industry was nationalised, attention has focused on the industrial relations implications of ownership change (Croney, 1996; Parry, Waddington and Critcher, 1997).

This study can be viewed as a contribution to the debate on the patterns of industrial relations which have emerged in the coal industry since privatisation, and therefore to the wider questions concerning the relationship between ownership and labour relations. As such, it is likely to be of interest to management, who may have anticipated the opportunities presented by the new commercial environment engendered by privatisation; to the trade unions, which were concerned that privatisation might undermine their bargaining position; and to individual workers, many of whom feared that privatisation might have a detrimental impact upon their terms and conditions of employment.

This study is concerned with the extent to which the emergent patterns of industrial relations in the privatised industry represent continuity or change with the past. Because the years of public ownership were characterised by having two distinct phases of labour relations, however, it also has a significant comparative dimension, since labour relations developments following privatisation are compared with both the earlier periods which are identified.

In Chapter Two, the patterns of industrial relations which have prevailed within the coal industry since nationalisation in 1947 are considered, and the 1984-85 strike is identified as a watershed. This chapter then explains how the restructuring of industrial relations which followed the 1984-85 strike was inextricably linked to the restructuring of both operations and ownership.

Chapter Three places the restructuring of the coal industry within the context of global capitalist restructuring. The privatisation programme instituted by the Conservatives during the 1980s and early 1990s is regarded as a manifestation of economic restructuring within the UK, and following an examination of the theoretical debate concerning the likely influence of privatisation upon industrial relations, labour relations developments in a number of privatised industries are considered. Two alternative hypotheses are then outlined which relate to the possible influence of privatisation upon industrial relations in the coal industry, and the implications of this for organised labour. A model is also presented which illustrates how patterns of labour relations in the privatised industry might be characterised by continuity or change, as a result of the interaction of management industrial relations strategies, and the responses of the mining unions to those strategies.

In Chapter Four, consideration is given to the methodology to be employed in order to test the hypotheses presented within Chapter Three. The merits of a case study approach are considered, after which the research design is outlined, and the operationalisation of the research is explained. This chapter also details how problems relating to access necessitated a review of methodology, which led to the adoption of a somewhat unorthodox case study approach, in which three of the four cases selected for study are holistic, whilst the final case is characterised by an embedded design.

Chapters Five, Six, and Seven are concerned with the empirical findings from three holistic case studies conducted at Cwmpridd colliery, Abergoed colliery and Workham colliery respectively. The structure of these chapters is identical, and reflects the analytical framework which was utilised when the case reports were being prepared. Each of these chapters therefore begins with an introduction to the case which is being considered, before developments in management industrial relations strategies are examined. The role of the trade unions is then analysed, followed by a consideration of the institutions of collective bargaining. Developments within the labour process are then assessed, and finally, some conclusions are offered as to whether the emergent patterns of labour relations are characterised by continuity or change.

The structure of Chapter Eight is slightly different from that of chapters Five, Six and Seven, since it is concerned with empirical evidence drawn from the final case study which has an embedded, rather than holistic design. This chapter therefore begins with an introduction to Coal UK, the company which forms the initial unit of analysis. Following this, the four subsections are each concerned with a different colliery owned by the company. The structure of these subsections is identical to that of chapters Five, Six and Seven, in that developments in management industrial relations strategies, the role of the trade unions, the institutions of collective bargaining and the labour process are analysed. The conclusions presented at the end of this chapter consider whether the patterns of industrial relations which are evident at both corporate and colliery level represent continuity or change.

In Chapter Nine the empirical findings detailed in the previous four chapters are compared, and some explanations are given for the emergent patterns of labour relations within the privatised coal industry. Finally, in Chapter Ten, the hypotheses and model presented at the end of chapter three are reconsidered, and their validity is assessed.

2 Background to Contemporary Change in Coal Mining

On 1 January 1947, the UK coal industry was taken into public ownership by the Labour government returned by the first post war election. Collective bargaining had been in evidence within the industry long before the advent of public ownership, with negotiations being largely conducted on a district basis, since the miners' union was then comprised of a number of autonomous local organisations, loosely combined within the Miners' Federation of Great Britain (Ashworth, 1986). However, industrial relations took on a more formal and institutionalised character in the era of nationalisation.

The Miners' Federation of Great Britain was replaced by the National Union of Mineworkers (NUM), on 1 January 1945, although the federal structure was retained, and local areas continued to exercise considerable autonomy (Page Arnot, 1979). Furthermore, local traditions remained pertinent and indeed, divisions between the politically militant coalfields of Scotland, South Wales, Kent, and later Yorkshire and the more moderate districts of Nottinghamshire and the Midlands were to have a significant impact on industrial relations in the industry in later years. Collective bargaining nevertheless gradually became the prerogative of the national union under nationalisation.

The terms and conditions of nationalisation reflected the corporatism of the post war consensus. The Coal Industry Nationalisation Act 1946 (section 46) obliged the newly created National Coal Board (NCB) to negotiate and consult with trade unions representing large sections of the workforce in order to establish joint structures for the negotiation of employment terms and conditions (Winterton and Winterton, 1993a: 71), and following nationalisation, joint consultative machinery was introduced at national, district, area and colliery levels in accordance with the Act (McCormick, 1979: 58).

Formal conciliation machinery had already been established under wartime control. This had resulted in the creation of a National Board which consisted of a Joint National Negotiating Committee (JNNC), which provided for union representation, and a National Reference Tribunal which was composed of independent people, and which made binding awards when the JNNC failed to reach agreement. After nationalisation, conciliation machinery was also introduced at colliery level (McCormick, ibid).

Industrial relations then, were both highly regulated and pluralistic (Goodman, 1984: 65-68) in character during the early decades of nationalisation. The institutional framework which was developed to support collective bargaining was based on an acceptance that capital and labour within the industry had competing interests that required accommodation, and indeed, the conciliation procedures were highly effective in relation to the resolution of disputes throughout the period of nationalisation (Winterton, 1981: 16). Furthermore, the existence of tripartite arrangements for strategic planning within the industry, involving the government, NCB management and the mining unions, arguably enabled the contraction of the industry during the 1960s to be managed more sensitively than were the closures of the 1980s and early 1990s.

In 1985, the defeat of the year long strike by NUM members opposed to pit closures facilitated sweeping changes in patterns of industrial relations within the industry, and the reassertion of managerial power. The 1984-85 strike was a watershed in terms of industrial relations in coal, although the origins of the changes which occurred can be traced back to the early 1970s.

Following the first oil shock of 1973, when oil prices trebled, global demand for coal began to rise, and throughout the 1970s global supply was increased in order to meet this, with new reserves in Colombia, South Africa and Australia being exploited (Rutledge and Wright, 1985: 307).

In the UK the implementation of the 1974 *Plan for Coal*, a tripartite agreement negotiated by the Labour government, the NCB and the NUM, following the union's victory in the 1974 wage dispute, resulted in the development of new capacity to replace collieries lost through exhaustion. *Plan for Coal* also committed the industry to 'operate at optimum efficiency' (NCB, 1974), and as a result new technologies and operational techniques were adopted at both new and existing collieries, which served to increase both output and productivity (Winterton and Winterton, 1995), although the ambitious projected output targets outlined in *Plan for Coal* were not met in full, and were revised downwards by the 1977 tripartite agreement *Coal for the Future* (Edwards and Heery, 1989: 199). As a result of the long development times inherent to coal extraction, many of the expansionist projects designed to increase coal production in both the UK and the world were only just beginning to come on stream when the recession of 1981 depressed global demand for coal.

By the beginning of the 1980s demand and supply side changes had resulted in international coal markets facing a crisis of over supply, which necessitated major restructuring in the global coal industry. In the UK industry this entailed the closure of uneconomic, i.e. surplus, capacity, which implied the closure of collieries on grounds other than exhaustion (Winterton and Winterton, 1989). This was not a situation envisaged by *Plan for Coal*, and was diametrically opposed to NUM policy which committed the union to resisting closures on grounds other than exhaustion.

By the early 1980s however, there were also a number of political factors which pointed towards major restructuring in the UK coal industry, some of which, like their economic counterparts, had their origins in events which transpired a decade earlier.

During the early decades of the nationalised era, the coal industry was noted for being relatively strike prone, with various theories being advanced in order to explain this (Clegg, 1979; Lynch, 1978; Winterton, 1981). Somewhat paradoxically however, the industrial relations strategies adopted by the NUM at national level following nationalisation, focused on co-operation rather than confrontation with NCB management. In part this was because the NUM saw co-operation with the NCB as the most appropriate strategy for ensuring the success of coal nationalisation, although it was also a consequence of the miners being divided, because pay was determined at area rather than national level (Allen, 1981), until the implementation of a series of wage structure agreements, comprising the 1955 Revision of Wages Structure Agreement, the 1966 National Power Loading Agreement (NPLA) and the 1971 Third Day Wage Structure Agreement, which created centralised pay bargaining in the industry (Winterton, 1981: 13-14).

The increased demand for coal generated by the 1973 oil shock however, served greatly to increase the bargaining power of the NUM at a time when there was a resurgence of militancy within the coalfields. This had been demonstrated in 1969, when unofficial strike action took place in several coalfields following a claim for a reduction in the hours worked by surface employees (McCormick, 1979). Moreover in 1971, the NUM national conference supported a rule change which reduced the majority necessary for strike action to be called from 66 per cent to 55 per cent, which paved the way for the first national stoppage for over forty years in 1972 in support of a pay claim.

The increasing militancy of the miners during the late 1960s and early 1970s, was in part a consequence of the establishment of centralised pay bargaining which enabled the NUM to unite over this issue. It was also a reflection of the rising power of the political left within the NUM, most crucially within the Yorkshire Area.

In 1967, the Barnsley Miners' Forum had been established to campaign for the election of left wing candidates to posts within the NUM (Winterton and Winterton, 1989), and indeed in 1973, the election of Arthur Scargill and Owen Briscoe as President and Secretary respectively of the Yorkshire Area NUM, affirmed the ascendancy of the political left within the UK's largest and therefore most strategically important coalfield. Left wingers such as Mick McGahey were also elected to the National Executive Committee (NEC) of the NUM during the early 1970s, and by the end of 1973, the left was within a handful of votes of ending the traditional right wing dominance of that body (Allen, 1981), although the Presidency of the national union did not fall to the left until the election of Scargill in 1982.

In November 1973, the NUM implemented a national overtime ban in pursuit of a pay claim, which was escalated into an all out stoppage in February 1974. The national strike of 1974 precipitated the downfall of the Conservative government led by Edward Heath. However, the overtime ban which preceded it also prompted a review of industrial relations policies within the upper echelons of NCB management, and a secret report prepared by Wilfred Miron, former Chairman of the NCB East Midlands Division, for Sir Derek Ezra, then NCB Chairman, in December 1973 outlined a strategy to reduce the influence of the political left within the NUM.

Miron's scheme rested firstly on a return to local wage bargaining, in order that moderate areas could be divided from more militant ones, as had been the case prior to the implementation of the 1966 NPLA, and secondly, on the adoption of new technologies, which would reduce the staffing levels required within the industry, and reduce the miners' control of the labour process at the point of production (Winterton and Winterton, 1989: 9-12). The Miron Report then, advocated a radical restructuring of both the labour process within coal mining, and of the industrial relations policies which had prevailed within the industry since nationalisation.

The analysis and objectives of the Miron Report were arguably reflected in a number of NCB policies which emerged during the 1970s and 1980s. By 1978, area incentive schemes were in operation in every UK coalfield (Ashworth, 1986: 674-675), despite mineworkers having twice rejected the introduction of such schemes in national ballots (Richards, 1996: 51). Furthermore, between 1973-74 and 1981-82, average staffing levels at UK collieries fell by almost 20 per cent (Ashworth, 1986: 674-675). The NCB's goal of restructuring, and the reassessment of industrial relations policies in the public sector however, were given added impetus by the election of a Conservative government in 1979.

The Conservative government led by Margaret Thatcher rejected the corporatism of the post war consensus (Beynon and McMylor, 1985), and instead was committed to the neo-liberal values of free market economics. Organised labour was seen by the Conservatives as a barrier to the operation of the free market, and as a consequence, a series of legislative measures beginning with the 1980 Employment Act were introduced, which restricted the powers of trade unions, by removing legal immunities and protection against unfair dismissal, restricting the right to picket and the operation of the closed shop, and by introducing pre-strike ballots. Furthermore, social security legislation introduced in 1980, reduced the level of welfare benefits paid to strikers (Jones and Novak, 1985).

The Conservative government, however, was also committed to returning many of the nationalised industries to the private sector, and to ensuring that those industries which remained within the public domain operated within a 'clearer financial discipline', (Conservative Party, 1979: 15). Indeed, the 1980 Coal Industry Act required the NCB to break even without government support by 1983-84, although government policy was revised in 1981, following threatened strike action by the NUM over pit closures (Robinson, 1985).

The coal industry had been identified as a key battleground for the implementation of government policy by Nicholas Ridley, in a report of the Conservative Party's policy group on the nationalised industries, which was leaked to the *Economist* in 1978. The report predicted that as a result of government policy, a major conflict with a public sector trade union was inevitable, and that the coal industry was the most likely arena for this to take place (*Economist*, 27 May 1978). The report, however, also outlined a number of measures for combating industrial action in the industry, which included building up coal stocks at power stations, making contingency plans for the importation of coal, utilising non union lorry drivers for the transportation of coal, ensuring that dual coal/oil burn facilities were available at all power stations, and deploying well equipped mobile police units against pickets.

Crucially, the report suggested that the confrontation, when it occurred, should be on favourable ground chosen by the government, and indeed the reversal of government policy following threatened industrial action by the NUM in 1981, was later attributed by David Howell, Energy Secretary at the time, to inadequate preparation (Crick, 1985: 88). In 1984 however, following the appointment of Ian McGregor, a man with a reputation for union busting as a result of his activities within the AMAX corporation (Adeney and Lloyd, 1986: 55), to the position of NCB Chairman, further reductions in capacity were announced by the NCB which included the closure of Cortonwood Colliery in South Yorkshire. This precipitated the year long strike by NUM members opposed to pit closures, in which the union was decisively beaten.

2.1 Operational Restructuring

Government energy policy after 1979 was driven by a commitment to increase competition in this sector, in order to improve efficiency, and oil and gas were privatised in the early 1980s as a consequence. Plans to privatise the coal industry however, though tacitly acknowledged within both the government and the NCB (Moore, 1983; Rost and Pargeter, 1985: 39), were not made public until 1988. Nevertheless, government preparations for privatisation centred on facilitating increased efficiency within the industry by increasing competition, initially by way of relaxing restrictions on the importation of coal, and the deregulation of opencast and licensed mining operations (Robinson and Marshall, 1985).

Government policy gave added impulse to increasing efficiency within the industry, to which the NCB had been effectively committed

10

since 1974, under *Plan for Coal.* New technology was to play a key role in NCB strategy for both increasing efficiency and restructuring, in preparation for privatisation.

Microelectronic technology developed during the 1970s, had enabled coal mining, which was already extensively mechanised, to be automated. The application of systems engineering led to the development of MINOS, and its associated sub-systems, MIDAS, IMPACT and FIDO, which enabled both new and existing capacity to be increasingly organised around huge, highly productive, multi-colliery complexes (Burns et al, 1983).

The application of new technology during the 1970s and early 1980s was uneven, and appeared piecemeal, although the strategy concentrated operations in the central coalfields of Yorkshire, Nottinghamshire, Derbyshire and the Midlands, because MINOS had been designed around the favourable geological conditions which prevailed in these districts. The peripheral coalfields of Scotland, South Wales, Kent and the North East, by comparison received little technological investment, as MINOS was not suited to the heavily faulted and steeply inclined seams which characterised these coalfields (Burns et al, ibid). The development of superpits, such as the Selby Complex in North Yorkshire however, ensured that other mines operating without systems control, were, because of their higher costs and lower productivity, classed as uneconomic capacity, and earmarked for closure. Indeed by the mid 1980s, as a result of the application of new technology, entire coalfields in the periphery were threatened with closure on economic grounds (Burns, Newby and Winterton, 1985).

At colliery level, the application of systems control technology, and the resultant changes in work organisation, served firstly, to increase management control over the labour process, and secondly, greatly to intensify work at the point of production by increasing machine running time. The implications for employment at colliery level then, were no less serious, and indeed the Selby Complex, which was developed as a highly automated mine, required 75 per cent less labour than a colliery with comparable output operating with conventional longwall mining (Burns et al, 1983).

Prior to the 1984-85 strike, the NUM, though opposed to the closure of capacity on economic grounds, had no co-ordinated policy in relation to the introduction of the technology which would facilitate this process.

This was in part because attitudinal differences towards new technology existed between the central and peripheral coalfields, as the application of new technology impacted in different ways in these areas, and because the federal structure of the NUM exacerbated these divisions. The gradual introduction of new technology however, also enabled the role of this within the NCB's overall restructuring programme to be disguised (Burns, Newby and Winterton, 1985).

The defeat of the NUM in the 1984-85 strike, demonstrated that the balance of power within the industry had tilted decisively in favour of management, and with worker resistance to restructuring effectively crushed, the pace of this dramatically increased. Indeed the defeat of the NUM was crucial in order that the full potential of new technology could be realised, since this facilitated the intensification of work, which in turn resulted in greatly increased productivity. Between 1984-85 and 1991-92, 70 per cent of UK collieries were closed, and the workforce was reduced by 74 per cent, whilst in the same period overall productivity rose by 97 per cent (Table 2.1). Further colliery closures occurred before the industry was offered for sale, and in December 1994, when the industry was returned to the private sector, only four collieries were operated by British Coal outside the central coalfield.

2.2 Restructuring Industrial Relations

Changes to the established patterns of industrial relations in the coal industry following the 1984-85 strike, in many respects reflected more general changes which had occurred in UK industrial relations over the decade.

Table 2.1 British Coal deep-mine operating statistics 1983-1994

Year	Collieries	Employment (000s)	Output (MT)	Total OMS (tonnes)	Face OMS (tonnes)
1983/84	170	191.7	90.1	2.43	10.32
1984/85	169	171.4	27.6	2.08	10.54
1985/86	133	138.5	88.4	2.72	12.03
1986/87	110	107.7	88.0	3.29	14.40
1987/88	94	89.0	83.4	3.62	16.20
1988/89	86	80.1	85.0	4.14	19.05
1989/90	73	65.4	75.6	4.32	20.52
1990/91	65	57.3	72.3	4.70	22.62
1991/92	51	43.8	71.0	5.36	25.28
1992/93	50	31.7	61.8	7.20	34.00
1993/94*	18	10.6	43.1	9.00	45.00

* Calculated from BC operating results for week 40.
Sources: NCB, BC Report and Accounts, and operating statistics (various).

During the 1980s there was a steady decline in trade union membership, which fell from a peak of 13.3 million members in 1979, to 9.9 million members in 1990 (*Employment Gazette,* June 1994). This was largely a result of the contraction of heavy industry and manufacturing, sectors traditionally associated with high levels of unionisation (Purcell, 1993: 9), although it was to some extent a consequence of the growing rejection of collective ideals. In addition however, management in many sectors adopted a more unitary approach to industrial relations. Incidences of trade union de-recognition and exclusion became more commonplace (Claydon, 1989; Smith and Morton, 1993; 1994; Gall and McKay, 1994), and trade unions experienced increasing difficulty in gaining recognition in newly established businesses (Disney, Gosling and Machin, 1995; Millward, 1994: 120).

As a result of these developments, the proportion of workers covered by collective bargaining fell during the decade, with lower levels of coverage being reported in both the manufacturing and service sectors, and amongst both manual and non-manual grades (Purcell, 1993: 14).

Where trade unions continued to operate, single union deals, which often incorporated no strike agreements increased in significance. In such deals, pioneered by the electricians' union (EETPU), and the engineering workers union (AUEW), which subsequently merged to form the Amalgamated Electrical and Engineering Union (AEEU), sole recognition was accorded to one union in exchange for compliance with management objectives (Millward, 1994: 35, 121-122).

Decentralised bargaining, became an emergent feature of UK industrial relations during the 1980s, particularly in the private sector (*IRRR,* 1989b), and similarly greater emphasis was placed on flexible working, as management sought to cut costs with the removal of job demarcation, and with changes to the established patterns of work (*IRRR,* 1987). The utilisation of temporary and subcontract labour also grew during the decade (*IRRR,* 1986b), reflecting the growing division of the workforce into core and peripheral sectors.

The changes which occurred in UK industrial relations during the 1980s, were to some extent prompted by increasingly intense international competition, which necessitated changes in work organisation (Edwards et al, 1992). However, they were also greatly facilitated by the creation of a legal framework and political climate which supported the re-assertion of managerial prerogatives, by a Conservative government hostile towards organised labour, and indeed Claydon suggests that union de-recognition represented an 'opportunist response' to these developments, rather than a coherent change in managerial industrial relations strategy (Claydon, 1989: 222).

Within the coal industry during the 1980s however, managerial approaches to industrial relations were both opportunistic and strategic, reflecting the long term objective of operational restructuring, and the restructuring of industrial relations in preparation for privatisation. The political and legal climate created by the Conservative government nevertheless facilitated the defeat of the NUM in 1984-85 which presented NCB management with an opportunity to operationalise this strategy.

In the aftermath of the strike the NCB objective of achieving financial break even resulted in the formulation of a production cost ceiling of £1.50/Gigajoule (Winterton and Winterton, 1993a: 82-83). This policy was developed unilaterally by NCB management, and represented an abandonment of the corporatism which had characterised the industry since nationalisation. It was however, also indicative of the intention of the NCB to remove the influence of the NUM from questions of long term industrial strategy (Edwards and Heery, 1989: 225).

The NCB unilaterally adopted a unitary approach (Goodman, 1984: 61-65) to industrial relations at all levels of the industry following the 1984-85 strike. This was illustrated within days of the return to work, by Ian McGregor's statement that, 'people are now discovering the price of insubordination and insurrection. And boy are we going to make it stick'. (*Sunday Telegraph*, 10 March 1985). At national level however, management strategies centred on the continued promotion of the collaborationist Union of Democratic Mineworkers (UDM), and the institutionalisation of dual unionism within the industry. The UDM had been formed in October 1985, by former Nottinghamshire Area NUM delegates who had supported strike breaking in the Nottinghamshire coalfield in 1984-85 in defiance of the policy of the national union. The organisers of the breakaway were opposed to a proposed revision of NUM rules which was designed to make the Nottinghamshire Area more accountable to the national union, and which provided for disciplinary action to be taken against them for their actions in 1984-85. The breakaway was later joined by former NUM members in other small coalfields such as South Derbyshire and Leicestershire who had also worked during the strike (Winterton and Winterton, 1989: 226-230).

Moreover, NCB policy received government support, since the Coal Industry Act 1987 ended the exclusive right of the NUM to represent and negotiate on behalf of mineworkers by permitting the UDM to act as workforce representatives (Winterton and Winterton, 1993a: 88).

The UDM was recognised by the NCB as soon as it was formed, and in December 1985, the NCB notified the NUM of its intention to replace the conciliation machinery established by the Coal Industry Nationalisation Act 1946 (Section 46), with a new scheme which recognised that the UDM then represented a substantial proportion of the workforce. The new conciliation arrangements were based on the majority/minority principal (Clapham, 1990), whereby the union with the majority of members within a particular area would be granted sole bargaining rights for the entire workforce in that area, with management being the arbiter of which union represented the majority of the workforce (Taylor, 1988).

The NUM rejected these arrangements because it objected to NUM members in areas such as Nottinghamshire, where the majority of the workforce belonged to the UDM, being denied the right to be 'represented by a trade union of their choice' (NUM, 1987a: 40). The involvement of the NUM in national negotiations was made conditional by the NCB on its acceptance of the new conciliation arrangements, however, and the union was therefore excluded from national negotiations from September 1986, when the UDM accepted the new scheme (Leman and Winterton, 1991: 57). Some commentators have however, suggested that although the stance of NUM national officials was understandable, particularly in the immediate aftermath of the strike, such intransigence was untenable in the long term, and indeed has led to the continued exclusion of the NUM, which has not now negotiated a pay settlement since 1983.

In addition to utilising strategies which aimed to institutionalise dual unionism at national level, NCB management also sought to exploit the internal divisions within the NUM in order to fragment collective bargaining. NCB policy regarding the proposed development of new capacity at Margam in South Wales exemplified this, since the NCB stated that this was conditional upon the South Wales NUM accepting six day working and greater labour flexibility. This both highlighted and exacerbated the policy differences of the national and South Wales NUM, since the national NUM was opposed to such developments, whilst the South Wales NUM was willing to negotiate, and indeed in February 1987, the South Wales Area Delegate Conference voted to accept six day working in defiance of the national union (Taylor, 1988: 228-229).

At local level the reassertion of management prerogatives, and moves by NCB management to marginalise the NUM took a variety of different forms. The existing local conciliation machinery was unilaterally withdrawn after the 1984-85 strike by NCB management, who proposed a replacement which incorporated both the dual union structure and the majority/minority principal of the new national arrangements. This scheme was accepted by the UDM in February 1987, but the NUM opposed the new arrangements, and as a consequence was excluded from formal conciliation procedures at local level (Leman and Winterton, 1991: 58).

The four months immediately following the strike were regarded as a 'punishment period' by many NUM branch officials, because they were required to resume three shift working, and were denied time off for union duties, whilst at many collieries, management refused to talk to branch officials (Winterton and Winterton, 1989: 222-223). In addition union officials were disproportionately represented amongst over seven hundred employees dismissed by the NCB for strike activities. Indeed in the Scottish area, 43 per cent of the sacked employees were elected union officials, and 71 per cent had been leaders of official strike committees (Rose, 1985).

Management's unitary approach at local level was also evident in unilateral changes made to working arrangements at individual collieries. Such changes usually involved the removal of long standing locally negotiated concessions, and at a number of pits this provoked unofficial strike action by NUM members. A new Disciplinary Code of Conduct was similarly imposed by NCB management in 1987. This applied to mineworker grades represented by the NUM or UDM, but not to supervisory staff who were represented by the National Association of Colliery Overmen, Deputies and Shotfirers (NACODS) or the British Association of Colliery Management (BACM) (NUM, 1987b: 522 and 524). The code extended the definition of gross industrial misconduct to activities occurring away from NCB premises, and provided for the summary dismissal of offenders. In addition it also gave management the power to veto the presence of union representatives at disciplinary hearings (Winterton and Winterton, 1989; 1993a). Whilst the UDM 'took note' of

17

the new code, its application in NUM strongholds resulted in a series of unofficial strikes (Taylor, 1988: 228; Richards, 1996: 216).

Management tactics which aimed to marginalise the influence of the NUM at local level included the extension of pit based incentive schemes, like the Doncaster Option, which served to fragment collective bargaining in the industry (Leman and Winterton, 1991: 61-62). In addition, NCB management adopted a variety of Human Resource Management techniques designed to undermine the NUM at individual collieries. Direct communication with the workforce, established during the 1984-85 strike was continued, with letters, and colliery/company news sheets which were sent to the homes of employees, and with videos and teletext messages on NCB premises (Richardson and Wood, 1989: 42), whilst team briefings were also introduced in some coalfields (*IRRR*, 1986a).

NCB management additionally made increasing use of subcontract labour which was employed initially on ad hoc contracts for specific tasks (Leman and Winterton, 1991: 61). Such contracts were frequently negotiated directly with the workers involved, and were intended to enable the NCB to circumvent the unions, although the use of subcontractors also enabled the NCB to introduce non union labour, the objective of which was to dilute NUM membership and further fragment the workforce (NUM, 1989a).

Despite the intensity of the managerial assault on union organisation at local level, the success of these initiatives was somewhat limited. This was partially a consequence of the relative autonomy afforded to individual colliery managers, since this enabled them to determine how zealously they pursued the unitary approach to industrial relations adopted centrally by the NCB, although the need for workforce co-operation to achieve productivity targets also acted as a counterbalance to the objective of restoring managerial prerogatives. In addition, however, NUM branches remained intact and the union was thus able to mount some resistance to the managerial offensive at colliery level (Clapham, 1991). Indeed, as Richards (1996), has pointed out, during 1986 only 15 of the 125 collieries owned by British Coal remained unaffected by industrial action (Richards, 1996: 215). Furthermore, the NUM also had some success in organising sub contract labour (Prowse and Turner, 1996).

Since the new pattern of industrial relations established in the wake of the 1984-85 strike was designed to promote the UDM, whilst weakening the

the NUM, it is unsurprising that the two organisations responded differently to these developments.

After the strike, the UDM confirmed its collaborationist credentials by its acceptance of the NCB's revised national and local conciliation schemes, and by its acquiescence to the Disciplinary Code. The willingness of the UDM to comply with managerial objectives however, was further underlined by its endeavours to gain sole recognition at the new developments of Margam and Asfordby in return for negotiations over flexible working (Taylor, 1988: 229).

The UDM leadership remained hostile towards the NUM, and indeed at the 1987 UDM Conference, the UDM President Roy Lynk insisted that the UDM would dictate the terms of any future reconciliation (Taylor, ibid). Lynk was ousted as UDM President in November 1992, although the attitude of his successor, Neil Greatrex was equally uncompromising towards the NUM, as he suggested shortly after his election, that there was 'no chance whatsoever' of reconciliation (*Guardian,* 1 December 1992). A more conciliatory approach to rapprochement with the NUM was favoured within some quarters of the UDM however, and indeed Horace Sankey, who adopted such a platform when he opposed Lynk in the UDM Presidential election of 1988, received the support of 37 per cent of UDM members (Waddington and Wykes, 1989: 26).

NUM responses to the post strike industrial relations were more complex, largely because the union was divided over how best to respond to the NCB's unitary approach, and to the emergence of the UDM. The national union was opposed to the new conciliation scheme, the Disciplinary Code, flexible working and the use of subcontractors (NUM, 1987b). A number of influential left wingers, notably Mick McGahey of Scotland and Des Dutfield from South Wales however, argued that such an uncompromising position was untenable, given that the balance of power within the industry had tilted away from the union as a result of their defeat in 1984-85, and believed that a reassessment of NUM strategy was therefore necessary (Edwards and Heery, 1989: 234).

At a Special National Delegate Conference in January 1988, the Derbyshire and South Wales areas unsuccessfully called for the union to accept the new conciliation arrangements in order to end its effective derecognition (*South Wales Miner,* June 1988). Similarly the North Western area called equally unsuccessfully at the 1989 Annual Conference, for a membership ballot, to determine whether opposition to consultation with British Coal should be continued (NUM, 1989b: 442-448). Indeed between the introduction of the new conciliation scheme and the 1989 Annual Conference, no fewer than twenty one unsuccessful attempts were made to change union policy on this issue (NUM ibid).

The South Wales NUM also opposed national policy on flexible working, partly in recognition that the new commercial objectives of the NCB made this necessary, if older mines with workings far from the shaft were to remain viable. Acceptance of flexible working at Margam and Asfordby, however, was also advocated in order to prevent the UDM expanding from its Nottinghamshire base (*South Wales Miner*, March 1987), and indeed the South Wales and Leicestershire areas ultimately agreed to negotiate over flexible working (Taylor, 1988).

Though the divisions within the NUM were primarily over policy questions, they were also a reflection of growing criticism of the leadership of Arthur Scargill. Scargill was an uncompromising advocate of national policy, and was both hostile towards, and contemptuous of, the UDM. Moreover, he unjustly accused those endeavouring to re-evaluate NUM strategy of collaboration with NCB objectives (*South Wales Miner*, April 1987). Like his UDM counterpart, Scargill was opposed in the 1988 NUM Presidential election by a candidate who advocated rapprochement between the two organisations. John Walsh, Scargill's opponent also called for the NUM to adopt more moderate policies to facilitate this goal, and suggested that it was Scargill's intransigence which was the major barrier to re-unification (*Independent*, 20 January 1988). Scargill was re-elected to the NUM Presidency, polling 53.8 per cent of the votes cast. The narrow margin of his victory however, indicated that ordinary NUM members were, like their officials, divided over the direction of the union's post strike strategy.

2.3 Privatising Coal

In May 1992, the Queen's Speech signalled the intention of the newly re-elected Conservative government to return the coal industry to the private sector. This followed Cecil Parkinson's pledge to the Conservative Party Conference in 1988, that this, the 'ultimate privatisation', would take place if the Conservatives won the next election.

Preparatory legislation for coal privatisation had included measures to remove the constraints on the small private sector which had continued to exist after most of the industry was nationalised in 1947 (Robinson and Sykes, 1987). The British Coal and British Rail (Transfer Proposals) Act 1993, enabled British Coal to participate in the privatisation process (DTI, 1993), and additional legislation established a new public sector body, the Coal Authority, with responsibility for licensing all mining operations (Robinson and Sykes, 1987). The Coal Authority also took over some of British Coal's liabilities in relation to subsidence when it came into being in October 1994, although British Coal itself was set to remain in existence until all its liabilities were settled (*Financial Times*, 26 October 1994). This was largely because the question of liabilities had threatened to undermine the sell off by deterring potential buyers (*Times*, 26 April 1994). The process of coal privatisation however, was most profoundly influenced by the earlier privatisation of the electricity supply industry (ESI).

By the early 1990s the UK coal industry was heavily dependent upon the market provided by the electricity generators. Coal had been largely eclipsed as a domestic fuel following the discovery of natural gas in the North Sea, and the use of diesel on the railways had removed another important market. In addition, industrial markets had diminished as a result of the contraction of heavy industry, particularly within the iron and steel sector, and indeed by the early 1990s, almost 80 per cent of UK coal sales were to the electricity generators (DTI, 1993: 18-19).

The privatisation of electricity in 1990 created two major generating companies, National Power and PowerGen, in addition to a number of regional electricity companies (RECs) whose business was electricity supply (Green, 1994). The market for coal was at first protected, as National Power and PowerGen were obliged by initial three year subsidised contracts to purchase 65 to 70 million tonnes of coal each year from British Coal, despite their requirements for indigenous coal being much lower than this (Robinson, 1992). The RECs also signed back to back contracts to buy the power produced by the generators (*Guardian*, 10 October 1992). Ultimately privatisation also enabled the industry to seek the most economically competitive fuel sources, which precipitated a scramble by both generators and RECs alike to diversify into other fuels, at a time when demand for power was falling due to the recession. As a result, stockpiles of coal increased, and by the time of the 1992 coal crisis more than eighteen months supply was held at power stations and pitheads (*Sunday Times,* 18 October 1992).

Following electricity privatisation, the generating companies invested in import terminals capable of handling increased quantities of foreign coal. This was cheaper than UK coal because it was extracted from opencast rather than deep mines in countries where labour costs were low, and where pricing policies were influenced by the need for hard currency. Imported coal had the additional advantage of having a lower sulphur content then coal mined in the UK. Coal imports did increase marginally after electricity privatisation, from 1.5 million tonnes in 1990, to 1.8 million tonnes in 1993, and in 1993, 2 per cent of electricity was generated from imported coal, a rise of 1 per cent on the corresponding figure for 1989 (DTI, 1994).

Nuclear power also assumed an increasing significance following the privatisation of electricity, since Nuclear Electric, the privatised nuclear generator, was protected from market competition by government subsidies which amounted to £1.2 billion per year, the equivalent of £50 per tonne of coal, whilst subsidies for the coal industry had been gradually withdrawn (*Guardian,* 9 and 14 October 1992). Indeed largely because of the subsidies granted to the nuclear industry, it was able to increase its share of the electricity generation market from 22 per cent in 1989 to 28 per cent in 1993 at the expense of UK coal (DTI, 1994).

The biggest threat to the market for UK coal however, came neither from coal imports, nor from nuclear power, but from the unregulated investment in gas burning generating facilities.

The 'dash for gas', was to some extent caused by the impact of EC environmental regulations. In 1988, the Large Combustion Plant Directive required governments of member states to outline plans for the reduction of sulphur dioxide and nitrogen dioxide emissions. As a consequence the UK agreed to reduce sulphur dioxide from existing plant to 20 per cent below the 1980 level by 1993, to 40 per cent below by 1998, and to 60 per cent below by 2003. Nitrogen Dioxide emissions were to be reduced by 15 per cent by 1993 and by 30 per cent by 1998, on the same basis (Newbery, 1993).

Flue gas desulphurisation equipment could have been installed at existing plants in order to reduce emissions, however this was seen as a more expensive option either than the importation of low sulphur foreign coal, or the construction of highly efficient Combined Cycle Gas Turbine generating facilities (Newbery, ibid). The use of gas as a generating fuel was prohibited by the EC, as it was deemed that this should be conserved due to it being a finite resource. When the ban was lifted in the late 1980s however, the 'dash for gas' began in earnest (*Sunday Times*, 18 October 1992).

The nature of the privatisation of the ESI itself, however, was also in part responsible for the 'dash for gas', since this created an effective duopoly in generation. The RECs desired to break the market dominance of National Power and PowerGen, because they saw that they were in a position to inflate prices. As a consequence the RECs were willing to enter into agreements with the smaller independent generators whose existence was permitted under the terms of privatisation, and to co-finance the construction of gas fired capacity. The independent generators in return, were then able to offer the RECs fifteen year contracts. Furthermore, as the RECs were permitted to pass on the extra costs resulting from their investment in gas fired capacity to their customers under the post privatisation pricing regime, the attractions of gas were great indeed (*Guardian*, 10 and 14 October 1992).

By the time of the coal crisis in October 1992, sixteen gas fired power stations had been built or were under construction, and a further twenty were planned (*Financial Times*, 15 October 1992). As a result, by 1993, 10 per cent of electricity generated in the UK was provided by gas fired capacity, whereas in 1989, the corresponding figure was just 1 per cent (DTI, 1994).

The privatisation of the ESI then, distorted the energy markets and allowed gas, and to a lesser extent imported coal and nuclear power to encroach into the electricity generation market formerly dominated by UK coal. Indeed between 1989 and 1993, the share of the market belonging to UK coal fell from 64 per cent to 51 per cent, representing a reduction of 20 per cent (DTI, 1994). These developments threatened the very existence of the UK coal industry and attracted widespread criticism from British Coal, the mining unions and opposition politicians as a result. Furthermore, because the privatisation of the electricity supply industry was also able to contaminate the privatisation of coal, even advocates of privatisation in the energy sector suggested that the process had been badly mishandled (Robinson, 1992).

The privatisation of the electricity supply industry set the parameters for the privatisation of coal, as the size and shape of the industry offered

23

for sale was largely determined by the shrinking electricity market, which necessitated further restructuring in the coal industry.

The initial subsidised contracts between the power generators and British Coal expired in March 1993. During the summer and Autumn of 1992 however, negotiations over new contracts stalled because the generators wanted to reduce the amount of UK coal they purchased. This was a consequence of their inability to agree back to back contracts with the RECs, who were concerned that the higher price of electricity generated from UK coal would attract penalties from the electricity regulator OffER (*Times,* 30 September 1992 and *Daily Telegraph,* 19 October 1992). The delay over the signing of new contracts between British Coal and the generators precipitated the coal crisis of October 1992, when Michael Heseltine announced the closure of thirty one collieries, because the government was unwilling to intervene and increase the demand for coal with the extension of subsidies (*Financial Times,* 14 October 1992). Heseltine did, however, instigate a review of energy policy in order to quell backbench rebellion and placate public outrage.

The delay influenced the timing of coal privatisation, and indeed in the wake of the October announcements some commentators suggested this could be abandoned altogether (*Independent,* 30 October 1992). Coal privatisation was delayed in the first instance, because the government had to ensure that contracts with the generators were in place in order that the market for coal was large enough to attract potential buyers. The government also decided to postpone coal privatisation until the review of energy policy was complete (*Times,* 30 October 1992).

In December 1992, Eastern Electric signed a five year electricity supply contract with PowerGen paving the way for a series of back to back agreements between the RECs, the generators and British Coal. The new contracts however, reduced the amount of coal supplied to the generators from 65 million tonnes in 1992 to 40 million tonnes in 1993 and 30 million tonnes in each of the following years. The market for coal therefore was to be effectively halved within two years, and as a result restructuring in the coal industry continued, albeit at a slower pace than that anticipated by the October announcements. Nevertheless, by April 1994 when the industry was offered for sale, some 34 collieries had closed, vindicating critics of the government's energy review, who argued that this was little more than a cynical exercise designed to circumvent public opinion whilst providing only a stay of execution for the threatened collieries.

In advance of privatisation proper, British Coal offered all the collieries it had closed following the coal crisis of 1992 for sale on lease or licence as individual units. A small number of mines were also placed on a care and maintenance basis subject to market testing (DTI, 1993). Private sector buyers had acquired 11 of these mines by the time the core collieries were returned to the private sector. Coal Investments, a company headed by Malcolm Edwards the former Commercial Director of British Coal, bought 5, RJB Mining purchased 3 collieries, 2 mines were acquired by management buyout teams whilst a further 1 was the subject of an employee buyout (Table 2.2). In April 1994, the 16 remaining core collieries were offered for sale in five regional packages which also included opencast sites, stockpiles and existing contracts with the electricity generating companies. British Coal had opposed the break up of the industry, arguing that it would be weakened as a result. The government however, favoured this option because retaining the coal industry intact would have replaced a public monopoly with a private one, without introducing competition to the industry (Robinson and Sykes, 1987). Therefore, though the government stated its willingness to consider selling all five regions to a single bidder, this was not a likely prospect.

The lack of interest displayed by international mining companies in the privatisation also influenced the decision to break up the industry, since few UK companies had the resources either to purchase or manage the entire industry, small though it was (*Financial Times,* 14 April 1994).

A number of collieries closed or mothballed in the months immediately preceding privatisation were also offered for sale in parallel as individual stand alone units. This element of privatisation was intended to be an entirely separate sale from that of the regional packages, however the sales occurred simultaneously, because the timetable for coal privatisation had been affected by the ramifications of the privatisation of electricity. This situation was further confused because bidders for certain regions were only allowed to purchase stand alone collieries within those regions under certain conditions, and because British Coal's non mining interests were the subject of a further separate sale (*Financial Times,* 12 September 1994).

Some twenty five companies pre-qualified in May 1994 to enter the bidding proper in September, although not all were expected to do so (*Times,* 13 September 1994). RJB Mining and Coal Investments had emerged in the preceding months as the companies most likely to emerge as the government's preferred bidders. RJB Mining was selected by the government as the preferred bidder for three regions, Central North, Central South and the North East. Mining (Scotland) a company part owned by Coal Investments was chosen for the Scottish region, and Celtic Energy was named as the preferred bidder for the South Wales region. RJB Mining also purchased two of the collieries offered for sale on a stand alone basis, whilst Coal Investments purchased one, with a further one being the subject of an employee buyout (*Financial Times*, 13 October 1994).

Table 2.2 Collieries transferred to the private sector 1992-1994

Leased or licensed before privatisation proper

Colliery	Area	Purchaser
Rossington	Central North	RJB Mining
Clipstone	Central South	RJB Mining
Calverton	Central South	RJB Mining
Hem Heath	Central South	Coal Investments
Silverdale	Central South	Coal Investments
Markham Main	Central North	Coal Investments
Coventry	Central South	Coal Investments
Trentham	Central South	Coal Investments
Betws	South Wales	BAL
Hatfield	Central North	HCC
Monktonhall	Scotland	MM

Sold to private sector in regional packages

Colliery	Area	Purchaser
Kellingley	Central North	RJB Mining
Prince of Wales	Central North	RJB Mining
North Selby	Central North	RJB Mining
Ricall	Central North	RJB Mining
Stillingfleet	Central North	RJB Mining
Wistow	Central North	RJB Mining

Table 2.2 continued

Whitemoor	Central North	RJB Mining
Maltby	Central North	RJB Mining
Point of Ayr	Central North	RJB Mining
Asfordby	Central South	RJB Mining
Daw Mill	Central South	RJB Mining
Bilsthorpe	Central South	RJB Mining
Harworth	Central South	RJB Mining
Thoresby	Central South	RJB Mining
Welbeck	Central South	RJB Mining
Longannet	Scotland	Mining Scotland

Sold to private sector as 'stand alone' units

Colliery	Area	Purchaser
Annesley/Bentinck	Central South	Coal Investments
Thorne	Central North	RJB Mining
Ellington	North East	RJB Mining
Tower	South Wales	GTA

Source: various.

The privatisation of coal was then characterised by confusion, but the process was finally completed in December 1994, with RJB Mining becoming the owner of around 65 per cent of the collieries that survived the restructuring, which had preceded the sale.

NUM and UDM members were likely to be affected in similar ways by privatisation, as a result of the restructuring associated with this process, and because of the anticipated reassertion of the profit motive under private ownership. The traditions of the two organisations however, determined that they responded somewhat differently to the prospect of the industry being returned to the private sector.

The position of the UDM was that privatisation was undesirable, but inevitable, and that it would therefore seek to gain influence with those parties likely to acquire a stake in the industry (*Financial Times*, 4

September 1992). In practice, the UDM position amounted to little more than tacit collusion with British Coal and government objectives. This was demonstrated by the UDM's engagement of consultants in October 1991, who advised the organisation on its own role in the privatisation process (*Times*, 5 October 1992). Characteristically, Roy Lynk recommended to the government that the industry be privatised as two regions, in order to reduce the effectiveness of any industrial action which might be taken by the unions (*Independent*, 14 December 1992).

Lynk's enthusiasm for privatisation was not shared by all his members, and in November 1992, he was replaced as UDM President by Neil Greatrex, who was more sceptical on this issue (*Financial Times*, 1 December 1992). Following Greatrex's election however, there were no significant changes to UDM policy in relation to privatisation and the UDM continued to explore the possibility of mounting a bid to take over the industry. During 1991 and 1992, the organisation had been linked with a number of commercial interests, including East Midlands Electricity, opencast companies and financial institutions (*Guardian*, 18 August 1992). A joint bid with BACM was also mooted, although BACM, unlike the UDM argued for the industry to be privatised as a single unit in order that a viable structure could be maintained (*Financial Times*, 8 October 1992). The UDM however, eventually joined forces with Coal Investments. The company submitted bids for several of the regional packages when the industry was offered for sale, although all were unsuccessful (*Financial Times*, 13 October 1994).

Official NUM policy regarding privatisation contrasted sharply with that of the UDM. The NUM opposed privatisation on ideological grounds, and at the 1992 Annual Conference, an Emergency Resolution submitted by the NEC, calling for the union to take 'any action necessary' to prevent privatisation, gained unanimous support (NUM, 1992: 109). The NUM however, also opposed privatisation because of fears that safety standards and working conditions would deteriorate under private ownership, when profitability was likely to assume an increasing significance (NUM, ibid). Such concerns were also voiced by NACODS (*Independent*, 15 February 1993), particularly as the government had signalled that it intended to relax mines safety legislation as part of the Coal Privatisation Bill (*Times*, 4 May 1993).

The NUM was also concerned that trade union rights would be eroded under private ownership, especially as many subcontractors employed by

BC were making increasing use of non-union labour (NUM, 1991: 65). Indeed, the use of subcontractors was viewed by the NUM as back door privatisation, and in April 1992, NUM members in Yorkshire supported calls for industrial action over their employment at Markham Main colliery (*Times*, 18 April 1992).

In the coalfields, responses to privatisation proper were characterised by a pragmatism born of an increasingly desperate struggle to prevent further colliery closures in areas already devastated by restructuring. As a result, a number of NUM branches at collieries threatened with closure, including Thurcroft in South Yorkshire, Monktonhall in Scotland and Tower in South Wales considered mounting employee buyouts (*Guardian*, 30 May 1992 and *Financial Times*, 1 December 1992), and the Scottish NUM similarly signalled its interest in an employee buyout scheme for the Longannet Complex. In addition, the Cokemen's and white collar sections of the NUM joined forces with BACM, two other trade unions and Unity Bank, to investigate the possibility of an employee buyout for the Coal Products Division (*Financial Times*, 4 September 1992).

At the 1992 NUM Annual Conference, two Emergency Resolutions condemning employee buyouts were unanimously supported. The privatisation debate however, served only to highlight the ambiguity of the NUM's position. Indeed some of the delegates supporting the resolutions were involved in buyout proposals themselves, not because they supported privatisation, but rather because they recognised that privately owned collieries were a preferable alternative to colliery closures. (NUM, 1992: 109-137). Two collieries, Monktonhall (*Guardian*, 10 June 1992), and Tower (*Times*, 3 January 1995) were ultimately acquired by employee buyout teams. The majority of the bids submitted by employee buyout teams were however, unsuccessful.

3 Towards a Theory of Restructuring and Industrial Relations

3.1 Capitalist Restructuring

The contemporary changes which have affected the UK coal industry, and which have been manifest in the restructuring of operations, industrial relations and ownership are inextricably intertwined with the process of capitalist restructuring.

Restructuring is an inherent feature of capitalist development, since it is this which facilitates the continual expansion of profit accumulation, which is required by capital (Bradbury, 1985: 39). Restructuring may involve the regeneration of the prevailing regime of accumulation, by way of the modernisation of capacity designed to increase the efficiency of both capital and labour, by the closure of unprofitable capacity (Bradbury, ibid), and by the development of new capacity in growth sectors (Tailby and Whitston, 1989: 1). However, as any regime of accumulation will eventually exhaust the potential for expansion and the generation of surplus value, periodic crises occur, which necessitate more fundamental structural change (Grahl, 1983: 118), designed not only to regenerate the existing regime of accumulation, but also to create a new regime, and thus a new source of surplus value.

For much of the twentieth century, the dominant regime of accumulation in the developed capitalist nations has been Fordism. Fordism is based on an equilibrium between the mass production of standardised goods manufactured using assembly line techniques, and the mass consumption of those goods. Levels of consumption, and therefore markets were supported by Keynesian policies, which were adopted by individual governments in order to maintain aggregate demand (Martin,

31

1988: 210), and by wage regulation, which linked pay to productivity and prices (De Vroey, 1984; Lipietz, 1982). In addition, the position of the unemployed as consumers was maintained by social security systems (Aglietta, 1979: 382-383). Small scale production however continued, and indeed continues, to operate in tandem with Fordist mass production, reflecting the fact that capitalist development has been both complex and uneven.

Due to the interaction of a number of factors, the prevailing regime of capitalist accumulation entered a period of crisis in the 1960s. At this time stagnating productivity served to undermine the Fordist mode of production (Lipietz, 1984: 99). Moreover, the systems of wage regulation which had been established to sustain this, were increasingly called into question because organised labour was willing to disrupt production, and therefore the process of accumulation in pursuit of its demands (Martin, 1988: 216). In addition, the profits of many companies operating in the capitalist heartlands of North America, Europe and Japan began to fall (Lipietz, 1982; 1984).

Though the crisis of capitalist accumulation was essentially multi-dimensional in character, the crisis of profitability in particular necessitated that new sources of surplus value be developed (Lipietz, 1984: 100). This provided an impulse for restructuring, and the development of a new regime of accumulation. The need for restructuring moreover, received added impetus from the economic crises of the 1970s, the most notable of these being the oil shocks of 1973 and 1979 (Thrift, 1988: 8).

3.2 Restructuring: The Global Dimension

The restructuring undertaken by capital in response to the crises of the 1960s and 1970s impacted globally, but had differing implications for different parts of the globe.

As Froebel, Heinrichs and Kreye have pointed out, global economic divisions which concentrated the production of manufactured goods in the first world, and the production of raw materials in the third world, were apparent from the sixteenth century, and were consolidated during the era of capitalist production (Froebel, Heinrichs and Kreye, 1980: 10-12). The restructuring which commenced in the 1960s however, resulted in the emergence of a new regime of accumulation based on the centralisation and internationalisation of capital (Andreff, 1984: 58), embodied in the growth of trans-national corporations (TNCs), and on the creation of a global market for labour and production sites (Froebel, Heinrichs and Kreye, 1980: 44). Encompassed within this process was 'the export of capitalist relations of production' (Thrift, 1988: 8), to the third world, as many capitalist enterprises relocated some of their manufacturing operations to those regions.

The relocation of manufacturing operations primarily involved labour intensive assembly processes, notably in the textiles and electronics sectors (Lipietz, 1982: 39), and was facilitated by developments in transport and communications (Froebel, Heinrichs and Kreye, 1980: 36). The fragmentation of tasks and the consequent de-skilling associated with the division of labour in capitalist manufacturing industries (Braverman, 1974), however, also facilitated relocation, since it ensured that an inexperienced labour force would achieve optimum productivity within a short space of time, and with the minimum of training (Froebel, Heinrichs and Kreye, 1980: 35-36).

Relocation facilitated the objective of capital, which was to generate new sources of surplus value to replace that lost as a result of the crisis of Fordism in the capitalist heartlands of the first world, because it enabled capitalist enterprises to access new and cheaper sources of energy and raw materials (Jenkins, 1984: 44). In addition however, relocation permitted the exploitation of an almost inexhaustible supply of cheap third world labour (Froebel, Heinrichs and Kreye, 1980: 34-35), which, unlike that in the capitalist heartlands was largely unorganised, and unprotected by the statutory regulation of employment terms and conditions (Elson and Pearson, 1981). Moreover, labour costs were further reduced by the employment of disproportionate numbers of young women, who, in addition to being cheaper to employ as a result of their position in the secondary labour market, were also favoured by capital because they were considered to be easier to control than their male counterparts (Elson and Pearson, ibid).

Relocation also facilitated the penetration of markets closed to imports by protectionist policies (Thrift, 1988: 10), although the relative importance of this factor in relation to the generation of surplus value is open to question, given that much of the production of capitalist enterprises operating in the third world is destined for re-export to the capitalist heartlands (Froebel, Heinrichs and Kreye, 1980: 45).

Nevertheless, the emergent regime of accumulation, of which relocation is an integral part, has had some success in creating increased surplus value, as since 1973 the profit rates of TNCs have increased, whilst those of companies not operating internationally have fallen (Andreff, 1984: 63).

The emergence of a new regime of accumulation has led to the reconstruction of pre-existing global economic divisions within the third world, which is, as a consequence, increasingly fragmented into proto capitalist and non capitalist segments (Lipietz, 1984: 102-103). The new regime furthermore, has resulted in the export of Fordist and Taylorist systems of work organisation from the capitalist heartlands, to parts of the third world (Lipietz, 1982). The consequences of the emergence of a new regime of accumulation however, have been equally profound in those nations which comprise the capitalist heartlands.

The creation of a global economy, as an integral feature of the new regime has resulted in the economies of individual nations becoming interrelated to such a degree, that no nation, or region, is now independent of developments in another (Bradbury, 1985: 54; Froebel, Heinrichs and Kreye, 1980: 8). Whilst foreign investments by corporations based in the capitalist heartlands have increased, domestic investment levels have stagnated. Moreover, that investment has been used to rationalise, rather than expand domestic capacity (Froebel, Heinrichs and Kreye, 1980: 2-3). The de-industrialisation of former manufacturing centres in the capitalist heartlands, and the resultant emergence of persistently high levels of unemployment and underemployment in those regions, can therefore be seen as a consequence of the inability of domestic capacity to compete with re-located capacity, which is able to take advantage of the low wage rates of the third world (Martin, 1988: 203-204).

An alternative model of capitalist restructuring which has been advanced, involves the development, in the capitalist heartlands, of a new mode of production, based upon the flexibility of production techniques, labour and patterns of consumption (Martin, 1988 ibid). Fordism as a mode of production, it is argued, is being replaced by flexible specialisation. This is said to be 'a strategy of permanent innovation', which seeks to accommodate change (Piore and Sabel, 1984: 17), since it developed in response to increasingly volatile markets, characterised by intense competition (Sabel, 1989: 18), and rapidly changing customer demands.

Flexible specialisation is said to represent a renaissance of craft production, since it embraces the use of technologically sophisticated, flexible machinery, and highly skilled, functionally flexible labour, in order to achieve the re-integration of the conception and execution of tasks, for the purpose of producing specialised rather than standardised goods, for niche rather than mass markets (Piore and Sabel, 1984; Sabel, 1989). Flexible specialisation, moreover, is said to be underpinned by the mutually dependent relationships of companies, who must co-operate on a regional basis in order to successfully meet market demands (Sabel, 1989), and indeed, it has been argued that the adoption of flexible specialisation in a number of 'mature industrial areas,' such as the 'Third Italy' and Baden Wurttemburg in Germany (Piore and Sabel, 1984: 205-206), and parts of Denmark, Sweden, Japan, France and the USA (Sabel, 1989: 22-23), has led to their re-generation.

It has also been claimed that as flexible specialisation represents a resurgence of craft production, so it also heralds a new era of liberation for workers who are re-skilled as a consequence, and who, especially through the use of computer based technology, are able to gain control of the labour process (Piore and Sabel, 1984: 261), which was lost under Fordism.

Technological developments able to facilitate the emergence of flexible specialisation have been made, particularly in computer controlled production, robotics and flexible manufacturing systems (Martin, 1988: 218; Williams et al, 1987: 429). Moreover, there is evidence to suggest that some capitalist operations, particularly those of medium and large size, are utilising such technology, if to a limited extent (Williams et al, 1987). However, the tentative emergence of innovative production methods and marketing strategies does not equate to the development of a new regime of flexible accumulation in the capitalist heartlands, nor is it a viable model of capitalist restructuring.

The notion of Fordism being displaced by flexible specialisation is open to question, not least because flexible production methods are themselves ill defined, and, are consequently hard to differentiate from the mass production they are allegedly replacing (Williams et al, 1987: 414-417; Pollert, 1988: 58). Indeed, Tomaney argues that 'What post-Fordist writers take to be signs of the end of mass production, are better seen as rather more incremental developments in the organisation of large scale industry' (Tomaney, 1991: 97). Moreover, the fragmentation of mass markets, which is said to have led to the emergence of flexible specialisation, is exaggerated, since mature products can be updated, new products can be developed, which are compatible with existing productive capacity and huge markets also exist for replacement goods (Williams et al, 1987: 424-425).

Much of the flexible specialisation literature is concerned with manufacturing industry, when this remains a declining sector throughout the capitalist heartlands, and employs, in the case of the UK, just 25 per cent of the workforce (Hyman, 1988: 52). Indeed, flexible specialisation theorists largely overlook one of the major features of contemporary capitalist development, namely, the growth of manufacturing in the third world, and the corresponding emergence of persistently high levels of unemployment in the capitalist heartlands. Furthermore, they do not recognise that these developments exclude large sections of the population in the capitalist heartlands from the markets for specialised products (Hudson, 1988: 161-162). In a further criticism of flexible specialisation, Hyman suggests that the notion of flexible enterprises co-operating to ensure mutual survival implies that the adoption of flexible production creates 'no losers, only winners' (Hyman, 1988: 53), and this he quite correctly argues, is untenable given the dynamics of capitalist market competition.

Labour flexibility, unlike flexible technology or production methods, is widely acknowledged to be an established trend within the capitalist heartlands, and the theoretical debate surrounding this issue, largely focuses on the extent to which this has developed, and its significance (Atkinson, 1984; Atkinson and Gregory, 1986; Hakim, 1987a; Pollert, 1988). Functional flexibility has been introduced in the UK primarily as a result of advances in technology, and most commonly involves skilled workers, although supervisory and technical grades have been affected to a more limited extent. The objective of functional flexibility from a management perspective, has been the removal of demarcations, particularly between electrical and mechanical skills, and between production and maintenance functions, in order to reduce idle time by speeding up the repair process following breakdowns (IDS, 1984; 1986; 1994).

Far from representing a renaissance of craft production which has positive implications for labour functional flexibility has, in reality, resulted merely in the intensification of work. Moreover, as the range of skills acquired by functionally flexible workers are generally plant, or firm specific, their position in the external labour market is considerably weaker than that of the traditional craft worker (Hyman, 1988: 53). The emergence of functional flexibility then, cannot be said to be indicative of the replacement of Fordism by flexible specialisation. Rather, it points to the reconstruction of Fordist and in some cases Taylorist modes of production, albeit in modified forms (Tomaney, 1990), whereby additional surplus value is generated by the more intensive exploitation of labour which results from the intensification of work. Similarly, the increasing incidence in forms of numerical and temporal flexibility (ACAS, 1988), represent the re-introduction of 'old hire and fire strategies' (Hudson, 1988: 155).

The emergence of labour flexibility in the capitalist heartlands has been facilitated by the existence of mass unemployment within those regions. This has seriously undermined the bargaining power of organised labour, and thus the ability, and even the willingness of workers to resist such developments (IDS, 1984: 4). Flexibility has therefore been established on capital's terms (Tomaney, 1990: 54), and under such circumstances, assertions that flexibility represents an emancipation for workers appear somewhat hollow.

3.3 Capitalist Restructuring and Coal

The process of capitalist restructuring, and its impact on global economic divisions, has been reflected in developments within the coal industries of the world since the early 1970s. Throughout this period, non OECD nations were responsible for the majority of world hard coal production. However, the proportion of total global production supplied by these countries has increased steadily, from 58 per cent in 1971, to 66 per cent in 1993. Moreover, whereas only one third world nation was represented amongst the world's top five producers of hard coal in 1971 (Table 3.1), by 1993, three of the top five producers were third world nations (Table 3.2). The expansion of coal production in the third world is, furthermore, forecast to continue, and China, India, Indonesia, Colombia and Venezuela are all expected to have dramatically increased production by the turn of the century (ILO, 1994a: 11).

Table 3.1 Leading hard coal producers 1971

	Output (MT)
USA	501.0
USSR	487.5
China	392.0
UK	150.4
Poland	145.5

Source: IEA Coal Information, 1994.

Table 3.2 Leading hard coal producers 1993

	Output (MT)
China	1154.0
USA	776.4
Former USSR	418.6
India	249.0
South Africa	182.2

Source: IEA Coal Information, 1994.

The expansion of coal production in the third world, and in other non traditional mining regions such as Australia, has been driven to a large extent by the activities of American and European oil companies, who invested in the development of new coal reserves following the oil shock of 1973 (Rutledge and Wright, 1985). It has also been facilitated by developments in opencast technology, which have enabled surface mines to operate at much greater depths than had previously been the case. This has permitted the new reserves to be exploited by companies using

38

opencast techniques and unskilled labour, and as a consequence third world mines have much lower operating costs than existing deep mines in the capitalist heartlands (Rutledge and Wright, 1985).

Like third world manufacturing, mining operations in the third world are frequently labour rather than capital intensive. The Chinese and Indian coal industries employed 5,500,000 and 672,200 people respectively in 1992 (ILO, 1994a: 22), and in the same year productivity was comparatively low, at less than 1.5 tonnes per manshift in each case (ILO, 1994b), reflecting the lack of capital investment in those industries.

Workers in the coal industries of the third world are, in general, well paid by third world standards (ILO, 1994a), and the living costs in those regions are lower than in the capitalist heartlands. Low labour costs nevertheless contribute to the low operating costs of third world mining, because miners in those regions are paid considerably less than their counterparts in the capitalist heartlands. Colombian mineworkers, for example, typically earn 75 per cent less than miners in the USA (ILO, 1994a: 92; *The Guardian,* 21 November 1992). Moreover, employment terms and conditions, and health and safety standards in third world mines are generally poorer, and are the subject of less statutory regulation than is the case in the capitalist heartlands (ILO, 1994a).

The exploitation of new coal reserves in the third world then, has been accompanied by the export of the highly exploitative productive relationships which prevailed in the mining industries of the capitalist heartlands at the turn of the century. This coupled with the adoption of low cost opencast mining techniques, has enabled capitalist operation in the energy sector to generate new sources of surplus value to replace that lost following the 1973 oil shock.

The corollary of the expansion of coal production in the third world has been the contraction of coal mining in many parts of the capitalist heartlands, and also in the former Eastern Bloc. This contraction has been particularly evident since the mid 1980s, when rationalisation programmes were introduced in many nations. Indeed, since then, the UK, Germany, Japan and France, alongside the former Soviet Union, Czechoslovakia and Poland have experienced significant falls in production, whilst in Belgium, coal mining has ceased altogether (ILO, 1994a). The USA is a notable exception to the general trend of contraction in the capitalist heartlands, as production in that nation has increased since the mid 1980s, although employment levels have fallen (ILO, 1994a).

Between 1988 and 1993, some 182,000 mining jobs were lost in the coalfields of Western Europe, whilst over 24,000 jobs were lost in the USA (ILO, 1994a). Many coalfield areas in the capitalist heartlands then, have, like their manufacturing counterparts, been blighted by de-industrialisation and high levels of unemployment, as indigenous industries have been unable to compete with the low operating costs and cheap labour advantages of third world mining.

The contraction of the coal industries in the capitalist heartlands, has however been accompanied by significant improvements in productivity, which have been generated by a combination of work intensification and the application of new technology.

The effects of work intensification can be seen because reductions in employment levels in Europe have been proportionately larger than reductions in output, whilst in the USA, employment levels have fallen, although output has increased (ILO, 1994a). Far fewer miners then, are producing slightly less, or in the case of the USA, slightly more, coal. New technology has also contributed to the improvements in productivity experienced by the industries of the capitalist heartlands, since this has enabled machine running time to be increased (Tomaney, 1990: 49-50). The adoption of forms of functional and temporal flexibility have also facilitated productivity improvements, as this was similarly designed to reduce constraints on machine running time (ILO, 1994b: 10), and to reduce the porosity of the minerworkers' working day. The relative importance of these factors however, has varied, not only between nations, but also between individual coalfields within nations, as Tomaney and Winterton (1995), have demonstrated.

The increases in productivity generated by the intensification of work and new technology suggests that the flexible specialisation model of restructuring cannot be applied to those parts of the coal industries in the capitalist heartlands which have survived contraction. Indeed it would appear that work organisation in those industries is being reconstructed around what are essentially Taylorist principles, in order that increased surplus value can be generated from the more intensive exploitation of labour power. This has been facilitated by the contraction of the industries, and the resulting high levels of unemployment in mining areas, which has rendered organised labour less able to mount any effective opposition to these developments. In the case of the UK industry, management strategies and government policies also contributed to the inability of the mining unions to offer any effective resistance to changes in work organisation.

3.4 Restructuring: The UK Dimension

It has been suggested that state intervention in the nations within the capitalist heartlands may have served to delay the onset of restructuring in some of those countries (Grahl, 1983: 119), and indeed, during the 1960s and 1970s the UK economy was sheltered from many of the negative consequences of capitalist restructuring, largely as a result of government policy.

Successive governments during those years endeavoured to prolong the post war boom with a continued commitment to those policies which had generated it. All political parties consequently subscribed to Keynesian economics, the maintenance of the welfare state, and to a form of industrial corporatism which drew organised labour into a 'deepening relationship with government' (Tailby and Whitston, 1989: 10). As the economic crises of the 1970s deepened however, the economic and political orthodoxies of the post war consensus were increasingly challenged by advocates of neo liberalism, whose influence had been growing within the Conservative Party during the decade (Veljanovski, 1987).

The central tenets of neo liberalism were the introduction of free market competition to all sectors of the economy, and the creation of the minimalist state, although somewhat paradoxically, these objectives also rested upon the concentration and centralisation of state power (Green, 1989: 6). In 1979 a Conservative government led by Margaret Thatcher was elected on a manifesto which committed the party to the neo liberal agenda (Conservative Party, 1979). In its rejection of the post war consensus however, the Conservative government also implicitly embraced restructuring. Indeed, Conservative policies have accelerated this process, and furthermore, have guided it in a particular direction (Green, 1989: 20), not least because organised labour had been identified as one of the primary obstacles in the way of economic regeneration (Tailby and Whitston, 1989: 10-11).

Privatisation was a major theme in Conservative policy, which came to dominate government legislative programmes once neo liberal ascendancy had been firmly established within both party and cabinet (Foster, 1992: 108- 110).

Privatisation took a number of different forms, ranging from highly visible and well publicised asset sales, to more subtle manifestations, such as the extension of commercial practices into public sector operations (Young, 1986). All these measures however, were consistent with neo liberal philosophy, as they sought to decrease the role of the state within the economy, and increase that of the market, whilst increasing the efficiency of those operations remaining within the public sector.

It has been suggested that a number of more specific aims, which embraced ideological, economic, financial, managerial and party political concerns, were also operationalised within the wider objectives of privatisation (Vickers and Wright, 1988). These aims however, received differing emphases at differing stages of the development of the policy (Marsh, 1991: 463).

A number of the subsidiary aims of privatisation have had important implications for public sector industrial relations. The neo liberal critique of the nationalised industries condemned the prevailing corporatist arrangements (Pendleton and Winterton, 1993: 1-10), and privatisation was viewed as a means of breaking with these, and of distancing the government from public sector industrial relations (Foster, 1992: 111; Marsh, 1991: 472). It has been suggested that privatisation was also seen as a way of releasing the nationalised industries from their statutory obligation to be 'good employers' (Heald, 1988: 31), which was seen as a barrier to the development of effective business practice (Moore, 1983: 6-7). Privatisation, however, was also explicitly seen by its exponents, as the *Ridley Report* made clear, as a means of curbing excessive public sector pay awards, by restricting the power of organised labour in the public sector, which it was argued, had grown too powerful (Moore, 1983 ibid). The emphasis placed by advocates of privatisation on improving efficiency in the public sector similarly had an industrial relations dimension because of the implications for employment levels, as public sector inefficiencies, though attributed to that sector's isolation from market disciplines (Redwood, 1980; Moore, 1983), were often equated with overstaffing (Redwood, 1980; Pryke, 1981).

Opponents of privatisation also suggested that this policy had important implications for public sector industrial relations. They argued that privatisation was likely to lead to a worsening of the terms and conditions of employment for workers in the public sector (Bickerstaffe, 1983: 7; McCarthy, 1988: 74), and that it would be detrimental to trade union organisation (Whitfield, 1983: 2). Indeed, as Thomas has suggested, the trade unions had as much to lose from privatisation as they had gained from nationalisation, since legislation enacting nationalisations commonly obliged employers to promote collective bargaining. Moreover, closed shop agreements were more common, and union density was consequently higher in the public sector than in private manufacturing (Thomas, 1986: 299-300).

Veljanovski (1987), has pointed out that privatisation represents,

> ...more than a change of ownership from the government to a small number of private individuals. It is a complex change in the objectives, property rights and business environment of each firm, and - in the case of the utility industries - a change in the system of controls they face and in their relationship with the government (Veljanovski, 1987: 19).

Other commentators have concurred with this analysis, and have suggested that this indicates that privatisation is likely to have a more complex influence on patterns of industrial relations in the former public enterprises than the participants in the political debate have anticipated.

Ferner and Colling (1991), like Veljanovski, have suggested that the environment in which the management of the former public enterprises formulate corporate strategy and industrial relations policies has changed as a result of privatisation. This they argue, is because firstly, the government no longer has any direct influence over such matters, secondly, former public enterprises have new responsibilities towards shareholders and regulators, and thirdly, privatisation has enabled some former public enterprises to diversify into other business areas. Ferner and Colling contend however, that these contextual changes are likely, especially in the first two instances to have an essentially ambiguous influence on industrial relations in the former public enterprises.

The decline in governmental influence over industrial relations policies in the privatised industries has been seen by Ferner and Colling as a development which may lead to the adoption, by management, of a more conciliatory approach to industrial relations. According to their argument, the Conservative governments of the 1980s actively encouraged public sector management to restore managerial prerogatives, and to adopt a confrontational approach in their dealings with trade unions. With this pressure effectively removed then, Ferner and Colling suggest that managerial decisions concerning industrial relations issues, 'will now be dictated by strategic business considerations rather than the need to accommodate to political pressures' (Ferner and Colling, 1991: 395).

Given that the NUM was regarded as something of a *bête noire* by the Conservatives following their successful strike in 1974, which toppled the Heath government, and that the Thatcher government was prepared to underwrite the not insubstantial cost of defeating the NUM in the 1984-85 strike, at least in part to avenge that defeat, Ferner and Colling's argument is persuasive. Now that the 'ultimate privatisation' has taken place moreover, there is some reason to believe that managerial approaches to industrial relations will become less confrontational, not least because, unlike in the past, management will have to meet the cost of industrial action taken by the unions (Edwards and Heery, 1989: 205).

The re-emergence of commercial considerations as the primary determinant of industrial relations policies in the former public enterprises may not, however, be as benign an influence as Ferner and Colling suggest, since the interests of labour are likely to be at variance with those of capital in such circumstances. Indeed the re-emergence of commercial imperatives may dictate that management in the coal industry, as in other former public enterprises, adopts a stance as uncompromising towards industrial relations issues as that taken by their ideologically coerced public sector predecessors. Ferner and Colling recognise this possibility however, as their consideration of the closure of Ravenscraig steelworks demonstrates.

Ferner and Colling (1991) suggest that the new responsibilities which privatised concerns have towards their shareholders, and their relationships with other financial institutions, may generate pressures for cost reductions, and that this may result in operational restructuring designed to reduce labour costs. Further pressure to reduce staffing levels, they argue, may also come from the regulatory bodies established in the wake of privatisation, to monitor competition, quality and pricing in some of the former public enterprises, since the pricing formulae operated by the regulators provides something of an incentive for restructuring.

Ferner and Colling also contend however, that these pressures are counterbalanced by the need both to provide and to maintain quality of service. This they suggest, has in the short term reduced the apparent

44

attractiveness of cutting staff levels, although in the longer term they argue that the tension between the need to cut costs and quality of service issues is likely to produce 'oscillating' priorities in terms of industrial relations.

As there is no coal industry regulator, and as quality of service is not as important in the industry as it is in others, it unlikely that industrial relations in the privatised coal industry will be influenced by these factors. Commercial considerations then, are most likely to be the primary determinant of managerial industrial relations policies in the coal industry.

Ferner and Colling (1991) also point out that some of the privatised operations, notably British Telecom and British Gas, have taken the opportunity presented by the removal of state control to diversify into other non-core areas of business. They contend however, that these developments, unlike those previously described, are likely to have less ambiguous, and from the point of view of the trade unions, less benign, implications for industrial relations in the former public enterprises.

Ferner and Colling suggest that a two tier pattern of industrial relations is likely to emerge in the former public enterprises, since new operations are predominantly organised as separate concerns, where management consequently 'feels freer to adopt new industrial relations strategies unfettered by the assumptions and constraints of the past' (Ferner and Colling, 1991: 405). They also suggest that union recognition is likely to be a more problematic issue, than in traditional spheres of activity.

As yet, the companies which emerged as the major players in the privatised coal industry have announced no plans to diversify into other areas of business. The influence of this factor on industrial relations in the coal industry then, remains to be seen. RJB however, had significant interests prior to the privatisation of coal in opencast mining in the UK; an industry with very different industrial relations traditions from its deep mining counterpart. It is possible that RJB may seek to import industrial relations practices commensurate with opencast mining into the deep mines the company has acquired. It must be remembered however, that the most significant, and sustained attempt to change the industrial relations culture in deep mining was instigated by British Coal during and after the 1984-85 strike, when the industry was being prepared for privatisation.

Ferner and Colling then, maintain that privatisation has, on balance, had an essentially ambiguous influence on industrial relations in the former public enterprises. Other, more optimistic assessments however, have focused on the de-centralisation associated with privatisation, and have suggested that, because of these developments, trade unions, in spite of their misgivings, may stand to benefit from privatisation in some respects.

Fairbrother (1994) has suggested that because privatisation has been accompanied by organisational restructuring, many of the former public enterprises have business structures which are significantly less centralised than was the case when they were under state control. He argues moreover, that the locus of industrial relations has consequently moved away from the national arena, and that emergent patterns of industrial relations in the former public enterprises are centred on local bargaining, often at workplace level.

Fairbrother concedes that these developments have taken place on capital's terms, since they have been instigated by management in response to commercial pressures, and have been accompanied by changes in work organisation, which have resulted in a greater emphasis being placed on flexible working, and in the intensification of work. He suggests however, that the changing locus of bargaining nevertheless provides an opportunity for union re-generation at local level, because a broader range of issues are dealt with by local representatives. Fairbrother, moreover, argues that de-centralisation opens up the possibility for trade unions to develop new structures at local level based on wider membership participation. Fairbrother though, also warns that trade unions which retain structures emphasising decision making at national and regional level are in danger of becoming increasingly irrelevant given the changing locus of bargaining.

Edwards and Heery have made much the same point in relation to the coal industry, since they contend that de-centralisation 'could enhance the power of the NUM officials by bringing many more decisions within their sphere of potential influence' (Edwards and Heery, 1989: 192).

The NUM has a federal structure, and local branches continued to function in spite of management efforts to undermine the union at local level (Clapham, 1991). There is therefore, some possibility of union renaissance at local level as Fairbrother and Edwards and Heery suggest. Whether this will embrace wider membership participation however, is another matter. Unemployment in mining areas remains significantly higher than the national average following restructuring (Edwards, 1993), and given managerial attitudes towards union activities over the past decade, there may be some unwillingness on the part of mineworkers to become actively involved in union activity. Fairbrother's claims, in relation to the coal industry at least then, seem a little utopian.

Colling and Ferner (1992) have also suggested that privatisation has provided a major impulse for de-centralisation in the former public enterprises, and like Fairbrother they have argued that the trade unions could benefit from these developments. Indeed Colling and Ferner have advanced two major reasons why this should be the case.

Firstly, they suggest that de-centralisation will create tensions between the concerns of corporate level management, and the objectives of local line managers, and that this can be exploited by the trade unions. Moreover, they argue that this presents an opportunity for tacit alliances to be formed between senior union officials and corporate personnel managers, which can then be used to shore up central bargaining.

How relevant these factors will be in relation to the coal industry will depend on the organisational structures of the companies operating within the industry. Clearly however, they are likely to be of more importance in a large company like RJB, which owns several collieries, than in a small concern where one colliery was acquired by a worker, or management, buyout team.

Secondly, Colling and Ferner argue that the break up of some of the former public enterprises into several competing private companies may serve to increase the bargaining strength of trade unions at local level, since those companies would be more vulnerable to localised industrial action, as each business unit would represent a larger proportion of their income.

Edwards and Heery made a similar point to this in relation to the coal industry, when they suggested that operational restructuring in the industry had the potential to 'enhance the strategic position of the workforces in the collieries that survive' (Edwards and Heery, 1989: 188). They have argued that in a smaller industry, the output of each colliery represents a greater proportion of aggregate output, and that industrial action at individual mines therefore has a greater disruptive potential. In addition, Edwards and Heery have suggested that the creation of a highly productive, technologically advanced industry may serve to strengthen the influence of the unions, firstly, because union influence over pay was strongest in the most productive collieries, and secondly because retreat mining techniques fostered solidaristic working relationships, which in turn enhanced union solidarity (Edwards and Heery, 1989).

The points raised by Colling and Ferner and Edwards and Heery may have some validity at a theoretical level. Their arguments however, overlook the existence of high levels of unemployment, which may serve to temper trade union militancy, and the presence of a legislative framework designed to strengthen the position of capital relative to that of labour. The restructuring of the coal industry, which led firstly to its contraction, and then to its return to the private sector was, moreover, accompanied by the restructuring of industrial relations in the industry. The objective of this institutional restructuring was to enable managerial prerogatives to be re-asserted. It could be argued however, that this also aimed to lessen the likelihood of industrial action in the industry, although it has only been partially successful, since localised industrial action occurred in the industry in the late 1980s. After privatisation, NUM members voted in favour of industrial action in support of a pay claim, and company wide collective bargaining at collieries owned by RJB (*Financial Times,* 17 May 1995), although this action was prohibited by a ruling made by the Court of Appeal (*Financial Times*, 13 June 1995). Indeed, no stoppages took place within the industry during 1995, making this the first recorded strike free year in the industry for some one hundred years (*Times,* 6 June 1996).

The vision of increasing union influence in the wake of privatisation presented by Colling and Ferner, Edwards and Heery, and Fairbrother, hereafter referred to as the optimists, then is not wholly justified. Whilst some of their arguments, particularly in relation to the possibilities of trade union renaissance at local level have some validity, these can nevertheless be challenged because the factors that these authors suggest may contribute to that renaissance, are counterbalanced by other factors which point to any rejuvenation being somewhat limited. Furthermore, whilst the optimists focus on the positive *possibilities* afforded to the trade unions by privatisation, they present scant evidence of positive *outcomes* from a trade union point of view.

Recent empirical studies have found that widespread change, anticipated by both advocates and opponents of the privatisation programme, has indeed occurred in patterns of industrial relations in the former public enterprises, although some degree of continuity is also highlighted. The studies have nevertheless pointed to a number of major developments, notably reductions in labour requirements, organisational de-centralisation and the de-centralisation of industrial relations, which, in addition to changes in working practices, and in managerial industrial relations strategies to varying degrees, have been common to the majority of those concerns at some point in their transition from public sector organisations to privately owned companies.

In many former public enterprises operational restructuring was undertaken in the years preceding privatisation. This commonly resulted in significant reductions in employment levels. Thus between 1980 and 1988, employment fell by 51 per cent in steel (Blyton, 1993: 177), whilst in electricity supply and distribution staffing levels were reduced by 24 per cent and 15 per cent respectively over the same period (Ferner and Colling, 1993: 113). Similarly between 1979 and 1988, 20 per cent of jobs were lost in gas (*IRRR*, 1989a: 14), as were 13 per cent of jobs in water between 1985 and 1989 (Ogden, 1993a: 49). The most dramatic reductions in staffing levels however, occurred in the coal industry, where no less than 74 per cent of the workforce was made redundant between 1984-85 and 1991-92 (discussed previously in Chapter Two).

A number of factors contributed to the employment reductions seen in the former public enterprises. Government financial targets and performance objectives imposed during the 1980s provided a major impulse for cost reductions, which in turn impacted upon staffing levels. Similarly, changes in working practices, which aimed to increase labour productivity, thus reducing aggregate labour requirements, were introduced in the majority of these concerns (Pendleton and Winterton, 1993: 233-235). Other factors which contributed to the reductions in staffing levels in the former public enterprises however were more industry specific. Thus the introduction of new technology reduced labour requirements in telecommunications (*IRRR*, 1989a: 12), and in coal (discussed previously in Chapter Two), whilst regulatory pressures provided an incentive for employment reductions in water (Ogden, 1994: 69), and electricity (Ferner and Colling, 1993: 121). Furthermore, a number of industries, notably steel and coal, were the subject of systematic rationalisation programmes (Pendleton and Winterton, 1993: 233).

In some of the former public enterprises, such as British Gas, staffing levels continued to fall following privatisation, whilst in other industries, employment levels stabilised, or indeed increased, following their transfer to the private sector. Such was the case at British Steel and British

Telecom respectively (Bishop and Thompson, 1993: 25). These post-privatisation developments arguably reflect the responses of individual companies to the tensions between quality of service issues and the need to cut costs, which was anticipated by Ferner and Colling (1991). However, they also indicate that optimum labour requirements were established within most of the former public enterprises before, rather than after, privatisation (Pendleton and Winterton, 1993: 240).

As mentioned earlier, changes in working practices designed to increase labour productivity have also been introduced in many of the former public enterprises. Empirical studies have highlighted how an increasing emphasis has been placed on labour flexibility in a number of these concerns, and how the employment of non-standard and sub-contract labour has grown, especially in new and subsidiary areas of business (Blyton, 1992; Colling, 1991; O'Connell Davidson, 1990; 1991; Ogden, 1994).

In the coal industry in recent years changes to working practices have similarly focused on increased flexibility. The 1986 Wheeler Plan advocated the introduction of flexible working as a means of achieving cost objectives determined by management following the 1984-85 strike, and though most emphasis has been placed on temporal flexibility, in order that productivity improvements could be made by increasing machine running time, functional and numerical flexibility has also been pursued, if to a lesser extent (Winterton, 1991).

In many former public enterprises changes in working practices were introduced in the years preceding privatisation. In some, however, the pressure for change has intensified since floatation (Ogden, 1993b: 159-160; 1994: 74), especially since some companies have used the threat of replacing direct labour with outside contractors in order to accelerate change (O'Connell Davidson, 1991: 251).

Changes to working practices were closely linked to reductions in staffing levels since, as Blyton has pointed out, the objective of the introduction of labour flexibility was to enable companies to meet the shortfall arising from this (Blyton, 1992: 646). Indeed changes in working practices have consequently resulted in an intensification of work in a number of the former public enterprises (Nichols and O'Connell Davidson, 1993: 721; O'Connell Davidson, 1990: 545).

Many of the former public enterprises now exhibit much higher levels of organisational de-centralisation than was the case when they were under state control. In some industries such as steel and electricity, moves to establish less centralised business structures, and to devolve managerial decision making to lower levels were initiated prior to privatisation (Blyton, 1992: 640; Colling, 1991: 122). Privatisation however, resulted in the former public enterprises being exposed to a more competitive environment. It therefore provided a strong impulse for de-centralisation, because de-centralised business structures and devolved managerial authority were considered to be more appropriate than the bureaucratic, centralised structures of the public sector in such a climate (Colling and Ferner, 1992: 211). Moreover, the adoption of de-centralised business structures was seen to be of symbolic importance in marking the end of state ownership (Colling and Ferner, 1992). In addition, the privatisations of water, electricity, buses and the docks resulted in the dismemberment of those industries, and in the establishment of a number of separate businesses (Pendleton and Winterton, 1993: 236), thus giving an added fillip to the pressures favouring de-centralisation.

To a large extent organisational de-centralisation was accompanied by the de-centralisation of industrial relations within many of the former public enterprises. The Conservative governments encouraged management in the former public enterprises to de-centralise pay bargaining (Ogden, 1993a: 46; *IRRR*, 1989a: 14), and some enterprises sought to bring industrial relations structures in line with new organisational structures (Pendleton and Winterton, 1993: 236). Modest steps were taken towards the de-centralisation of bargaining in steel and water in the years before privatisation (Avis, 1990; Blyton, 1992; 1993; Ogden, 1993a; 1994), and in coal, although managerial strategies here were designed to undermine the influence of the NUM (discussed previously in Chapter Two). Privatisation nevertheless provided a major stimulus for a shift in the locus of industrial relations in the former public enterprises.

Privatisation was seen by management in many of the former public enterprises as an opportunity to break with the formalised industry wide bargaining machinery of the public sector past (Ferner and Colling, 1993: 121), and to link bargaining instead to the business performance of individual operating units (Ogden, 1993a: 46). The break up of a number of nationalised industries following privatisation moreover, facilitated the abandonment of industry wide bargaining, and indeed in those industries single employer bargaining has replaced national bargaining (Pendleton

51

and Winterton, 1993: 236). In addition, individual contracts were introduced for managerial grades in several of the former public enterprises following privatisation, including gas and telecommunications (*IRRR*, 1989a: 12 and 14), and electricity (Ferner and Colling, 1993: 123), which has served to both de-centralise and de-collectivise bargaining at that level.

The enthusiasm with which management in the former public enterprises moved to change the locus of industrial relations has varied considerably however, both between, and indeed within, industries. Thus whilst patterns of industrial relations in British Gas exhibited much continuity, with 'no change in the company's bargaining structure since privatisation' (*IRRR*, 1989a: 14), in electricity, concerted efforts were made to de-centralise bargaining following privatisation (Colling, 1991: 125), although some managers questioned the wisdom of such developments (Ferner and Colling, 1993: 124). Similarly in water, the water authorities were divided over whether to abandon or retain national bargaining, although the former option eventually prevailed (Ogden, 1993a).

Significant changes have also taken place in managerial industrial relations strategies within many of the former public enterprises. Successive Conservative governments encouraged managers in both public and private sector companies to re-assert managerial prerogatives, and to adopt less conciliatory approaches in relation to trade unions, and unitary approaches to industrial relations certainly became more common amongst management in the former public enterprises during the years of Conservative rule. There was however considerable variation in how zealously managerial prerogatives were re-established, and whilst confrontational management styles were readily adopted in coal (Winterton and Winterton, 1993a), steel (Blyton, 1993), and on the docks (Turnbull, 1993), in other industries such as electricity and gas, more consensual approaches have generally prevailed (Ferner and Colling, 1993; *IRRR*, 1989a).

Pendleton and Winterton have suggested that such variations can be partly explained by the industrial relations traditions of particular industries. Thus those industries where 'macho management' styles were adopted, were those which already had long histories of relatively bitter industrial conflict (Pendleton and Winterton, 1993: 238), and indeed, in coal, steel and on the docks, the re-assertion of managerial prerogatives occurred in the wake of unsuccessful national strike action. They also argue however, that government industrial relations policies have been contradictory, and that managerial caution has been urged, notably in electricity, when this has been politically expedient (Pendleton and Winterton, 1993).

In many cases changes in managerial approaches to industrial relations in the former public enterprises were discernible long before privatisation. The environment created by privatisation nevertheless gave added impetus to the re-assertion of managerial prerogatives in some industries. Thus in electricity 'there was a strong perception that the transfer to the private sector opened a "window of opportunity" for competent aggressive management' (Colling, 1991: 122), and indeed, following floatation consultations with the unions occurred less frequently (Colling 1991). Similarly in water, the introduction of single table bargaining by a number of the new plcs was accompanied by the effective de-recognition of several trade unions (Ogden, 1993b: 162), and union de-recognition generally became more common in the water industry following privatisation (Saunders and Harris, 1994: 113). Furthermore, in enterprises such as British Telecom and a number of the water companies, which took the opportunity presented by privatisation to diversify into other areas of business, recognition has not been granted in subsidiary activities (Ogden, 1994: 76-77; *IRRR*, 1989a: 13), thus enabling the emergence of the two tier pattern of industrial relations anticipated by Ferner and Colling (1991).

In addition to these developments however, privatisation has also enabled significant variations in management industrial relations strategies to emerge within individual industries. Thus whilst management in some of the new water companies have sought to marginalise the influence of trade unions, and to unilaterally impose changes to bargaining arrangements, in other companies, management have endeavoured to involve the unions in the process of change (Ogden, 1994).

Although widespread change is clearly discernible in patterns of industrial relations in the former public enterprises, a number of commentators have suggested that attributing this to privatisation is somewhat problematic. Ferner and Colling (1991) have argued that this is firstly because those changes which have occurred have not been universal, secondly, because changes in industrial relations practices have not been confined to privatised companies, and thirdly, because those changes which followed privatisation were not necessarily caused by this. Pendleton and Winterton (1993), similarly suggest that the influence of privatisation should not be overstated, because factors which promoted continuity in industrial relations practices were also in operation during the privatisation process, and also, because many of the changes which did occur, pre-dated privatisation, often by many years.

The studies of industrial relations in the former public enterprises which were considered earlier tend to support many of these points. They have revealed that there has been much variation in the nature and pace of change, both between and within the privatised industries, and that privatisation was but one of a number of factors which contributed to this. They have also demonstrated that pressures for continuity have existed alongside pressures for change, and have thus lent weight to the argument advanced by Ferner and Colling (1991), which maintained that privatisation was likely to have an ambiguous influence on industrial relations.

Studies of the former public enterprises have also shown that changes in industrial relations practices within those concerns were often visible long before privatisation. Such change however, cannot be divorced from privatisation itself, since government plans to sell off particular industries were announced, in most cases, several years before privatisation occurred, and were often tacitly acknowledged, as in the case of the coal industry, prior to this information being made public. Management in the former public enterprises consequently had a number of years in which to prepare their industries for operation in the private sector. Privatisation therefore, arguably represents a relatively long process of transition, with the actual transfer of ownership marking the mid point, rather than the beginning of this.

3.5 Focus of the Research

The theoretical perspectives contained within the existing body of literature relating to industrial relations in the privatised industries, have facilitated the development of a number of hypotheses regarding the possible influence of privatisation upon industrial relations in the coal industry. Underpinning each of these hypotheses are a number of more focused sub-propositions, which relate to particular aspects of industrial relations, such as managerial strategies, the role of the unions, collective bargaining and the labour process. It is these propositions which will form the focus of the research, since an analysis of how specific facets of industrial relations in the coal industry have developed following privatisation, will enable the broader hypotheses relating to the influence of privatisation upon patterns of industrial relations in the industry to be addressed also.

One hypothesis which may be posed following a review of the relevant literature, is that the privatisation of the coal industry may be beneficial to organised labour within the industry. This is because private ownership might precipitate changes in the existing pattern of industrial relations, by facilitating the emergence of relationships between management and the trade unions which are less conflictual than was the case between 1984 and 1994. This hypothesis then, accepts the position taken by the optimists. In order for more conciliatory industrial relations to develop however, changes would need to occur in managerial industrial relations strategies, the role of the unions and in the institutions of collective bargaining. Change would possibly also be visible within the labour process. A number of sub-propositions can therefore be made concerning each of these particular aspects of industrial relations, which buttress the broader hypothesis.

It could thus be proposed, that changes in managerial industrial relations strategies following privatisation might include the abandonment of the unitary approach which prevailed during the last decade of state ownership. This could be replaced by a pluralist or collaborative approach, in which management would seek to involve rather than marginalise the unions. Furthermore, management may seek to re-establish collective bargaining in the industry.

It might also be expected, given changing managerial strategies, that there would be a corresponding change in the role of the unions after privatisation. Thus all the mining unions might expect to have the same relationship with any given company within the industry, and no union would be favoured by any one company. The re-establishment of collective bargaining would also increase the influence of all the unions in relation to the determination of pay and conditions of work. A further proposition might be that the role of the unions at local level might expand under private ownership, and both the strategic position and influence of workplace branches would be enhanced, since the fragmentation of the industry resulting from privatisation would increase the importance of local bargaining.

Although industry wide bargaining would not be possible after privatisation, given the break up of the industry, it may be that new institutions of collective bargaining will emerge, which would facilitate the establishment of company wide bargaining. Similarly, company wide conciliation procedures might be introduced following privatisation.

In relation to the labour process, it might be proposed that management would recognise the negative health and safety implications of flexibility and work intensification. Under such circumstances management would perhaps seek more sophisticated methods of increasing productivity, and would thus not seek to extend new working arrangements.

An alternative hypothesis which could be presented rejects the view of the optimists, and suggests instead that privatisation may be detrimental to organised labour, because it could result in continuity with the patterns of industrial relations established since 1984. For continuity with the existing patterns of industrial relations to be evident however, changes in managerial strategies, the role of the unions, the institutions of collective bargaining and the labour process, would be negligible. The pessimistic hypothesis is therefore similarly underpinned by a number of sub-propositions relating to these issues.

It could be proposed in support of the pessimistic hypothesis, that managerial industrial relations strategies following privatisation might be centred on the maintenance of managerial prerogatives, and on the continued marginalisation of the unions. It might also be expected that management would continue to employ policies aimed at creating division in the workforce, and a culture of individualism amongst employees.

Given such managerial strategies, it may also be proposed that, following privatisation, the union considered by management to be most likely to comply with corporate objectives, might be accorded greater recognition than the other unions, which would continue to be marginalised. In this scenario, moreover, the increased importance of local bargaining would arguably not be accompanied by a corresponding increase in the influence of the unions at local level, and indeed, branch organisation would remain largely ineffective.

The continued emphasis on the maintenance of managerial prerogatives, may indicate that institutional structures to support collective bargaining would be unlikely to emerge after privatisation, and that bargaining would instead take place on an ad hoc basis at local level. Wage structures might come to reflect this, with pay being increasingly linked to individual performance.

It might also be expected that management would seek to extend new working practices, if the pursuit of profit came to be the main determinant of business strategy following privatisation. Similarly, management might adopt additional measures in order to further improve productivity by reducing the porosity of the working day.

The development of industrial relations in the coal industry following privatisation may, alternatively, be more complex than either the optimistic or pessimistic hypotheses suggest. Privatisation has resulted in the fragmentation of the industry, which instead of having one owner, as was the case when it was under state control, is now owned by a number of separate companies. It is possible therefore, that differing patterns of industrial relations might develop within the industry, which reflect the emergence of multiple ownership. Thus industrial relations within some companies might come to be characterised by continuity with the patterns established between 1984 and 1994, whilst in others, significant change might be apparent.

The coal companies which emerged as a result of privatisation have the same product, and are subject largely to the same market pressures, however, the origins and corporate objectives of these companies are markedly different. RJB is the most commercially orientated of the companies, having operated for some years in the private opencast sector, whilst Coal Investments, and those companies formed as a result of management buyout initiatives retain elements of the public sector tradition, as many of these companies' senior managers formerly held positions within British Coal. By contrast Goitre Tower Anthracite is under co-operative ownership, and a number of former NUM branch officials are now part of the senior management team. Significant variation therefore may be visible in the managerial industrial relations strategies of the different companies, which might be expected to be reflected in the development of industrial relations within each company.

Figure 3.1 A typology of industrial relations in the privatised coal industry

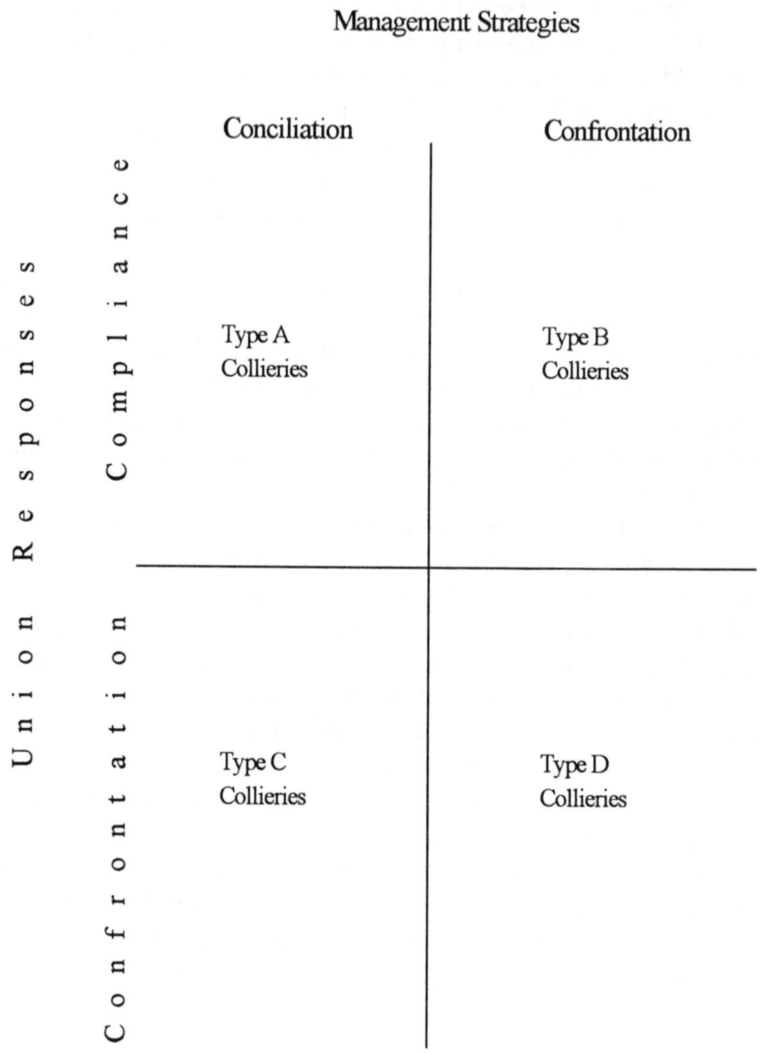

Management Strategies

	Conciliation	Confrontation
Compliance	Type A Collieries	Type B Collieries
Confrontation	Type C Collieries	Type D Collieries

Union Responses

The traditions of the major unions representing workers in the new coal companies are also somewhat different. The UDM has, since its foundation in 1985, demonstrated its willingness to comply with managerial objectives. The NUM by contrast, has remained unwilling to assume such a position, although the union is divided between those who wish to adopt a confrontational approach to managerial strategies, and those who favour a greater degree of pragmatism (discussed previously in Chapter Two). Differences might therefore be expected in the responses of the various unions to managerial strategies which develop in the wake of privatisation, which may also influence emergent patterns of industrial relations in the industry. The coalfields which have remained in production following restructuring are characterised by differing industrial relations traditions, which reflect historical developments, and which overlap with the positions of the unions to a large degree. Thus Nottinghamshire, the stronghold of the UDM has enjoyed relatively tranquil industrial relations, whilst Yorkshire, South Wales and Scotland, bastions of NUM support have experienced bitter and conflictual industrial relations in recent years. These variations in coalfield industrial relations traditions then, might similarly exert an influence over patterns of industrial relations in the privatised coal industry.

The possible consequences of the interaction of the variables discussed above, may perhaps be best expressed the model outlined in figure 3.3   This model anticipates that continuity with the patterns of industrial relations established during the final decade of public ownership will be most likely to occurr at Type D collieries, where both management and the trade unions have adopted a confrontational approach to labour relations.   By contrast, the model expects that change, manifest in the establishment of more consensual relationships between management and the trade unions would be more likely to emerge at Type A collieries.

The empirical research which will form the basis for the remainder of this study will test the hypotheses presented above. Managerial industrial relations strategies, the role, and responses of the unions, the development of the institutions of collective bargaining and changes in the labour process, will thus be closely examined, in order that the emergent patterns of industrial relations in the coal industry can be analysed, and the implications for organised labour assessed. The following chapter will consequently consider the methodological approach which will best facilitate these objectives.

4 Methodology

4.1 The Case Study Approach

As Yin (1994) has pointed out, the selection of a methodological approach for any given research project is dependent, firstly upon the nature of the research question, that is, upon whether the study is descriptive, exploratory or explanatory in character, secondly, upon the degree of control the researcher has over the behaviour of actors, and thirdly, upon whether historical or contemporary events constitute the focus of the research. A research project which seeks to examine and account for the development of patterns of industrial relations in the coal industry following privatisation, clearly has both exploratory and explanatory elements. It is also obviously focused on contemporary events over which the researcher has no control. In such circumstances, case study methodology has a number of specific features which make it a particularly appropriate approach for the prosecution of such a study.

The case study approach facilitates the investigation of contemporary phenomena within their real life context, and is therefore especially useful when the boundaries between phenomena and context are relatively indistinct (Yin, ibid). These are important considerations in relation to a study of industrial relations in the privatised coal industry, since the phenomenon to be examined, namely the emergent patterns of industrial relations cannot be divorced from its contextual conditions, these being the patterns of ownership which emerged in the industry after privatisation, the nature of labour representation in the industry, and the accumulated industrial relations traditions of the surviving coalfields.

Case study methodology moreover, offers 'the strengths of experimental research within natural settings' (Hakim, 1987b: 61), because it permits the isolation of selected contextual conditions, thus enabling relationships between those conditions and the phenomenon under study to be explored and accounted for. Case studies, unlike experiments, do not seek to divorce phenomenon and context (Yin, 1982: 52). The similarities that case study methodology has with experimental research however, make it a particularly useful approach when the researcher has no control over events, nor over the behaviour of actors within the field of study, since it enables the same phenomenon to be examined under different conditions. Thus the researcher is able to allow for contextual factors which may influence the phenomenon under study (Mitchell, 1983: 192).

The careful selection of cases for a study of the development of industrial relations in the privatised coal industry then, would enable the emergent patterns to be considered, and the influence of differing forms of ownership, differing forms of trade union representation, and the different industrial relations traditions of individual coalfields upon these patterns to be analysed. Similarly, thoughtful case selection would facilitate the testing of the hypotheses outlined at the end of Chapter Three, which relate to the nature of the relationship between the development of industrial relations in the coal industry following privatisation, and the context in which this occurs.

Despite the benefits afforded by case study methodology to particular types of research, this approach has nevertheless been the subject of serious criticism.

It has been suggested that case study methodology does not have an inbuilt corrective against researcher bias, and that as a consequence the approach lacks rigour. Indeed it is claimed that because of this, the internal validity and reliability of case study research is questionable (Stoecker, 1991: 91). Whilst it may be true, as Yin (1994) has pointed out, that no research strategy can completely guarantee against bias, the problem of researcher bias within case study research, and the attendant threat to internal validity can be countered by the use of multiple sources of evidence. Case study research is, indeed, uniquely able to facilitate this, for unlike other methodologies which are oriented towards the use of a single source of evidence (Yin, 1982: 85-86), 'the fieldwork for case studies may incorporate the analysis of administrative records and other documents, depth interviews, larger scale structured surveys, participant and non-participant observation and collecting virtually any type of evidence that is relevant and available' (Hakim, 1987b: 63). The internal validity of case studies can also be buttressed by having the draft case study report reviewed by the subject of the research (Yin, 1994: 144-146).

Research into the development of patterns of industrial relations in the privatised coal industry then, could employ depth interviews with both managerial and trade union representatives, in order to elicit high quality data, in addition to a large scale workforce survey designed to generate a larger volume of lower level data. Documentary evidence could also be examined. This strategy could be adopted, in the knowledge that 'when we find the same results through different methods we can be much more confident of our results' (Stoecker, 1991: 106). Alternatively however, this approach could illuminate differing perspectives and viewpoints held by the various actors in the industry, which would then have to be accounted for. Key respondents furthermore, could be asked to review the draft case reports.

The problem of establishing reliability, which is also associated with case study research can similarly be overcome. The use of a well designed case study protocol ensures that fieldwork procedures are consistent, this being of particular importance in relation to multiple case designs, and thus guards against the possibility of errors and bias entering the research (Yin, 1994). Similarly, the systematic and methodical documentation of fieldwork procedures ensures that the research can be replicated by a later investigator, who is likely to arrive at the same findings as a result (Yin, ibid).

Another criticism which has been levelled at case study research is that the findings of such projects cannot be generalised to wider populations, and that as such, there is no assurance of external validity (Stoecker, 1991: 91). Such arguments are based upon 'the common assumption that the only valid basis of inference is that which has been developed in relation to statistical analysis' (Mitchell, 1983: 197). Case study methodology however, has a different rationale to that of quantitative research, since cases are selected on theoretical grounds rather than because they are representative. Thus, 'cases may be chosen to replicate previous cases or extend emergent theory, or they may be chosen to fill theoretical categories and provide examples of polar types' (Eisenhardt, 1989: 539). Moreover, irrespective of whether cases are selected in order to achieve literal or theoretical replication, the researcher would be seeking to generalise his or her findings to some broader theory rather than to some wider population (Yin, 1994: 36), and because of this, any inferences subsequently made about wider populations would be 'based on the validity of the analysis rather than the representativeness of the events' (Mitchell, 1983: 190).

Case study research also stands accused of being a time consuming and cumbersome process, which generates voluminous quantities of impenetrable data. As Yin (1994) has suggested however, the timetable and prosecution of any case study will be influenced by the research strategies employed. Thus, whilst case studies utilising an ethnographic or anthropological approach may require lengthy periods of fieldwork, this is less likely to be the case with other research strategies. Case study research into the development of industrial relations in the coal industry following privatisation, which sought to make use of depth interviews with key respondents, workforce surveys and documentary evidence, would arguably fall into the latter of these categories.

4.2 Case Selection

In case study research, the unit of analysis has to be established before cases can be selected for study. With regards to research into the development of industrial relations in the coal industry following privatisation, a number of considerations led to the colliery being identified as the most suitable unit of analysis.

The privatisation of coal resulted in the fragmentation of the industry, and in the emergence of a number of separate coal companies. The coal industry then, cannot now be considered as a single entity, and the choice of the unit of analysis had to take this into account. These considerations therefore precluded the selection of the industry as the unit of analysis.

Recent literature has revealed that organisational de-centralisation, and the de-centralisation of industrial relations often accompanied privatisation (discussed previously in Chapter Three). It is possible therefore, that change, or indeed continuity, in the patterns of industrial relations in the coal industry would be more readily discernible at local, that is colliery, rather than corporate level. Indeed in the case of individual collieries acquired by management or employee buyout teams, such developments would only be visible at colliery level.

The selection of the colliery as the unit of analysis also permits the isolation of a greater number of contextual variables than would be the case if the company was selected for this purpose. Implicitly then, the selection of the colliery as the unit of analysis, was accompanied by the decision to adopt a multiple case design, in order that the emergent patterns of industrial relations in the privatised coal industry could be examined under different contextual conditions.

Having selected the colliery as the unit of analysis, cases were selected in order that theoretical replication could be achieved. Collieries were selected for study therefore, not because they were representative of other collieries, or of the industry as a whole, but rather, because they corresponded to the theoretical categories identified in the model presented at the end of Chapter Three.

In the initial selection of cases, two collieries owned by Coal UK (CUK), a large corporate enterprise were chosen for study (Table 4.1). Dearnley colliery, which supplies coal to the electricity supply industry was closed by British Coal following the 1992 coal crisis, when the entire workforce was made redundant. It was acquired by CUK under the lease/licence arrangements, and was returned to production in March 1994. Dearnley is located in the traditionally militant Yorkshire coalfield, and the workforce is represented by the NUM. Dearnley consequently conforms to the theoretical type D colliery identified in the model. Nottston colliery, like Dearnley also produces coal for the electricity supply industry. Unlike Dearnley, however, Nottston was not closed by British Coal, and remained in production throughout the privatisation process. Nottston is situated in the more moderate Nottinghamshire coalfield, and the UDM is the majority union. This colliery then, conforms to the theoretical type B colliery.

Two collieries owned by English Coal, a management buyout which acquired a number of the mines formerly owned by British Coal, were also selected for study. Wakeford colliery, which supplied coal to the electricity supply industry is located in the Yorkshire coalfield. The NUM is the majority union, and the mine therefore corresponds to the theoretical type C colliery. Workham colliery similarly produces coal for the electricity market. This mine was closed by British Coal in April 1994, when the entire workforce was made redundant. The mine was acquired by English Coal under the lease/licence arrangements however, and returned to production in April 1995. Workham is situated in Nottinghamshire, and the majority of the workforce are represented by the UDM. Workham then, conforms to the theoretical type A colliery.

Table 4.1 Summary of preliminary case selection

Colliery	Ownership form	Location	Union	TUPE	Workforce	Product market	Period of closure
Dearnley	large enterprise	Yorks	NUM	no	320	ESI	Oct 92 - Mar 94
Nottston	large enterprise	Notts	UDM	yes	600	ESI	never closed
Wakeford	management buyout	Yorks	NUM	no	data unavailable	data unavailable	data unavailable
Workham	management buyout	Notts	UDM	no*	600	ESI	Apr 94 - Apr 95
Cwmpridd	co-operative	South Wales	NUM	no	280	Domestic/ industrial	Apr 94 - Dec 94

* Although Workham colliery was subject to the provisions of TUPE when it was acquired by EM after the collapse of EC, these regulations did not apply when EC purchased the colliery in the first instance.

Cwmpridd colliery, an NUM stronghold located in the traditionally militant South Wales coalfield was also selected for study. Cwmpridd, which supplies high quality anthracite to domestic markets and local steelworks, was closed by British Coal in April 1994, and the workforce was made redundant at this time. In December 1994, however, the mine was purchased by Welsh Anthracite (WA), a company formed by an employee buyout team. Because this colliery is co-operatively owned, the relationship between management and the unions is radically different from that at other mines selected as cases. Cwmpridd, then, also conforms to the theoretical type A colliery identified in the model. It was not included in the study in order to facilitate literal replication however, but for its atypicality, since the reasons for it corresponding to this theoretical category are somewhat different to those associated with Workham.

The selection of cases outlined above, would enable different combinations of ownership, trade union representation and coalfield industrial relations traditions to be considered, thus facilitating the analysis of the relationships between these factors and the emergent patterns of industrial relations in the industry.

The selection of Dearnley and Nottston as cases for study, would moreover, also permit the implications of the legal framework surrounding privatisation to be considered, and any influence that this factor might have had on the development of labour relations within the industry to be analysed. For whilst both Dearnley and Nottston were acquired by the same company, Nottston was purchased as a going concern as part of privatisation proper, and was therefore subject to the Transfer of Undertakings (Protection of Employment) Regulations 1981 (TUPE). Dearnley, however, was not subject to this legislation, since this mine was acquired by CUK under the lease/licence arrangements having been closed by British Coal.

CUK was the only coal company which acquired collieries which were subject to the TUPE regulations as well as mines where this legislation did not apply. The legal framework was therefore more likely to influence industrial relations developments at collieries owned by CUK than at collieries owned by other companies, and because of this, no allowance was made for this factor when selecting collieries for study which were owned by companies other than CUK.

Developments in the industry prior to the commencement of fieldwork, prompted a review of the selection of cases however. The collapse of English Coal in February 1996 placed doubt over the long term future of the mines owned by the company, and as a consequence the substitution of other collieries in place of Wakeford and Workham had to be considered.

After a period of uncertainty, the future of Workham was assured, when a management buyout team acquired this colliery, and another, in the process of establishing a new company, which was named English Mining (EM). The change of ownership at Workham did not, however, result in the emergence of a different form of ownership, since former British Coal employees were included in the senior management team of English Mining, as had been the case at English Coal. Workham therefore continued to conform to the theoretical type A colliery identified in the model, and for this reason the decision was taken to retain the mine as a case for study (Table 4.2).

The situation at Wakeford, the second mine owned by English Coal which was selected for study was somewhat different from that at Workham. Like Workham, Wakeford was offered for sale following the collapse of English Coal, however potential buyers were slow to come forward. An eleventh hour rescue package mounted by the colliery manager in August 1996 ultimately failed, and the mine closed in September 1996 as a result. Another mine had to be chosen for study therefore, which would conform to the theoretical type C colliery, and which could consequently be substituted for Wakeford as a case for study.

In terms of ownership, trade union representation and coalfield location, Abergoed closely resembles Wakeford, and thus constitutes a suitable replacement case, although this colliery produces high quality anthracite for the domestic market, rather than for the electricity supply industry. Abergoed was closed by British Coal in January 1993, when all the workers were made redundant. It was later acquired by Anthracite Cymru (AC), a company which was formed as a result of a management buyout initiative, and was re-opened in April 1994. Abergoed is situated in the South Wales coalfield where industrial relations have traditionally been adversarial in character, and the NUM has customarily represented workers at the mine. Abergoed then conforms to the theoretical type C colliery, and this colliery was consequently selected as a replacement for Wakeford.

Table 4.2 Summary of revised case selection

Colliery	Ownership form	Location	Union	TUPE	Workforce	Product market	Period of closure
Dearnley	large enterprise	Yorks	NUM	no	320	ESI	Oct 92 - Mar 94
Nottston	large enterprise	Notts	UDM	yes	600	ESI	never closed
Abergoed	management buyout	South Wales	NUM	no	117	domestic/ industrial	Jan 93 - Apr 94
Workham	management buyout	Notts	UDM	no*	600	ESI	Apr 94 - Apr 95
Cwmpridd	co-operative	South Wales	NUM	no	280	domestic/ industrial	Apr 94 - Dec 94

* Although Workham colliery was subject to the provisions of TUPE when it was acquired by EM after the collapse of EC, these regulations did not apply when EC purchased the colliery in the first instance.

As with all case study research, the selection of cases outlined above represented a compromise between the ideal study, and a study that was feasible to undertake given the twin limitations of time and resources. The study could arguably have been improved by the inclusion of a number of cases which would have allowed for literal replication, in addition to theoretical replication. For literal replication however, a minimum of four additional collieries, one corresponding to each of the theoretical categories A, B, C and D, would have had to have been selected as cases. This though, would have raised the total number of cases to nine, thus placing the study beyond the capabilities of a single researcher.

4.3 Operationalisation of the Research

In order to collect data with which to address the hypotheses presented at the end of Chapter Three, it was decided to conduct depth interviews with representatives of both management and the trade unions, at each of the collieries selected for study. From the management side, interviews were sought with colliery managers, personnel managers, where this function existed, and with the site managers of sub contracting firms operating at the collieries, whilst from the trade union side, interviews were sought with representatives of the NUM, UDM and NACODS. Interviews were also sought with representatives of BACM, however, it was decided to approach national officials rather than colliery representatives in the case of this organisation, since BACM members at colliery level would hold management positions, and their responses would possibly be coloured by this.

The purpose of the interviews was to elicit high quality, detailed information about management industrial relations strategies, and the responses of the various unions to these, in addition to data relating to any developments regarding the institutions of collective bargaining, and any changes in the labour process, at each of the collieries under study. To facilitate this, two complementary interview schedules were designed, one for use with management representatives, the other for trade union officials, in order to ensure that each set of interviews conformed to a standardised format, thus buttressing the construct validity and reliability of the research. The interview schedules for use with management and trade union representatives are reproduced in Appendix A and Appendix B respectively.

Drafts of both interview schedules prepared in advance of the pilot study contained initial sections which related to the labour process. Questions in these sections consequently sought to establish to what extent numerical, temporal, and functional flexibility had been adopted at the collieries under study, and whether there had been any change in the intensity of work, and in the way in which miners were supervised since privatisation. A number of questions in the these sections sought additionally to examine the degree of workforce fragmentation at the collieries under study. These questions consequently sought information concerning the extent of sub contracting, and the level of unionisation, and, by implication, the level of non unionism also. Other questions relating to the labour process sought to determine whether or not the different companies operating at the five collieries offered standardised terms and conditions to their employees, and whether or not there had been any change in health and safety standards since privatisation.

Both interview schedules also contained sections concerning managerial industrial relations strategies. Initial questions in these sections sought to establish whether or not recognition was granted to all, or indeed to any, of the unions operating at the collieries under study, and what form recognition took if this was the case. A number of questions however, anticipated the possibility that only one union would be recognised, or that one union would be given preferential treatment. These questions consequently sought to establish whether or not this situation had arisen, and if so, which unions were involved, what form preferential treatment took, and why those particular unions were favoured by management. Another group of questions took into account the possibility of the unions being refused recognition. These questions thus sought to ascertain the strategies of the unions in the event of such developments, and the reasons for de-recognition where this had occurred. Other questions relating to management strategies aimed to assess the extent to which managerial prerogatives were being enforced, and whether or not management was pursuing policies designed to marginalise the unions.

A section on the role and responses of the unions was also included in both interview schedules. Questions in these sections sought to establish whether there had been any change in the main locus of bargaining since privatisation, or in the range of issues dealt with by local trade union representatives. A number of questions also aimed to examine whether there had been any change in the degree or locus of union influence

71

following the return of private ownership. Other questions in these sections sought to establish whether or not the unions had been able to take advantage of the changed environment which resulted from privatisation, and whether there was any variation in the responses of the unions to management strategies.

In both interview schedules, the final sections were concerned with the institutions of collective bargaining at the collieries under study. Questions in these sections therefore sought to ascertain whether or not new institutions of collective bargaining had been established, and, if so, whether the unions had been involved in their construction. In anticipation of the possible absence of formal bargaining machinery however, one question in each schedule sought to examine how disputes were resolved in these circumstances. Other questions in these sections sought to determine whether or not company wide bargaining had been adopted in the industry, or, conversely, whether industrial relations had been de-collectivised to any great extent at colliery level.

In addition to conducting interviews with management and trade union representatives, it was also decided to undertake a large scale workforce survey at each of the collieries under study. The object of the surveys was to gather a large volume of lower level data relating to how management industrial relations strategies, the role of the unions, and developments in relation to institutions of collective bargaining, and the labour process, were perceived by the miners who worked at the five collieries.

A questionnaire was designed to facilitate the surveys. This duplicated many of the questions included in the interview schedules, although the wording of such questions was modified to reflect the fact that the questionnaire was designed to elicit information from individual respondents rather than from respondents representing organisations. An initial group of questions sought to establish the level of workforce fragmentation. It was also envisaged however, that cross referencing the responses to these questions with those to later questions, would illuminate whether or not particular groups of workers had been disproportionately affected by any emergent patterns in industrial relations. In addition, some of the questions required respondents to compare their experience of working for British Coal, with that of working for a private concern, the purpose of these particular questions being to analyse workforce perceptions of continuity and change. The questionnaire designed for use within the workforce survey is reproduced in Appendix C.

The primary concern in relation to the workforce questionnaire was ensuring a high response rate, and for this reason the questionnaire was reasonably short. In recognition of the relatively poor educational opportunities available to mining communities, questions were phrased in uncomplicated language, and the majority also offered a number of different answers to respondents. The strategy of utilising multiple choice questions was also adopted for ease of coding.

The strategy of gathering data from depth interviews with management and trade union representatives, and from large scale workforce surveys was designed to ensure that the attitudes and perceptions of all the actors in the industry were available for analysis. This use of multiple sources of evidence then, sought both to lessen the threat posed by researcher bias, and to bolster the internal validity of the research.

A pilot study was conducted at a colliery in Yorkshire, which was selected because of its location in the home town of the researcher. Several union officials at the colliery were known personally to the researcher, and obtaining their help and goodwill was therefore unproblematic. Pilot interviews were conducted with representatives of the NUM and NACODS at the colliery, and their responses were both frank and informative. The pilot interviews highlighted sensitivities which though obvious with hindsight, were nevertheless unforeseen in the first instance. As a result some changes were made both to the ordering and the phraseology of a number of questions on the trade union interview schedule. Pilot interviews were not conducted with management representatives, however, nor with UDM representatives, since there were no UDM members at the colliery concerned.

4.4 Access Issues

Had this research project been considered at any time between the end of the 1984-85 miners' strike, and the privatisation of the industry, problems relating to access would almost certainly have been encountered, because of the political sensitivities surrounding the industry at that time. Though such sensitivities have arguably declined since privatisation, it was nevertheless anticipated that gaining access would be problematic.

Unlike British Coal, which was the monopoly coal producer in the UK between 1947 and 1994, the companies which have emerged as a result of privatisation do not enjoy such a position. The possibility of some companies being reluctant to participate in the research due to sensitivities relating to market competition therefore had to be taken into account. Similarly it was acknowledged that companies might be hesitant to grant access, as the research involved gathering data from trade union representatives and workmen as well as from managerial representatives. In an attempt to overcome such problems, companies whose collieries had been selected for study were advised that all information would be treated in absolute confidence, and that the collieries selected for study would remain anonymous within the thesis. They were similarly informed that draft case reports would be available on request for validation with the respective respondents.

Because of the sensitivities surrounding industrial relations, particularly in relation to the issue of the legitimacy of managerial industrial relations strategies, the interview schedule designed for use with management representatives had to be carefully prepared. This was reflected in the ordering of the schedule, since it's initial section contained questions relating to continuity and change in the labour process, this being the least contentious area of the research. In addition, managerial terminology was utilised throughout the schedule, and questions relating to particularly sensitive issues were phrased in such a way as to decrease any misgivings. Such concerns were initially thought to be of less importance in relation to the interview schedule prepared for use with trade union officials, although it was recognised that gaining the trust of union officials was nevertheless a significant issue.

In the event, gaining access to the collieries owned by WA, AC and EM proved to be unproblematic, and chapters five six and seven, which follow, therefore comprise the findings of the holistic case studies which were undertaken at Cwmpridd, Abergoed and Workham collieries respectively.

CUK, by contrast, refused to grant access to their collieries. Whilst representatives of the company agreed that independent research would provide objective information which might be of use to the company, they stated that a number of internal research projects were currently being undertaken in similar areas, and that the proposed research would conflict with these. The company did however agree to grant access at group level.

4.5 A Review of Methodology

CUK's refusal to grant access at colliery level necessitated a review of methodology, since the decision of the company prevented interviews being conducted with management personnel at the collieries selected for study, moreover it also meant that the workforce questionnaire could not be utilised at collieries owned by the company. CUK's refusal to grant access at colliery level did not however, block access to the trade unions, since these bodies could be approached independently.

It was imperative that collieries owned by CUK were included in the study, since the company had emerged as the major player in the industry following privatisation. It was therefore decided to adopt an embedded case design for the study of this company, with the company itself forming one unit of analysis, whilst a second unit of analysis would be provided by a number of colliery level studies. Although it had initially been proposed to select two collieries owned by CUK for study, it was decided to increase the number of collieries studied to four in order that firstly, the influence of the legal framework could be fully examined in combination with each other variable which had been identified, and secondly, to compensate for the insufficiency of management respondents at colliery level.

Dearnley colliery had initially been selected as a CUK colliery for study because it was located in Yorkshire, was organised by the NUM, and was not subject to the provisions of TUPE. It was therefore decided to retain Dearnley within the study. It was however, necessary to choose another Yorkshire colliery organised by the NUM, which was, unlike Dearnley, subject to the provisions of TUPE. Donborough colliery, which supplies coal to the electricity supply industry was not closed by British Coal, and remained in production throughout the privatisation process. CUK therefore acquired Donborough as a going concern, and because of this the provisions of TUPE applied at the mine. This colliery was therefore chosen as an additional mine for study.

Nottston colliery had similarly been selected as a CUK colliery for study during the initial phase of case selection because it was located in Nottinghamshire, was organised by the UDM, and was subject to the provisions of TUPE. It was therefore decided to retain Nottston within the study, and to choose another Nottinghamshire mine organised by the UDM, which was, unlike Nottston, not subject to the provisions of TUPE. Mansthorpe colliery, which produces coal for the electricity market, was closed by British Coal in May 1993, when the entire workforce was made redundant. It was acquired by CUK under the lease/license arrangements, and was consequently not subject to the provisions of TUPE. This colliery was therefore chosen as an additional mine for study (Table 4.3).

In order to operationalise the CUK case study, it was decided to conduct interviews with corporate level managers, and with national and area union officials, so that information relating to developments in labour relations at corporate level could be gained. In addition, it was decided to utilise interviews with trade union branch officials in order to elicit information relating to developments at colliery level. The possibility of conducting focus group interviews with members of the workforce at each colliery selected for study, in order to gauge workforce perceptions of developments within the sphere of industrial relations was also considered. As such an approach would have been unauthorised by CUK, however, future research within the company could have been compromised. This strategy was therefore rejected.

No access problems were encountered when approaches were made to representatives of the mining unions in relation to the prosecution of the CUK case study. It was therefore possible to conduct the proposed research as planned, and the findings of the CUK case study comprise Chapter eight, which follows.

The review of methodology necessitated by the access problems associated with the CUK case resulted in the total number of collieries being selected for study rising from five to seven (Table 4.4). However, as workforce surveys were only to be conducted at four of the collieries chosen for study, it was believed that this increase in workload could neverthess be completed by a single researcher within the time available.

4.6 A Review of Fieldwork Procedures

Conducting depth interviews with management and trade union representatives at the three collieries which were the subject of holistic case studies proved to be unproblematic. Similarly, no problems were encountered in relation to conducting interviews with management within CUK, once the perametres of access had been established, nor with trade union representatives within that company.

Table 4.3 Summary of embedded units within CUK case

Colliery	Location	Union	TUPE	Workforce	Product market	Period of closure
Donborough	Yorkshire	NUM	yes	600	ESI	never closed
Dearnley	Yorkshire	NUM	no	320	ESI	Oct 92 - Mar 94
Nottston	Nottinghamshire	UDM	yes	600	ESI	never closed
Mansthorpe	Nottinghamshire	UDM	no	300	ESI	May 93 - Jan 94

By contrast, some difficulties were encountered in relation to the distribution of questionnaires at the three collieries where workforce surveys were conducted. At all three mines management were unwilling to release the names and addresses of members of the workforce. This made a postal questionnaire unfeasible, and other more unorthodox methods of distribution therefore had to be utilised.

At Abergoed, the colliery manager and representatives of all the recognised unions drew up a joint letter detailing the research, and explaining that the questionnaires would be analysed by a neutral academic researcher. The questionnaires, and pre- paid envelopes addressed to the researcher, supplied by management were then distributed to members of the workforce when they collected their wages. At Cwmpridd, the questionnaires were distributed, and collected by trade union representatives at the colliery, who then forwarded them to the researcher, whilst at Workham the questionnaires were distributed and collected by staff in the wages office, where they were collected by the researcher.

Such distribution strategies were obviously far from ideal, not least because at Cwmpridd and Workham distribution was incomplete. In addition, however, the principal of objective research was to some extent undermined at all three collieries. Such considerations were less significant at Abergoed, since the covering letter signed by members of management and the unions stressed that the questionnaire was to facilitate objective research, and the pre-paid envelopes supplied with the questionnaire ensured that confidentiality was maintained. The co-operation of management at Abergoed was dependent on them receiving the aggregate data from the questionnaires however, this presented no ethical questions for the researcher, since it had previously been agreed that the individual case report would be made available to respondents at the mine, in order that the research could be validated.

At Cwmpridd and Workham, however, considerations relating to objectivity were more significant, since the distribution strategies employed at theses mines could have given the impression that the research was being conducted on behalf of the trade unions and management respectively, even though this was not the case. Moreover because the completed questionnaires were collected at the workplace, respondents at these collieries did not have the same level of confidentiality as that afforded to respondents at Abergoed.

Table 4.4 Summary of final colliery selection

Colliery	Ownership form	Location	Union	TUPE	Workforce	Product market	Period of closure
Donborough	large enterprise	Yorkshire	NUM	yes	600	ESI	never closed
Dearnley	large enterprise	Yorkshire	NUM	no	320	ESI	Oct 92 - Mar 94
Nottston	large enterprise	Notts	UDM	yes	600	ESI	never closed
Mansthorpe	large enterprise	Notts	UDM	no	300	ESI	May 93 - Jan 94
Abergoed	mgt buyout	South Wales	NUM	no	117	domestic/industrial	Jan 93 - Apr 94
Workham	mgt buyout	Notts	UDM	no	600	ESI	Apr 94 - Apr 95
Cwmpridd	co-operative	South Wales	NUM	no	280	domestic/industrial	Apr 94 - Dec 94

The unorthodox methods of distribution are arguably reflected in the relatively low response rates at each of the collieries (Table 4.5), however considerations relating to objectivity and confidentiality might also explain why the response rates at Cwmpridd and Workham were lower than that obtained at Abergoed.

Table 4.5 Workforce survey response rates

Colliery	Response rate
Abergoed	48%
Cwmpridd	26%
Workham	18%

When access was being negotiated, it was agreed that copies of the relevant case reports would be forwarded on request to respondents, once these had been completed. Management respondents within CUK expressed no interest in the CUK case report, and did not request that copies of the report were forwarded to them. Because of this, the CUK case report was not made available to CUK management respondents. Copies of the report were, however, forwarded to each of the trade union branch officials involved in the CUK case, since these respondents expressed considerable interest in the findings of the research.

Copies of the Cwmpridd and Workham case reports were made available to the respective management and trade union respondents at each colliery, however the Abergoed case report was only made available to the colliery manager.   This was because this respondent, though wholly supportive of objective research, had made his co-operation conditional upon the report being made available to him alone.

4.7 Objectivity and Detachment

The researcher involved in the production of this work is a native of South Yorkshire, and has lived for the majority of her life in a small mining township within the county. Her partner is a former mineworker, and both were active participants in the 1984-85 strike. Because of this, the researcher came to this project with views sympathetic towards the NUM, and hostile towards the UDM. She was nevertheless acutely aware that her own sympathies could not be allowed to stand in the way of objective research, and therefore endeavoured to mentally detach her earlier experiences from current events, whilst continuing to bear in mind that the events of 1984-85 provided the context for much of what has followed. The researcher approached fieldwork in Nottinghamshire with some trepidation nevertheless. She met with no hostility from UDM respondents however, and discovered that there are some fine trade unionists at branch level in Nottinghamshire, who care deeply both about the future of the industry, and about those employed within it.

5 Cwmpridd Colliery

5.1 Introduction

Cwmpridd is located in what remains of the South Wales coalfield. The NUM has traditionally represented the miners at the collieries in South Wales, and the coalfield has a history of relatively bitter industrial relations. Cwmpridd itself is an NUM stronghold, like the other collieries in South Wales, indeed the Cwmpridd NUM lodge has customarily been controlled by the political left, and has, over the years, gained a reputation for militancy (Trade union representative).

When preparations were being made for the privatisation of the industry, Cwmpridd was initially classified by British Coal as a core colliery, however, British Coal later announced that the colliery was to close. The Cwmpridd lodge of the NUM mounted a campaign against the closure, but this was ultimately unsuccessful, and the mine ceased production in April 1994.

Following the closure of Cwmpridd, the Cwmpridd lodge of the NUM and two colleagues from the other mining unions represented at the mine, formed the Cwmpridd Employee Buyout Team (CEBOT), and initiated a bid to purchase the colliery. They were supported by over 200 former Cwmpridd employees, who each paid £8,000 of their redundancy money towards the bid. In October 1994, the government announced that CEBOT had been selected as the preferred bidder for the colliery, which was to be sold as an individual 'stand alone' unit, and in December 1994, Cwmpridd re-opened under co-operative ownership. The form of ownership which emerged at Cwmpridd as a result of privatisation then, is radically different to that at any of the other collieries which have survived restructuring. Several former union officials who were involved in CEBOT now hold senior management positions within the company, Welsh Anthracite (WA), which was established as part of the buyout bid. In addition, 80 per cent of the workforce are equal shareholders in Welsh Anthracite.

Cwmpridd represents something of an atypical case, because the co-operative ownership which has emerged at the colliery is so different to that at the other mines which have survived restructuring. Given the customary militancy of the NUM in South Wales, and the history and traditions of the coalfield, it might be anticipated that industrial relations at Cwmpridd would continue to be characterised by conflict. However, the possibility cannot be discounted that the relationship between management and the trade unions would reflect the nature of ownership at the colliery, and that this may facilitate the development of pluralistic patterns of industrial relations, or, alternatively, in the emergence of a shared unitary perpsective.

5.2 Management Strategies

The style of management which has emerged at Cwmpridd following its return to the private sector, is very different to that which prevailed in the last decade of public ownership. The unitary approach introduced unilaterally by British Coal management following the 1984-85 strike has been abandoned, and a more collaborative regime has been established at the colliery.

Managerial strategies are no longer centred upon the marginalisation of the unions. As a result, collective bargaining has been re-established at the colliery, and all the unions recognised by WA have full bargaining rights (Management representatives and trade union representatives). Moreover, WA stipulates that any contracting companies employed by them must also recognise and negotiate with the unions. As one trade union representative pointed out, 'The contractors would not have their contracts renewed if they blacked a union' (Trade union representative C). Indeed the Cwmpridd lodge of the NUM has a representative with special responsibilities for those employed by the contracting companies (Management representatives and trade union representatives). WA additionally provide office facilities, stationary and unlimited telephone access for all the recognised unions, and allow union officials time off with pay for union business (Management representatives and trade union representatives).

Changes in management style are also visible at Cwmpridd because the maintenance of managerial prerogatives no longer receives the same emphasis as was the case when British Coal owned the mine. Strategic decisions relating to the long term future of the colliery have to date been jointly made by management and the unions. The worker-shareholders who comprise 80 per cent of the workforce, however, have to ratify all major decisions, and indeed would be in a position to decide between competing strategies forwarded by management and the unions should this situation arise (Management representatives and trade union representatives).

The unions have no formal role in terms of the day to day running of the colliery, however, consultative meetings occur regularly, and are 'encouraged by the company' (Management representative B), and informal consultations take place 'on a daily basis' (Trade union representative A). In addition, trade union officials have unlimited access to management representatives, and do not have to wait for several days before discussions can take place with a senior manager, as was the case under British Coal procedure (Trade union representative).

Table 5.1 Which of the following best describes how decisions are made about the day to day running of your pit?

	%
Management impose their decisions without consulting the unions	10
Management consult the unions but still have the final say	41
Management and the unions come to joint decisions	47
No response	2

Source: workforce survey (n = 58).

The perceptions of the workforce confirm that the unions are involved in, rather than marginalised from, decisions relating to the running of the mine in spite of their lack of a formal role, as 47 per cent of respondents stated that management and the unions came to joint decisions about the running of the colliery, whilst a further 41 per cent stated that the unions were consulted (Table 5.1).

The perceptions of the workforce also confirm that the maintenance of managerial prerogatives is not the overriding priority for WA managers, since two thirds of respondents believed the managerial regime at the colliery to be firm but fair (Table 5.2).

Table 5.2 Which of the following terms best describes the overall attitude of management at your pit?

	%
Dictatorial	16
Hard line	5
Firm but fair	66
Relaxed	10
Easy going	0
No response	3

Source: workforce survey (n = 58).

Unlike their British Coal predecessors, management at WA have not endeavoured to foster division and individualism amongst the workforce in order to marginalise the unions; Indeed, one management representative described such tactics as 'taboo' (Management representative B). Management do communicate directly with members of the workforce on an individual basis, by way of newsletters, noticeboards and pit head briefings (Management representatives and trade union representatives). The rationale behind this strategy, however, is to remove the atmosphere of mistrust and suspicion created by the systematic use of misinformation by British Coal following the 1984-85 strike, and to create a culture of openness, because, as one management representative observed, 'Rumours are the worst thing in the world' (Management representative A).

Direct communication with individuals is therefore designed to augment rather than replace communication through collective channels, thus ensuring that the workforce is informed about the performance and prospects of the colliery, and indeed the new approach is welcomed by the unions: 'It's much better now. People are fully informed of what's happening' (Trade union representative C). Significantly however, communication is regarded as a two way process. One management representative commented that, 'Communication is also to get feedback from the men and improve innovation' (Management representative A). Members of the workforce are consequently encouraged to share their ideas for improving the performance of the colliery with management, this being indicative of the development of a more democratic management style at the colliery.

The management at WA have similarly demonstrated their support for collective representation by actively encouraging members of the workforce to join the appropriate trade union. As one management representative suggested, 'We have come from a unionised background, and encourage people to join the union for their own safety' (Management representative A). One trade union representative suggested that management policy relating to this issue had served to increase the membership of his particular organisation, and indeed, 96 per cent of respondents stated that they belonged to one of the unions recognised by WA (Table 5.3).

Table 5.3 Which union do you belong to?

	%
NUM	77
UDM	0
NACODS	12
BACM	7
Other	2
None	2
No response	0

Source: workforce survey (n = 58).

The changes in management style and strategy discernible at Cwmpridd, have been precipitated by privatisation, since this facilitated the establishment of co-operative ownership at the colliery, which was conducive to a democratic management style. The relationship between management and unions at the colliery has changed significantly as a result of this, since a number of former NUM lodge officials now hold senior management positions, and their approach towards the unions is coloured by their previous experience and ideological standpoint. Indeed one senior manager expressed the view that, 'You must put into practice what you've believed in all your life. There's no point otherwise' (Management representative A).

Another group of managers at Cwmpridd however, formerly held managerial positions within British Coal. As a result they subscribe to a different ideology, and indeed there is some suggestion that this group disapproves of the style of management established at the colliery, and would prefer to see managerial prerogatives restored. One trade union representative commented that, 'A small portion of the management resent information being available to the unions' (Trade union representative C), whilst another remarked, 'Sometimes they forget themselves. Three or four would like to squash us. They don't like the power we've got' (Trade union representative A). As this group is a minority within the management structure however, they are not in a position to exert significant influence on management styles. Indeed, one trade union representative observed, 'Their ideology hasn't changed, but they have to swallow it' (Trade union representative A).

The co-operative ownership established at Cwmpridd has also been reflected in the structure of WA, and this in itself has had implications for industrial relations at the colliery. Members of management, like members of the directly employed workforce are shareholders in WA. Each shareholder however, has shares of the same value, irrespective of their position in the company, or occupational grade, and as a consequence relations between management and the workforce are conducted on a more equal basis. The structure of WA then, has also served to constrain the industrial relations policies pursued by management, and has made the adoption of a unitary approach less tenable, since the worker-shareholders are also trade union members. As one management representative stated, 'It's very difficult to manage. A man can say to XX [the colliery manager]

"You can piss off! I've got £8,000 of shares same as you'" (Management representative D).

5.3 The Role of the Unions

WA has granted recognition to three of the unions which organise within the industry, these being the NUM, NACODS and BACM. Recognition however, has not been granted to COSA, the white collar section of the NUM, nor to APEX (Management representative). All the unions which are recognised have full bargaining rights, and WA has not sought to favour unions which are supportive of conventional managerial objectives. Indeed, the UDM, which has, since its establishment, consistently demonstrated both its deference to corporate policy and its political moderation, has not been recognised by WA. The decision not to recognise the UDM arguably reflects the ideological standpoint of those members of the management team who formerly held positions within the Cwmpridd lodge of the NUM, since one management representative observed, 'No, we don't recognise the UDM. The UDM is a scab union, always has been and always will be' (Management representative A), whilst another commented, 'Are they a union? No way would they be allowed on site!' (Management representative B). It could be argued however, that the presence of former NUM lodge officials within the senior management structure of WA, and the adoption of employee ownership and co-determination as corporate objectives, indicate that at this particular colliery the NUM is the union most likely to be supportive of corporate policy.

Collective bargaining has been re-established at Cwmpridd, and this has served to restore the influence of the trade unions at the colliery. The unions were involved in the development of procedural agreements (Management representatives and trade union representatives), and indeed have negotiated a number of substantive agreements in relation to the terms and conditions of the workforce, in the period since the buyout. These agreements are superior to those which exist in other parts of the industry (Management representatives and trade union representatives). Because of this, members of Cwmpridd NUM, unlike their counterparts in other collieries, were not balloted in December 1996, nor in February 1997, over industrial action in support of a pay claim and bargaining rights

(Trade union representative). The Cwmpridd workforce appears to acknowledge that the influence of the unions has increased under the current regime, since 41 per cent of respondents stated that the unions have more influence now, compared with when British Coal owned the colliery (Table 5.4).

The influence of the unions at Cwmpridd has also been affected by the nature and structure of WA. Management at the colliery is more sympathetic to the demands of the unions than was the case when British Coal owned the mine because a number of senior managers formerly held positions within Cwmpridd NUM. As a management representative remarked, 'They [the unions] are just bargaining with themselves' (Management representative C). Furthermore, as all the union officials are also shareholders they are additionally able to influence company policy by way of the shareholders meetings, this being recognised by the workforce, one of whom suggested that, 'The union can influence as a union, but also as shareholders' (Cwmpridd worker).

Table 5.4 Do you think the unions at your pit have more or less influence now than they did when the colliery was owned by British Coal?

	%
More influence now	41
About the same level of influence now	28
Less influence now	24
No response	7

Source: workforce survey (n = 58).

The nature and structure of WA has also precipitated changes in the range of issues handled by union officials at the colliery. As a consequence of managements' adoption of co-determination, the unions at Cwmpridd are now much more involved in strategic planning than was the case in the British Coal era, as one management representative acknowledged, 'They do have discussions on commercial issues as well, on marketing, on the equipment we buy. They never had those rights under British Coal' (Management representative A).

The role of trade union officials in terms of making day to day representations on behalf of the membership however, is much diminished. This is largely the result of management at the colliery being more responsive to union demands. Whilst the unions welcome these developments, they have nevertheless experienced some problems in adjusting to the loss of their traditional role. A union representative intimated that the unions had become accustomed to the adversarial style of industrial relations which characterised the last decade of public ownership, and that adapting to relationships based on consensus presented new challenges to the unions at the colliery, 'The problems we had under British Coal gave us a common enemy. Now we don't have an enemy to fight as such' (Trade union representative A). Such sentiments were echoed by one management representative, who remarked, 'If anything they're more content now, but in my opinion they miss the fight' (Management representative C), and by another, who suggested, 'Yes, they find it difficult. I think what we've done is taken their major enemy away from them...I think they find there's not that many problems at the colliery now, and so I think sometimes they feel a little bit in limbo' (Management representative A).

The policy of open communication adopted by management has also served to reduce conflict between management and the unions (Trade union representative), and the new mood of co-operation which has emerged between management and the workforce following the buyout, has also reduced the number of issues dealt with on a day to day basis by union officials. Indeed, one trade union representative expressed the view that, 'Now there are hardly any issues at all, because we are all equal shareholders, we are all working together, and the pit is doing well' (Trade union representative D).

Changes in the locus of bargaining are not in evidence at Cwmpridd, and as in the British Coal era, most contact between WA management and union officials takes place at colliery level. It is acknowledged by both management and the unions, that negotiations would only involve area or national level union officials in the event of serious problems, although as yet, such a situation has not occurred. One management representative commented, 'The nitty gritty of all problems is at colliery level. Problems would only go to area if it couldn't be solved locally' (Management

91

representative A), and similarly, a trade union representative suggested that 'The area [level of the union] was used as a trouble-shooter under British Coal, but this situation hasn't arisen since the take-over' (Trade union representative C).

The importance of local bargaining, and the effectiveness of the unions at local level, is apparently recognised by the Cwmpridd workforce, since 57 per cent of respondents stated that the unions were most influential at pit level (Table 5.5). A further 21 per cent stated that the unions had most influence at company level, however, and as WA owns only one colliery, these figures can be combined, giving a total of 78 per cent suggesting that the influence of the unions was greatest at local level.

Though the preference of both management and the unions is to retain bargaining at local level, the importance of local bargaining has been buttressed by the restructuring which has occurred in the industry. Operational restructuring in South Wales has reduced the number of operating collieries to two, and has effectively left the NUM South Wales Area without a role. Indeed, one management representative remarked that, 'The South Wales Area is struggling to justify itself' (Management representative D). Cwmpridd itself now accounts for more than 50 per cent of mining jobs in South Wales, and to some extent the Cwmpridd lodge of the NUM has replaced the South Wales Area as the focal point of NUM organisation in the locality. As one of the trade union representatives at the colliery stated, 'We are South Wales' (Trade union representative A).

The fragmentation of the industry which accompanied privatisation, and the growth of sub-contracting has also undermined national bargaining, since single employer bargaining has replaced industry wide negotiations. Although trade union structures at national level have remained intact following privatisation, their function is much diminished, and one management representative indicated that, 'National level exists only in name' (Management representative D). There is also some suggestion that the fragmentation of the industry, and the emergence of single employer bargaining has undermined the solidarity of the NUM. Indeed, one management representative suggested that the Cwmpridd lodge itself was now wholly concerned with local matters, and would consequently be unlikely to support NUM members in other collieries: 'The NUM here is nothing like the NUM elsewhere, there's no Arthur Scargill. They have no allegiance to any other pits up country, but they're

still a pain in the arse to me. They're just looking after themselves'
(Management representative C).

Table 5.5 At which level do you think the unions have most influence?

	%
National level	3
Company level	21
Area level	0
Pit level	57
Influential at all levels	3
Ineffective at all levels	10
No response	5

Source: workforce survey (n = 58).

5.4 Institutions of Collective Bargaining

When Cwmpridd was closed by British Coal in April 1994 the entire workforce was made redundant. Because of this, the acquisition of the colliery by WA did not represent a transfer of undertakings, and the provisions of the Transfer of Undertakings (Protection of Employment) Regulations, relating to collective agreements consequently did not apply. The institutional structures developed to facilitate collective bargaining during the nationalised era therefore, and the collective agreements negotiated by the mining unions and the NCB/British Coal were no longer in force at the colliery when it re-opened under the current ownership in December 1994.

New institutional structures are now in place at the colliery. These structures are based on the institutional arrangements which prevailed in the industry between 1947 and 1985. As one management representative stated, 'Everything was a clean start based on an old system' (Management representative C). The conciliation scheme currently in operation at Cwmpridd provides for disputes which cannot be resolved at colliery level to be referred to area union officials, and, in the event of continued disagreement, to an 'independent umpire' (Welsh Anthracite, Staff Handbook, January 1995, Section 12: 2). The disciplinary procedure in place at the mine similarly grants employees the right to be represented by a trade union official at all stages in the disciplinary process. Employees moreover, also have the right of appeal against management decisions in relation to disciplinary matters (Welsh anthracite, 1995). The nature of the institutional arrangements currently in operation at Cwmpridd is significant, since this is indicative of continuity with the structures of the 1947-85 period, rather than with those procedures developed to facilitate restructuring following the 1984-85 strike.

A formal pay structure is also in operation at the colliery. This is similarly based on the former British Coal pay structure, however, the productivity bonus has been abandoned in favour of a flat weekly wage, and differentials have been dramatically reduced (Management representatives and trade union representatives). Changes to wage rates have to date been made by a wages committee comprised of management, trade union and worker representatives (Management representative).

The emergence of institutional structures to support collective bargaining at Cwmpridd reflects the nature of ownership at the colliery. Indeed the conciliation scheme, disciplinary procedure, and pay structure, were all developed by CEBOT in conjunction with their advisors as part of the buyout bid (Management representatives and trade union representatives). Moreover, these structures were ratified by the worker-shareholders in advance of their implementation (Trade union representative).

Formal colliery level bargaining at Cwmpridd is augmented by informal bargaining, which is sometimes conducted without union involvement (Management representatives and trade union representatives). Such arrangements were widespread during the final years of public ownership, however the scope of informal bargaining has been reduced under the current regime. Thus whilst 'job and knock' agreements, which allow workers to go home early on completion of specific tasks, and informal bargaining over deployment, and working arrangements is permitted, informal financial deals are not tolerated under any circumstances (Management representatives and trade union representatives). The continued importance of informal bargaining is reflected in the perceptions of the Cwmpridd workforce, since only 5 per cent of respondents stated that reference was made to long standing formal agreements when changes were made to working arrangements (Table 5.6).

Table 5.6 How are changes to terms and conditions of work usually made at your pit?

	%
By reference to long standing formal agreements	5
By informal talks between management and the unions representing the workers concerned	48
By informal talks between management and the workers themselves	29
No response	17

Source: workforce survey (n = 58).

The institutional structures developed to facilitate collective bargaining at Cwmpridd apply to the 80 per cent of the workforce who are WA shareholders, but not to those workers employed by either of the two sub-contracting firms which operate at the colliery.

The largest of these firms, Coalcon, operates nationally, but employs 54 workers at Cwmpridd, primarily on development work. Coalcon has a conciliation scheme and a disciplinary procedure and, whilst those structures are similarly based on the institutional arrangements of the nationalised era, they were nevertheless developed without union involvement, and were imposed on the company's workforce (Management representative).

The pay structure operated by Coalcon was similarly developed without union involvement. Coalcon employees, unlike their WA counterparts receive a productivity bonus, and official Coalcon policy is that the wage levels paid by Coal UK are used as a benchmark by the company. As one management representative stated, 'In the last pay award, Coalcon paid in line with Coal UK's payment to the NUM' (Management representative D).

Informal bargaining, which is frequently conducted without trade union involvement, is a major feature of Coalcon's operations at Cwmpridd (Management representative), and there is some suggestion that this a reflection Cwmpridd's relative isolation from Coalcon's administrative headquarters in Yorkshire.   Indeed, one management representative commented, 'I can do private deals that I don't publicise, because the company gives me more leeway than they would if I was based up country. All agreements are supposed to be cleared with Coalcon management but they aren't' (Management representative D).

Unlike the informal bargaining which involves WA employees however, that involving Coalcon workers frequently embraces ad hoc financial agreements. Indeed it is not uncommon for different groups of Coalcon workers engaged on the same task to be paid different rates for the job (Management representative).This is significant, since it points to the emergence of a two tier pattern of industrial relations at Cwmpridd.

5.5 The Labour Process

Productive operations under the current regime at Cwmpridd are influenced by a different rationale to that which prevailed when British Coal owned the mine. The long term strategy of WA is not geared to increasing output, but is instead based on the controlled depletion of reserves, and the protection of employment.   One trade union representative expressed the view that, 'Having suffered the indignity of pit closures, the mood is now to keep the pit open for as long as possible, and to keep people in work for as long as possible' (Trade union representative C).   Marketing and production are consequently more closely integrated than was the case under public ownership, and as a result, a number of changes are visible within the labour process.

When British Coal owned Cwmpridd, there were three coaling shifts each day at the colliery. The policy of WA however, is to operate only two coaling shifts per day, with the third shift being utilised for maintenance, since this level of output is, at present, sufficient to meet sales (Management representatives and trade union representatives). Furthermore once weekly output targets have been realised, production ceases, and workers are transferred to routine maintenance tasks. Indeed it is not uncommon for production to be limited to four days per week. As one trade union representative pointed out, 'When production targets are met early we use Fridays for maintenance' (Trade union representative B).

Since WA acquired Cwmpridd in December 1994 less emphasis has been placed on improving productivity than was the case when British Coal owned the mine. In part this represents a recognition that excellent levels of productivity had already been achieved under British Coal ownership. A management representative alluded to this when he stated: 'We've taken no direct steps to improve productivity, because the men were working hard before the take-over' (Management representative A).

Though some flexible working practices have been adopted at the colliery in order to improve performance, such developments have been limited, and have been largely centred on functional flexibility.

Co-operation between workers has traditionally been a feature of coal mining. Indeed, as a management representative indicated, 'We have always been more flexible in comparison to, say, a factory' (Management representative D). To a large extent functional flexibility at Cwmpridd has merely formalised this tradition. WA employees are consequently encouraged to train for jobs other than their own, and plans are in place for all underground workers to be face trained in the future (Management representative).

There is some suggestion that the adoption of functional flexibility has been resisted by the WA workforce, as one management representative commented that, 'They're not very good at sticking their hands up to work on different jobs' (Management representative C). However, the perceptions of the workforce at Cwmpridd suggest that many are embracing the concept of multi-skilling, if reluctantly in some cases, since over half of respondents stated that they performed a wider variety of tasks in their current employment than they did in the employ of British Coal (Table 5.7).

Numerical flexibility has been adopted at Cwmpridd to a limited degree, since 20 per cent of the workforce at the colliery is employed by two sub contracting firms. The largest of these firms, Coalcon, was engaged by WA for development work, whilst the smaller company, was engaged by British Coal to operate the Cwmpridd washery (Management representatives and trade union representatives). The contractors at Cwmpridd then, perform strictly limited functions, and there are no plans to extend sub contracting at the colliery (Management representatives and trade union representatives).

**Table 5.7 Do you perform a wider or narrower range of
tasks in your current job than when you were
employed by British Coal?**

	%
Wider variety of tasks	53
About the same variety of tasks	34
Narrower variety of tasks	5
No response	7

source: workforce survey (n = 58)

WA's decision to sub-contract development work was taken because of the inherently transient nature of mining development. Since permanent posts for development workers could not be guaranteed, it was considered inappropriate to encourage such workers to become shareholders (Management representatives).   Indeed, all Coalcon employees are engaged on temporary contracts, although to date the labour requirements of the colliery have enabled all the workers to be re-engaged (Management representatives and trade union representatives).

Temporal flexibility is not a major feature of operations at Cwmpridd. WA and Coalcon employees are normally expected to work five shifts per week, each being of seven hours and thirty minutes duration, as was the case when British Coal owned the mine (Management representatives and trade union representatives).

WA employees are contractually obliged to work overtime on request. As the WA Staff Handbook states, 'Depending on requirements, from time to time you may be asked to work overtime or extra hours which you may not unreasonably refuse' (Welsh Anthracite, Staff Handbook, January 1995, Section 3: 1).   Similarly, Coalcon employees may be required to work additional hours if this is necessitated by operational requirements.   A management representative remarked that, 'The contractors have to work overtime if they fall behind schedule' (Management representative C). In practice however, overtime working is limited, with most additional hours being worked by specific groups of workers, such as winders and deputies, whose working time is influenced

98

by their statutory duties (Management representatives and trade union representatives). Excessive overtime is avoided in part because of management concerns relating to the effects of fatigue. Indeed, one management representative stressed that, 'It is our policy not to overwork the men' (Management representative B). Financial considerations also have some influence however, and one management representative made the point that overtime working was discouraged because of the cost to the company, 'We don't like overtime because of the money' (Management representative C). The relatively relaxed attitude towards overtime at Cwmpridd is confirmed by the perceptions of the workforce, since 83 per cent of respondents stated that overtime was voluntary, thus suggesting that there is indeed little pressure on the workforce to work excessive hours (Table 5.8). Furthermore, more than half of respondents stated that they normally worked 40 hours per week or less (Table 5.9).

Table 5.8 Is overtime working at your pit voluntary or compulsory?

	%
Voluntary	83
Compulsory	16
No response	2

Source: workforce survey (n = 58).

Management at Cwmpridd have not sought to increase productivity with the application of new technology, since the colliery had been the subject of large scale technological investment under British Coal administration, and MINOS was fully installed prior to the closure of the mine in April 1994 (Management representatives). The scope for technological improvement has therefore been marginal, and those improvements which have been undertaken have focused on increasing the efficiency of existing machinery rather than on reducing the porosity of the working day. Routine condition monitoring, for example, uses the analysis of oil samples from machinery to predict breakdowns, thus enabling repairs to take place during scheduled maintenance periods. Indeed, one management representative suggested, 'You can plan a repair before it happens' (Management representative E).

Table 5.9 How many hours do you normally work each week, including overtime?

	%
40 or less	53
41 - 50	33
51 - 60	9
60 or more	3
No response	2

Source: workforce survey (n = 58).

The relative neglect of measures to improve productivity by management at Cwmpridd is also a consequence of the emergence of a new form of ownership at the colliery, since WA employees are also shareholders in the company, and are therefore committed to the corporate objective of improving performance. As one management representative put it, 'It is in their own interest to produce the coal and not to waste materials. They're shareholders, so if the pit does well they get dividends, the power of the company increases, and so does their job security. If they want to act silly, they'll only affect their own business' (Management representative C). Such sentiments were echoed by one trade union representative who commented that, 'People are more aware now that it's their company...People have the will to make it succeed' (Trade union representative C), whilst another commented, 'There's a willingness to do whatever needs to be done to get the output required' (Trade union representative D).

Although productivity levels have been maintained at Cwmpridd, management at the colliery are nevertheless mindful of the negative health and safety implications of raising productivity through work intensification. Efforts to improve health and safety at Cwmpridd have

100

included the development of training programmes to facilitate multi-skilling. Indeed Cwmpridd's training programmes have gained national recognition, and Cwmpridd was the first mine in the country to be recognised as a BTEC approved centre (Management representative). In addition, risk assessments and method statements must be produced before the commencement of any new task, or before any change in working practices is authorised (Management representatives).

Both management and trade union representatives concede that Cwmpridd had a good safety record when it was owned by British Coal; nevertheless the accident rate has fallen since the colliery was acquired by WA. Nine major injuries occurred in the last year of public ownership, compared with just one in the first year since the colliery re-opened under the current regime (Management representative), these figures arguably being reflected in the insurance premiums for the colliery being reduced by half a million pounds over the same period (Management representative).

Table 5.10 Do you think that safety standards at your pit have improved or worsened since privatisation?

	%
Improved	74
No change	16
Worsened	5
No response	5

Source: workforce survey (n = 58).

The views of the workforce at Cwmpridd would appear to confirm that health and safety is given greater priority than was the case when British Coal owned the mine, since 74 per cent of respondents suggested that there had been an improvement in safety standards at the colliery under the current ownership (Table 5.10).

5.6 Conclusions

In the short period since Cwmpridd was returned to the private sector, industrial relations at the colliery have been transformed. The adversarial nature of labour relations which characterised the last decade of public ownership has been superseded, and the relationship between management and the trade unions at the colliery is now based on co-operation and conciliation rather than conflict. The emergent pattern of industrial relations at Cwmpridd then, represents a significant break with the recent past, and marks a return to the less conflictual relationship between management and the trade unions which characterised labour relations in the industry between 1947 and 1984.

Current managerial industrial relations strategies at Cwmpridd certainly bear more resemblance to the labour relations policies pursued by the NCB between 1947 and 1984, than to those which were operative in the final decade of public ownership. Collective bargaining has been re-established at the colliery, and management have not sought to marginalise the unions. Moreover, the maintenance of managerial prerogatives receives considerably less emphasis than was the case in the last decade of the nationalised era, and indeed, the unions are able to exert significant influence in relation to strategic decision making.

The experience at Cwmpridd then, appears to accord with some of the views forwarded by the optimists. Privatisation has, as Ferner and Colling (1991), anticipated, changed the environment in which corporate industrial relations strategies are developed, and the removal of the influence of government has enabled WA to develop new labour relations policies based on consensus and co-determination. Privatisation, however, has had a much more direct influence on the development of industrial relations at Cwmpridd than the optimists might have envisaged, since this facilitated the emergence of co-operative ownership at the colliery. This in turn gave rise to a more balanced relationship between management and the trade unions, and also between management and the workforce, thus making the unilateral adoption of a unitary approach to industrial relations by management both less likely and less viable, although an alternative interpretation might be that privatisation has resulted in the emergence of a shared unitary perspective.

The role of the unions at Cwmpridd has also changed profoundly in the period since privatisation. All the unions which organise at the colliery have been recognised, and the re-establishment of collective bargaining has restored their influence in relation to pay and conditions. The importance of local bargaining has increased following privatisation, and there has been significant change in the range of issues dealt with by Cwmpridd lodge officials.

Such developments similarly give some credence to the optimistic view advanced by Fairbrother (1994), and Edwards and Heery (1989), that the increased importance of de-centralised bargaining following privatisation would lead to the rejuvenation of trade unionism at local level. Two important qualifications have to be made however: firstly, local bargaining was already well established at Cwmpridd under public ownership; and secondly, the increasing influence of the Cwmpridd NUM lodge is in part, a reflection of the extent to which the role of the South Wales Area has been undermined by restructuring.

The transformation of industrial relations which has occurred at Cwmpridd since privatisation is also discernible in the institutional structures which were established to facilitate collective bargaining at the colliery. The structures which were developed following privatisation owe much to the institutional arrangements which were operative in the industry between 1947 and 1984. These new arrangements however, apply only to the 80 per cent of the workforce who are worker-shareholders, and not to those employed by the sub contracting firms which operate at the colliery. It can therefore be argued that a dual pattern of industrial relations is beginning to emerge at Cwmpridd.

Change is also evident in relation to the labour process at Cwmpridd, since productive operations at the mine are influenced by the strategy of controlled reserve depletion, and the preservation of employment. Less emphasis is placed on increasing output than was the case in the last decade of public ownership, and efforts to improve productivity by introducing flexible working arrangements and new technologies have similarly been marginal.

Because the new pattern of industrial relations at Cwmpridd represents a significant break with the recent past, and a return to the consensual relationships between management and the trade unions which characterised the industry between 1947 and 1984, it is possible to conclude that privatisation has had positive implications for labour at the colliery. The Cwmpridd workforce appear to recognise that the effects of privatisation at their colliery have been favourable, since 41 per cent of respondents regarded privatisation as a positive change for miners (Table 5.11).

Table 5.11 Do you think that privatisation has been a good thing or a bad thing for miners? Why is this?

	%
Positive response	41
Negative response	10
Positive at Cwmpridd, negative elsewhere	22
Acceptable alternative to closure	2
Positive for WA employees, negative for sub contractors	2
No response	22

Source: workforce survey (n = 58).

Perhaps the most telling comments however, were made by some of the 22 per cent of respondents, who, though acknowledging that the Cwmpridd workforce enjoyed an exceptional and advantageous situation, nevertheless suggested that privatisation had been a negative experience for the industry as a whole, particularly given the restructuring which accompanied this policy. As one respondent stated, 'For us at Cwmpridd it [privatisation] is a good thing as we now own the pit, but for others, no, as the pits have closed' (Cwmpridd worker).

6 Abergoed Colliery

6.1 Introduction

Abergoed is one of only two deep mines formerly owned by British Coal to have survived the restructuring of the South Wales coalfield. The workforce in South Wales has traditionally been represented by the NUM, and historically industrial relations in the coalfield have been adversarial in character. Like the other collieries in South Wales, Abergoed has been a bastion of NUM support, although the lodge has, over the years, gained a reputation for moderation and independence (Trade union representative and management representative).

At the time of the coal crisis in October 1992, Abergoed was earmarked for closure, and the colliery ceased production in January 1993. Following the government's coal review however, Abergoed along with a number of other collieries owned by British Coal, was offered for sale under licence to the private sector in advance of the privatisation of the core collieries. Three bids were received for Abergoed, including one from a management buyout team. The management buyout team was ultimately successful in its attempt to purchase the colliery, and in April 1994 the colliery re-opened under the ownership of Anthracite Cymru (AC), the company which was formed as part of the buyout bid. The colliery currently employs 117 people.

Because AC was established by the former British Coal management at Abergoed, it might be expected that the company would have inherited some of the long standing industrial relations traditions of the public sector, and that patterns of industrial relations at the colliery might come to be more pluralistic in character as a result of the removal of the influence of government. However, given the commercial pressures facing the new company, the customary militancy of the NUM in South Wales, and the recent history of the coalfield, it is also possible that the relationships between management and the unions at Abergoed might continue to be conflictual in character.

6.2 Management Strategies

The style of management to have emerged at Abergoed following the privatisation of the colliery is somewhat different from that which prevailed during the years of public ownership. The structure of AC is such that the positions of Company Chairman, Managing Director, Colliery Owner and Colliery Manager are all held by a single individual (Management representative). This concentration of managerial control has facilitated the emergence of an autocratic management style which has significantly influenced the development of industrial relations at the colliery.

Though there has been some change in the managerial style at Abergoed, there has nevertheless been a considerable degree of continuity in the industrial relations strategies pursued by management at the colliery following privatisation. The unitary approach to industrial relations adopted by British Coal during the last decade of public ownership has been perpetuated by the current management, and the maintenance of managerial prerogatives similarly continues to receive high priority.

The strategies adopted by the present management at Abergoed in relation to the trade unions which organise in the industry, continues to reflect the unitary approach to industrial relations adopted by British Coal, as AC has de-recognised BACM, NACODS and the NUM at both national and area levels (Management representatives and trade union representatives). The three unions are recognised locally however, and have been granted full bargaining rights (Management representatives and trade union representatives), although the unions have been able to gain few concessions from management thus far, and one trade union official described collective bargaining at the colliery as 'very one sided' (Trade union representative C). Management provide office and telephone facilities for the trade unions, and although the lodge officials are rarely allowed time off work for union business, they are paid the equivalent of one shift at surface rates to complete these duties in their own time (Management representatives and trade union representatives).

Strategic planning in relation to the long term future of the mine is wholly a managerial concern, and in practice the colliery manager is responsible for all major decisions. One management representative commented, 'He does confer with the Directors, but only to confirm his decision. Ultimately he makes the final decision' (Management

106

representative E), whilst another observed, 'It's a one man band really' (Management representative B). The trade unions have no meaningful input into strategic planning at Abergoed. They are consulted about matters of strategic importance, significantly however, such consultations occur after decisions have been taken, rather than as part of the decision making process itself, as one management representative pointed out, 'An opportunity is made after the decision is made for the unions to give their views' (Management representative A). Moreover another management representative candidly observed, 'You can consult somebody and listen to them, and you can consult somebody and not listen to them' (Management representative B). It can thus be seen that management strategies in relation to strategic planning are geared to exclude the unions from the decision making process, and indeed one trade union representative remarked that, 'We are told what is going to happen, and if we question anything we are told that they run the pit' (Trade union representative A), whilst another suggested, 'Some things are done and we're not consulted. We're told afterwards maybe' (Trade union representative C).

The role of the unions in relation to the day to day running of the colliery is also extremely limited, and indeed one management representative stated that, 'The unions are not involved to any great extent' (Management representative B). Management at the colliery have abandoned the formal consultative meetings which were a feature of public ownership (Trade union representatives), although union representatives do have the opportunity to express their views in relation to everyday operational matters, since they meet informally with management representatives on a weekly basis, in what was described by one management representative as an 'open forum' (Management representative C). One union representative however, suggested that issues raised by the unions in these meetings were seldom taken into consideration, 'We have a meeting every Wednesday where we bring our complaints up. Very rarely get satisfied, mind' (Trade union representative B). Another representative indicated that the authoritarian tone of the meetings precluded meaningful discussion, 'In the meetings it is a case of this is what we're going to do, and this is how we're going to do it, and this is what will happen if we don't do it' (Trade union representative A).

The workforce at Abergoed acknowledge that management at the colliery discuss everyday operational matters with representatives of the trade unions, since 75 per cent of respondents stated that the unions were consulted over such issues. Importantly however, they also recognise that the unions are excluded from the decision making process itself, since none of the respondents indicated that operational matters were the subject of collective decision making (Table 6.1).

Table 6.1 Which of the following best describes how decisions are made about the day to day running of your pit?

	%
Management impose their decisions without consulting the unions	25
Management consult the unions but still have the final say	75
Management and the unions come to joint decisions	0
No response	0

Source: workforce survey (n = 53).

The perceptions of the workforce moreover, also confirm the continued priority given to the maintenance of managerial prerogatives, as 45 per cent of respondents described the managerial regime at the colliery as dictatorial, whilst a further 19 per cent thought it was hard line (Table 6.2).

Management strategies in relation to communication with the workforce are not designed to undermine the position of the unions. Indeed one management representative stated, 'We don't think it's right to by-pass their role'(Management representative C). Management do communicate directly with members of the workforce by way of the occasional letter, and through team briefings. In addition, the colliery manager makes regular underground visits in order to speak to the men on an individual basis (Management representatives and trade union representatives). Nevertheless, the majority of communication at the colliery is directed through collective channels: 'Most of the communication with the workforce is done through the unions' (Management representative B).

Table 6.2 Which of the following best describes the overall attitude of management at your pit?

	%
Dictatorial	45
Hard line	19
Firm but fair	34
Relaxed	0
Easy going	0
No response	2

Source: workforce survey (n = 53).

It is significant that communication is regarded by management as a one way process, and that the unions are seen as vehicles for articulating the position of the company and gaining support for managerial decisions. As one management representative acknowledged, 'We know they understand the business, and would like them to present a fair view of the company to the men at all times' (Management representative C).   One union representative confirmed that the unions are now expected to perform a communicative role which is arguably more commonly associated with company unionism: 'The manager uses the union as a mouthpiece. That's what he thinks we're here for. He will say You will tell the men this, or You will tell the men that. He wants us to rubber stamp his decisions' (Trade union representative A). Another trade union representative also indicated that members of the senior management team do not appear to recognise that the unions have a responsibility to communicate the views of their members, and are consequently dismissive of any information that they receive from lodge officials, 'The colliery manager doesn't believe us when we tell him what the men are saying' (Trade union representative C).

The changes which have occurred in management style at Abergoed can be attributed to privatisation, since this resulted in the establishment of a new form of ownership at the colliery, which in turn gave rise to a new managerial regime.

The structure of the company which acquired Abergoed facilitated the development of an autocratic management style. In part this is because several of the most senior positions within the company are held by a single individual, and managerial control at the colliery is thus highly concentrated. As one management representative remarked, 'the colliery manager is quite happy to think that he can do everything himself' (Management representative B). In addition, because AC is a small company which owns only one colliery, there is no overarching corporate industrial relations policy which serves to constrain decisions taken at local level. Indeed, one trade union representative identified this factor as a major influence on industrial relations at Abergoed: 'The manager was hot-headed when he was the undermanager under British Coal, but there was someone to cool him down then. The problem is there isn't anyone like that now' (Trade union representative A).

Given the style of management to have emerged at Abergoed following the return of the colliery to the private sector, it is perhaps unsurprising that there has been no significant change in managerial industrial relations strategies, since a unitary approach to industrial relations is commensurate with an autocratic managerial regime. It is an apparent paradox, therefore, that in engendering the new regime, privatisation facilitated the continuation of existing industrial relations strategies.

6.3 The Role of the Unions

AC has de-recognised BACM, NACODS and the NUM at national and area level, although recognition has been granted to all three unions at local level, and all have been granted full collective bargaining rights at that level (Management representatives and trade union representatives).

AC has not sought to offer preferential treatment to unions which are prepared to support managerial objectives at the colliery. The perceptions of the Abergoed workforce suggest that management does indeed behave in an identical manner towards all three unions, since 88 per cent of respondents believed management at the colliery treated the unions on an equal basis (Table 6.3).

Table 6.3 Are all trade unions at your pit treated equally by management?

	%
Yes, management treats all unions in the same way	88
No, some unions are treated better than others	9
No response	4

Source: workforce survey (n = 53).

Comments made by members of the Abergoed workforce however, reveal that such equable treatment is regarded with cynicism by many of the employees. One remarked, 'Yes they are all treated the same, they are all treated like shit on their boots' (Abergoed worker), whilst another commented, 'All the unions are treated like dirt' (Abergoed worker), and a third expressed the view that, 'No union is treated good at Abergoed. They all get the same answer: fuck off' (Abergoed worker).

The UDM, which was founded on a platform of political moderation and deference to managerial prerogatives, has not been recognised by AC. The decision not to recognise this particular organisation however, arguably reflects a pragmatic realisation that the UDM has never enjoyed significant support in South Wales, and that management consequently had little to gain from recognising this particular body. As one management representative pointed out, 'Nobody is bothered with the UDM here. I'm sure we would recognise them if there was a demand, but no-one has shown any interest' (Management representative C).

For equally pragmatic reasons, management have not endeavoured to promote non-unionism at the colliery, and indeed a number of management representatives suggested that the presence of the unions offered a number of benefits to the company from a managerial perspective. One management representative expressed the view that collective representation made the task of managing the colliery more straightforward, 'I don't agree that it's to management's advantage if the workforce is non-union. With the union at least you're only dealing with one or two people. It's far easier to administrate' (Management representative D). These comments were echoed by another management representative who remarked, 'It's better to talk to one body than to half a dozen individual bodies' (Management representative F), whilst a third management representative indicated that the unions also provided something of a safety valve for workforce discontent: 'The men have someone to take their grievances to. It gives them a sense of well being if they can see that fairness is being enforced' (Management representative A). In addition, there was a general recognition amongst management that the workforce should be able to enjoy the benefits of trade union membership, particularly in relation to legal representation and accident cover.

The perceptions of the Abergoed workforce suggest that management at the colliery nevertheless have an ambivalent attitude towards members of the workforce becoming union members, since 60 per cent respondents stated that they were neither encouraged nor discouraged from joining a union. Workforce perceptions however, do confirm that the creation of a non-union labour force is not a managerial objective at the colliery, since none of the respondents stated that they were discouraged from becoming union members (Table 6.4).

Table 6.4 What is the attitude of management at your pit to trade union membership?

	%
Workers are encouraged to join the union of their choice	21
Workers are encouraged to join a particular union	19
Workers are neither encouraged nor discouraged from joining a union	60
Workers are discouraged from joining a union	0
No response	0

Source: workforce survey (n = 53).

112

Moreover, 97 per cent of respondents stated that they were members of one of the unions recognised by AC (Table 6.5).

Table 6.5 Which union do you belong to?

	%
NUM	75
UDM	0
NACODS	13
BACM	9
None	2
Other	0
No response	0

Source: workforce survey (n = 53).

Although collective bargaining has been re-established at Abergoed, this has not served to increase the influence of the unions in relation to pay and conditions, and indeed the unions have been able to gain few concessions from management in the three years since AC acquired the mine.

In part, the apparent lack of bargaining progress by the unions is because the commercial environment facing the company has limited the room for manoeuvre available to management. As one management representative remarked, 'In the present climate, with the price of coal going down rather than up, there's not very much to bargain about' (Management representative F). Another management representative similarly suggested, 'They've [the unions] got very little influence here because of the tight commercial situation facing the company. They don't have any freedom because there isn't any freedom to give. That's why I may come across as dictatorial' (Management representative A). A trade union representative similarly observed that the commercial environment served to undermine the unions' ability to bargain effectively, 'We request and demand better terms and conditions, but it is flatly denied on commercial grounds' (Trade union representative A).

113

Just as it furthered the development of an autocratic management style, then the structure of AC itself has also served to limit the effectiveness of the trade unions in relation to collective bargaining. Unlike when British Coal owned the colliery, there is no higher level of organisation to which the unions can appeal if they disagree with decisions taken at colliery level. Indeed one trade union representative alluded to this when he stated, 'We can ask for different things, but the answer ninety-nine times out of one hundred is no, and there is no other channel we can follow' (Trade union representative B).

The emphasis placed on the maintenance of managerial prerogatives at Abergoed has also had negative implications for the bargaining power of the trade unions at the colliery. Management representatives acknowledge that they use the threat of dismissal both to ensure the compliance of the workforce, and to prevent industrial action at the colliery. One management representative remarked, 'The men are fully aware that their livelihood depends on their co-operation and compliance with their contract of employment. They are fully aware of the consequences of withdrawing their labour' (Management representative C), whilst another unreservedly revealed, 'In the event of a dispute, the labour force would be dismissed and new labour recruited' (Management representative B). A trade union representative similarly suggested that it was not uncommon for management to use the threat of dismissal as a bargaining tool: 'We get it thrown at us that there are plenty outside the gates waiting for our jobs' (Trade union representative C).

The workforce at Abergoed appear to believe that the bargaining power of the trade unions at the colliery has decreased since privatisation, as 94 per cent of respondents stated that the influence of the unions at the colliery had declined under the current ownership (Table 6.6). One of the management representatives however, expressed the view that the influence of the unions prior to privatisation had been overstated: 'You can question the influence that the NUM had under British Coal. It wasn't as great as it was purported to be, especially after 1984' (Management representative B). Another management representative similarly suggested that the 1984-85 strike, rather than privatisation, represented a watershed in industrial relations in the industry: 'After the miners' strike their [the unions'] negotiating facility was non-existent' (Management representative E).

114

Table 6.6 Do you think the unions at your pit have more or less influence now than they did when the colliery was owned by British Coal?

	%
More influence now	2
About the same level of influence now	4
Less influence now	94
No response	0

Source: workforce survey (n = 53).

Changes in the locus of bargaining are evident at Abergoed, because AC has de-recognised BACM, NACODS and the NUM at area and national level, which has increased the importance of local bargaining. The majority of contact between management and union officials occurred at colliery level throughout the era of public ownership, but it is important to note that bargaining now is wholly a local preserve (Management representatives and trade union representatives).

The significance of local bargaining has also increased because privatisation was accompanied by the fragmentation of the industry. The establishment of a number of separate coal companies has led to the emergence of single-employer bargaining, which has served to undermine bargaining at national and area levels. As one management representative observed, 'There is no talk of national agreements now. The industry is so fragmented it wouldn't happen anyway. I think Coal UK are the only ones that have what you might consider to be national agreements' (Management representative C).

The increasing importance of local bargaining however, has not been accompanied by a corresponding increase in the influence of the trade unions at local level, nor has it resulted in a broader range of issues being the subject of negotiations. Though management do now inform the unions of commercial developments affecting the colliery (Management representatives and trade union representatives), the unions are unable to influence policy in this area, because they are excluded from the decision-making process, and indeed bargaining is centred around the same issues that were the subject of negotiation when the colliery was owned by

British Coal (Management representatives and trade union representatives). The perceptions of the Abergoed workforce indicate that there has been no rejuvenation of the unions at local level as a result of the increasing importance of local bargaining, and 57 per cent of respondents claimed that the unions lacked influence at all levels (Table 6.7).

Table 6.7 At which level do you think the unions have most influence?

	%
National level	8
Company level	6
Area level	6
Pit level	22
Influential at all levels	2
Ineffective at all levels	57
No response	0

Source: workforce survey (n = 53).

6.4 Institutions of Collective Bargaining

When Abergoed ceased production following the 1992 coal crisis, the workforce was made redundant. The subsequent acquisition of the colliery by AC therefore, did not represent a transfer of undertakings, and as a result, the provisions of the Transfer of Undertakings (Protection of Employment) Regulations 1981 did not apply at the mine. The institutional structures which were developed to facilitate collective bargaining during the era of public ownership, and the collective agreements which had been negotiated by the NCB/British Coal and the mining unions, were, therefore, no longer in force at Abergoed when the colliery re-opened in April 1994 under the current ownership.

Some institutional structures have emerged at Abergoed to replace those mechanisms which supported collective bargaining during the years of public ownership.

There is no formal conciliation scheme at Abergoed. However, as the grievance procedure at the colliery applies to 'both individual and collective grievances' (Anthracite Cymru. Code of conduct, disciplinary and grievance procedures, June 1995, Section A: 7), a mechanism does exist for the resolution of disputes. Because AC only recognises the trade unions at local level, however, this procedure, unlike the NCB conciliation scheme which operated until 1986, does not provide for disputes which cannot be resolved at colliery level to be referred to area and/or national union officials. Similarly it does not make provision for arbitration by an independent body (Anthracite Cymru 1995).

The disciplinary procedure currently in operation at the colliery provides for local trade union representatives to be present during disciplinary hearings, (Anthracite Cymru 1995), but employees have no right of appeal against management decisions in relation to disciplinary matters (Anthracite Cymru 1995).

A formal pay structure is also in operation at the colliery, and, as in the years of public ownership, the rate of pay received by each worker is related to his or her occupational grade (Management representatives and trade union representatives). In all other respects, however, the pay system in operation at Abergoed is strikingly different from that which was in operation during the nationalised period, since the wages received by Abergoed employees are also influenced by the operation of what is known at the colliery as the pool system.

The pool system was devised by members of senior management as part of the buyout bid, and was designed to ensure that stability was maintained both in the output level of the colliery, and in the level of the weekly wage earned by Abergoed employees (Management representatives). The output target for the colliery stipulated by management does not vary, and the workforce is required to produce the same amount of coal each week. When this target is exceeded, the surplus production is added to what is known as the pool. When the output target is not achieved, however, the shortfall is taken from the pool. The pool therefore subsidises any deficiencies in production. As a consequence of the operation of the pool, the weekly pay of Abergoed employees does not fluctuate with variations in production levels, as was the case under public ownership, although workers are paid a production bonus on a monthly basis if the weekly output target is consistently exceeded.

The pay structure and the disciplinary and grievance procedures currently operating at Abergoed were developed by members of senior management without union involvement (Management representatives and trade union representatives), although union representatives were asked for their comments after these arrangements had been finalised (Management representatives and trade union representatives). These procedures then, do not constitute collective agreements, and indeed all were imposed on the workforce (Management representatives and trade union representatives). As one management representative remarked in relation to the pay structure, 'The men were told, "This is the rate for the job. Do you want a job?"' (Management representative C). It could be argued, then, that those institutional structures to have emerged at Abergoed following privatisation, have more in common with the procedures developed unilaterally by British Coal following the defeat of the NUM in the 1984-85 strike, than to the collective agreements negotiated during the period 1947 to 1984.

Formal bargaining structures have emerged at Abergoed, but informal bargaining between members of junior management and trade union representatives continues to be a feature of industrial relations at the colliery, despite attempts by management to reduce the scope of such agreements.

'Job and finish' agreements, where workers are allowed to finish work before the official end of the shift on completion of particular tasks, were commonplace under public ownership. Such arrangements are no longer permitted at Abergoed because of a management belief that this practice would compromise health and safety standards at the colliery. As one management representative pointed out, 'I discourage that totally. I don't think that's a good thing. It encourages men to rush and to take short cuts, and that's when accidents can happen' (Management representative A). Ad hoc financial agreements between members of junior management and groups of workers are similarly prohibited (Management representatives and trade union representatives).

Informal bargaining in relation to deployment and shift times, however, does occur at the colliery (Management representatives and trade union representatives). Indeed, the continued importance of informal bargaining is acknowledged by the Abergoed workforce, since only 17 per cent of respondents stated that reference was made to formal agreements when changes were made to working arrangements (Table 6.8).

Table 6.8 How are changes to terms and conditions of work usually made at your pit?

	%
By reference to long standing formal agreements	17
By informal talks between management and the Unions representing the workers concerned	70
By informal talks between management and the Workers themselves	8
No response	6

Source: workforce survey (n = 53).

Interestingly, 70 per cent of respondents stated that trade union representatives were involved in informal bargaining, compared with 8 per cent referring to informal discussions directly between management and members of the workforce.   This is significant, since it indicates that informal bargaining is not utilised by management to undermine the trade unions, and there is some suggestion that informal arrangements made between members of junior management and trade union representatives serve instead to circumvent senior management at the colliery (Trade union representatives).

6.5 The Labour Process

The change in ownership which has occurred at Abergoed, has been accompanied by a radical transformation in production methods at the colliery, and as a result marked changes are also visible within the labour process.

British Coal operations at Abergoed exhausted large parts of the available reserves, and only small pillars of coal remained when the colliery ceased production in January 1993 (Management representatives and trade union representatives). The business plan developed by AC as part of the buy out bid therefore, centred on the abandoning the longwall mining technique utilised under public ownership, and re-introducing pillar and stall working (Management representative), a method of extraction which employs shorter coalfaces (For a full discussion of both longwall and pillar and stall working see Winterton, 1994). Though abandoned in much of the UK following technical and productive developments, pillar and stall working nevertheless remained commonplace in the small licensed mines of South Wales. Indeed it was these mines which provided the inspiration for the introduction of the pillar and stall method to Abergoed, as one management representative explained, 'What we've done is refine a very basic production method used in the private mines, and adapt it to the situation at Abergoed' (Management representative C).

In addition to changing production methods at Abergoed, AC has also initiated changes in relation to the technical base of the colliery. The capital costs both of installing and running coal cutting machinery on shortwall faces would have rendered the colliery unprofitable (Management representatives). For this reason hand filling has been introduced by the current owners, despite this mode of working having been phased out in UK collieries during the years of public ownership. Indeed one management representative observed, 'In a sense we've taken a backward step in time' (Management representative B), whilst a union representative similarly commented, 'We've gone back to the methods of the 1930s and 1940s. Every ounce that's filled here is filled with a shovel' (Trade union representative B).

Although the production process at Abergoed is no longer mechanised, modern conveyor systems are still utilised at the colliery to bring the coal to the surface (Management representatives and trade union representatives). Moreover, AC has recently invested in a number of small 'cob' conveyors, which transport coal from the stalls to the main belts, thus reducing the need to move coal manually (Management representatives). It can thus be seen that AC has incorporated both new technology and old techniques in their operations at Abergoed, in order that coal can be produced profitably in what remains a very difficult market.

Because the production techniques employed at Abergoed are labour intensive, the scope for increasing output is somewhat limited. As a

120

management representative explained, 'The level of output is determined by the skill and work of the men. Once a man's physical capacity is reached that's it' (Management representative A). Increasing output is not therefore a corporate objective, and operational policy at the colliery centres on maintaining aggregate production at a stable level.

In order to achieve the objective of maintaining stable production levels, senior managers at Abergoed developed the pool system described earlier. This links production levels to pay, but perhaps more importantly, in relation to the labour process, this system also links output levels to hours of work, because if the output target is not reached on a number of consecutive weeks, and the amount of coal in the pool falls below a stipulated level, management are at liberty to introduce extended shifts, and each employee must then work an additional one hour each day without additional payment, until output rises, and the amount of coal in the pool returns to a specified level (Management representatives and trade union representatives).

Although operational policy at Abergoed is not focused on increasing the output of the colliery, measures have nevertheless been taken to improve productivity.

AC has endeavoured to utilise recruitment policy in order to increase productivity, since management at the colliery have sought to recruit workers familiar with handfilling techniques and pillar and stall working. Recruitment strategies have consequently centred on attracting labour from the private mines of the locality where such techniques are employed (Management representatives). Indeed, around 70 per cent of the production workers currently employed at the colliery were formerly employed within the licensed mine sector, although the majority of these also had experience of working for British Coal (Management representatives and trade union representatives). There is, however, some suggestion that labour was recruited from the licensed sector because some of the former British Coal workers found the physical conditions of un-mechanised mining too arduous, and left the colliery as a result. As one management representative remarked, 'The British Coal boys were a bit soft' (Management representative B).

Flexible working has also been introduced at the colliery in order to improve performance, although such developments have centred on functional and temporal flexibility. Management have not sought to promote numerical flexibility at the colliery, and indeed less than 5 per cent of the Abergoed workforce is employed by sub contractors (Management representatives and trade union representatives).

Rigid job demarcation has never been a feature of operations at Abergoed, as one management representative pointed out, 'Even under British Coal it wasn't one man one job, not in this part of Wales anyway' (Management representative F). Demarcations have been further reduced under the current managerial regime, however, and indeed the summary of terms and conditions within the employment contract given to Abergoed workers states that, 'The company reserves the right to deploy you to do any other work for which you are able and competent' (Anthracite Cymru, Written Particulars of Main Terms and Conditions of Employment, March 1995: 2). Abergoed workers themselves recognise that multi-skilling is a major feature of operations at the colliery, since 77 per cent of respondents stated that they performed a wider variety of tasks in their current post than was the case when they were employed by British Coal (Table 6.9).

Table 6.9 Do you perform a wider or narrower range of tasks in your current job than when you were employed by British Coal?

	%
Wider variety of tasks	77
About the same variety of tasks	9
Narrower variety of tasks	9
No response	4

Source: workforce survey (n = 53).

Outbye and surface workers are encouraged to embrace multi-skilling, but faceworkers are not, and coal cutting remains their primary responsibility. As one management representative remarked, 'Colliers themselves in the main do not perform multiple functions. They are there to fill coal' (Management representative B). This is significant since it indicates that the functional flexibility of outbye workers is being utilised in order to reduce the porosity of the faceworkers' working day. One management representative suggested that, 'Flexibility is designed to maximise the time the colliers spend on the coal' (Management representative A), whilst a trade union representative similarly observed, 'The outbye teams give assistance to the colliers. They keep them supplied with props, powder and the like, to keep them on the coal as much as possible' (Trade union representative B).

The introduction of functional flexibility has also contributed to the intensification of work, because it has precipitated changes to the way in which miners are supervised at the colliery. The pit deputies at Abergoed are now incorporated into the production teams (Management representatives and trade union representatives), and are thus in direct contact with the workforce for a greater proportion of the time than was the case when British Coal owned the mine. As one trade union representative remarked, 'The deputy is not up and down the district anymore, he's on the shovel next to you' (Trade union representative A). The workforce is consequently more closely supervised under the current managerial regime, and it could be argued that as a result there are fewer opportunities for unscheduled breaks.

Temporal flexibility is a major feature of operations at Abergoed. Indeed it is an intrinsic characteristic of the pool system, and Abergoed workers are contractually obliged to work extended shifts to maintain output levels when this is deemed necessary by management (Anthracite Cymru, Written Particulars of Main Terms and Conditions of Employment, March 1995: 4), although overtime working is optional at all other times.

Abergoed workers acknowledge that there is an element of compulsion in relation to overtime working, since 40 per cent of respondents stated that overtime was compulsory, whilst a further 13 per cent indicated that overtime working was compulsory in some instances (Table 6.10).

The weekly output target at Abergoed does not take into account geological conditions within the mine (Management representatives and trade union representatives), nor are allowances made for absenteeism (Anthracite Cymru, Code of Conduct, Disciplinary and Grievance Procedures, June 1995, Section C: 9), and one management representative indicated that as a result, extended shifts were in operation, 'about 40 per cent of the time' (Management representative A). The introduction of temporal flexibility at Abergoed can therefore be seen as an essentially

Taylorist solution to the question of increasing productivity at the colliery, and indeed, one trade union representative stated that, 'They've got no answers except to keep men underground longer for no extra pay' (Trade union representative A).

Table 6.10 Is overtime working at your pit voluntary or compulsory?

	%
Voluntary	43
Compulsory	40
Compulsory in some instances	13
No Response	4

Source: workforce survey (n = 53).

Health and safety continues to have a high profile at Abergoed, and one management representative indicated that company policy is to maintain the standards of safety that prevailed at the colliery during the years of public ownership, 'The emphasis has been on maintaining Abergoed's safety record, which was excellent under British Coal' (Management representative C). The trade union representatives also appear to acknowledge that there has been no reduction in the priority accorded to safety, since one remarked, 'Safety is still paramount, I'll give them that' (Trade union representative A), whilst another stated, 'Safety is regarded as very important. It receives the same priority as under British Coal' (Trade union representative B). Nevertheless both management and trade union representatives concede that the production techniques currently employed at Abergoed have had a number of negative implications for health and safety at the colliery.

Because Abergoed is an un-mechanised mine, a larger proportion of the workforce is employed at the point of production, where the most potentially hazardous conditions are to be found. As one management representative commented, 'Most of our employees are at the sharp end if you like' (Management representative C), and another management representative indicated that because of this, there is a relatively high incidence of minor injuries at the colliery, 'We have loads of cuts and bruises, but nothing really serious' (Management representative F). In addition, the use of explosives on the coalface has increased dust levels in the colliery (Trade union representatives), and although dust suppression systems have been installed on the coalfaces, there is some suggestion that members of the workforce are unwilling to utilise this equipment (Management representatives and trade union representatives). This reluctance is because the water used to suppress the dust makes the coal heavier to move, thus making it more difficult for the miners to achieve the weekly output target and avoid the imposition of extended shifts (Trade union representatives).

The perceptions of the Abergoed workforce suggest that overall safety standards have been maintained at the colliery since privatisation, as the majority of respondents indicated that safety standards had neither increased nor decreased since the colliery had been acquired by the current owners (Table 6.11). A significant minority of respondents however, stated that safety standards have worsened, indicating that there is some recognition of the existence of problem areas in relation to health and safety at the colliery. It is not clear however, whether these problems are thought to result from changing production methods, work intensification, or a combination of these factors.

Table 6.11 Do you think that safety standards at your pit have improved or worsened since privatisation?

	%
Improved	6
No change	62
Worsened	30
No response	2

Source: workforce survey (n = 53).

6.6 Conclusions

Industrial relations at Abergoed have not undergone any profound change in the three years since the colliery was privatised, and considerable continuity with the patterns established during the period 1984-94 is evident. The unitary approach to industrial relations adopted by British Coal management following the 1984-85 strike continues to be favoured by the current managerial regime, and the adversarial relationships between management and the trade unions which were characteristic of the final decade of public ownership similarly continue to be a feature of labour relations at Abergoed today.

Privatisation has led to some change in managerial style at Abergoed. These developments have not, however, been accompanied by changes in the industrial relations strategies pursued by management at the mine. As in the last decade of the nationalised era, considerable emphasis is placed upon the maintenance of managerial prerogatives. Furthermore, all the mining unions have been de-recognised at area and national level, and although the unions have been granted recognition at local level, they have been excluded from decision making at the colliery, and are consequently unable to exert any significant influence in relation either to operational or strategic matters.

Developments at Abergoed in relation to management industrial relations strategies do not then, support the argument presented by Ferner and Colling (1991), that a more conciliatory management approach would emerge from the new environment engendered by privatisation. Commercial pressures have replaced the influence of government as the main determinant of management industrial relations strategies at Abergoed, but this influence has not been benign, and has encouraged management at the colliery to adopt as uncompromising a stance towards labour relations issues as that taken by their public sector predecessors. Privatisation has also had a more direct influence on managerial industrial relations strategies at Abergoed however, since it has engendered a new form of ownership at the colliery in which management control is highly centralised. These developments have led to the emergence of an autocratic management style at the colliery, and have thus facilitated the maintenance of a unitary approach to industrial relations by AC.

The role of the unions has similarly undergone little change since privatisation. Although BACM, NACODS and the NUM have been de-recognised by AC at area and national level, it could be argued that this development has, particularly in relation to the NUM, merely formalised the de facto situation which existed during the final decade of public ownership. The unions have been granted recognition and full collective bargaining rights at local level, although this has not served to increase their influence in relation to the terms and conditions of Abergoed employees. Furthermore, changes in the locus of bargaining have not been accompanied by changes in the range of bargaining issues handled by local lodge officials, and indeed branch organisation at Abergoed continues to be largely ineffective.

At Abergoed then, there is no evidence to support the view presented by Fairbrother (1994), and Edwards and Heery (1989), who suggest that the increasing importance of de-centralised bargaining following privatisation would lead to the renewal of local trade union branches. It would however, be wrong to attribute the current weakness of the trade unions at Abergoed wholly to privatisation, since labour relations within the industry were comprehensively restructured during the final decade of the nationalised era, when the position of capital was strengthened relative to that of labour. Privatisation has nevertheless led to the consolidation of these developments at Abergoed.

Continuity with the patterns of industrial relations established during the period 1984-94 is also evident at Abergoed, because those institutional structures developed to support bargaining at the colliery, owe more to those procedures introduced by British Coal following the 1984-85 strike than to those agreements negotiated by the NCB/British Coal and the mining unions in the period 1947-84. The procedures currently in operation at Abergoed were developed unilaterally by AC management, and were imposed upon the workforce. Unlike the institutional structures which operated between 1947 and 1984 then, they do not constitute collective agreements, and consequently cannot be said to represent a return to consensus at the colliery.

The production methods at Abergoed have been transformed in the three years since privatisation, and because of this, operational policy has centred on maintaining stable levels of production rather than on increasing output. Management at the colliery have nevertheless continued to seek productivity improvements, and the measures employed in pursuit of this objective have continued to be largely focused on the intensification of work and on reducing the porosity of the working day.

Because the emergent patterns of industrial relations at Abergoed exhibit more of the features associated with industrial relations during the final decade of public ownership, than with those patterns established during the period 1947-84, it can be argued that privatisation has had a deleterious impact upon organised labour at the colliery. The perceptions of the Abergoed workers suggest that they themselves recognise this, since 79 per cent of respondents thought privatisation had been disadvantageous for miners (Table 6.12). Furthermore, more than a third of those who stated that privatisation had been a detrimental development, suggested that this was because it had resulted in the consolidation of managerial control at the colliery. Indeed one Abergoed worker remarked, 'The miner today has virtually lost all his rights of negotiation. You either do as you are told or are down the road. All that the mineworker fought for has now gone' (Abergoed worker). Similarly, another employee commented, 'Management seem under privatisation to think that people in their employment should be grateful for being given work. British Coal was overmanned and badly run, but the pendulum has definitely swung too much towards the owners' (Abergoed worker).

**Table 6.12 Do you think that privatisation has been a good thing or a
bad thing for miners?**

	%
Positive response	9
Negative response	79
Privatisation has had both negative and positive features	2
No response	9

Source: workforce survey (n = 53).

7 Workham Colliery

7.1 Introduction

Workham is one of six collieries formerly owned by British Coal that remain in operation in the Nottinghamshire coalfield. Nottinghamshire miners and their representative bodies have been associated with political moderation for many decades, and labour relations in the coalfield have not been as conflictual as in those coalfields where workers have traditionally subscribed to a more militant brand of trade unionism. In common with the other Nottinghamshire collieries, the majority of the Workham workforce has been represented by the UDM since its foundation in 1985, although the NUM continues to have a small presence at the colliery.

Workham was not selected for closure during the coal crisis of 1992, however British Coal later decided to mothball the mine, and the colliery ceased production in April 1994 (Management representatives and workforce representatives). Workham was one of six collieries retained on a care and maintenance basis which were offered to private-sector bidders as 'stand alone' packages, in sales which ran parallel to the privatisation of the core collieries. English Coal (EC), a consortium which included a group of individuals who formerly held positions within the senior management structure of British Coal, and the UDM, made a bid for Workham during the summer of 1994, and in October 1994, the government announced that this company had been selected as the preferred bidder for the colliery.

Workham was re-opened by EC in April 1995, but the collapse of the company in February 1996 placed the future of the colliery in doubt. In June 1996 however, Workham and another mine formerly owned by EC, were acquired by English Mining. English Mining (EM), was established by a group of senior EC managers, but despite the change in ownership, managerial continuity was preserved at Workham, as many of those involved in the formation of EM had also previously held senior

129

management positions within British Coal. EM has continued to operate Workham, and the colliery now employs some 600 workers.

Because a number of former British Coal managers hold positions within the management structure of EM, it might be anticipated that the company would be influenced by the long-standing industrial relations traditions of the nationalised era, and that management at Workham would consequently seek to adopt a more conciliatory approach to labour relations, especially since the influence of government has been removed from this sphere. Moreover, given the political moderation of the UDM, and the history of the Nottinghamshire coalfield, it might be expected that the co-operative relationships between management and the unions which were characteristic of the period 1947-84, would be re-established at the colliery. It is also possible however, given the market pressures facing EM, that industrial relations at the colliery would become more adversarial in character than has previously been the case.

7.2 Management Strategies

The style of management adopted by EM at Workham following their acquisition of the colliery in June 1996 exhibits some continuity with that developed by British Coal nationally during the final decade of public ownership, as EM favours a unitary approach to labour relations and similarly places a significant emphasis on the maintenance of managerial prerogatives. There is however, much evidence to suggest that EM has sought not only to consolidate those patterns of industrial relations developed by British Coal between 1984 and 1994, but also to intensify them.

The strategies adopted by the current management at Workham in relation to the trade unions which operate in the industry reflect the unitary approach to labour relations favoured by British Coal following the 1984-85 strike. However, whilst British Coal strategies in the last decade of public ownership were designed to maintain dual unionism in the industry, and led to the de facto de-recognition of the NUM, the strategies embraced by EM at Workham have arguably been designed to de-collectivise industrial relations at the colliery, since EM has withdrawn recognition from all the trade unions which operate in the industry (Management representatives, workforce representatives and trade union representatives). Moreover EM provides neither office nor telephone facilities for union officials, has refused to grant the unions check off facilities (Management representatives, workforce representatives and trade union representatives), and has refused to allow the unions to display posters on colliery premises (Management representative and workforce representative). In addition, EM only permits branch officials time off work for union duties as the law requires (Trade union representative).

The three sub contracting companies which operate at Workham, employing around 20 per cent of the workforce, similarly do not recognise any of the unions which organise at the colliery. However, this can be seen as an opportunistic response to the position taken by EM, since two of these companies, Coalcon and Minecon grant recognition to the unions at their other sites. As one management representative pointed out in relation to Minecon, 'At Workham none of the unions are recognised. Nationally Minecon grants recognition where a majority of the workforce request it, but at Workham they follow the line established by EM' (Management representative E).

In addition to refusing recognition to the trade unions, however, management at Workham have also adopted policies designed to undermine trade union organisation at the colliery, as the current manager has sought to recruit labour from the Yorkshire coalfield rather than from Nottinghamshire. A management representative suggested that Yorkshire miners were being recruited because the manager was familiar with their skills, having been employed by British Coal at a colliery in Yorkshire before being appointed to his current position, 'The manager brought men from Yorkshire because he knew their skills and abilities. He had another pool of labour he could use' (Management representative B). However, a trade union representative, suggested that the Yorkshire recruitment was designed to dilute UDM membership at the colliery, 'I can't prove it, but I suspect they're bringing in lads from Yorkshire because they know damn well they won't join the UDM. They'd rather be in no union than join the UDM' (Trade union representative A). Similarly, one workforce representative intimated that workers were being recruited from Yorkshire in anticipation of any changes to employment legislation, which would require employers to grant recognition to trade unions where this was requested by the majority of the workforce, 'There's an effort to recruit anyone that's not UDM. As long as UDM membership stays below 50 per cent, they're not bothered where they're from or what union they're in' (Workforce representative C).

Management at Workham have arguably also sought to undermine trade union organisation at the colliery with the introduction of an accident insurance scheme available to all employees at the colliery. This is paid for by EM, and incorporates a twenty four hour telephone hotline which any employee can use in the event of an accident (Management representative and workforce representative). It can thus be seen that management at the colliery have sought to appropriate the major role of the trade unions at the colliery, given that recognition and collective bargaining rights have been denied, thus making the remaining benefits of trade union membership appear less attractive to the workforce. As one management representative candidly revealed, 'The thing about it is, it's completely free. Joining a trade union isn't' (Management representative B).

Though trade unions are not recognised at Workham, management at the colliery do discuss operational matters, safety issues and workforce grievances with a consultative committee comprised of elected workforce representatives (Management representatives and workforce representatives). The Consultative Committee (CC), was established as a concession to the workforce following an industrial dispute at Workham in December 1996. The dispute was ostensibly related to management's imposition of changes to working arrangements, and to the manner in which managerial prerogatives were being enforced at the colliery (Management representatives, workforce representatives and trade union representatives), however, the underlying issue behind the dispute was that EM's de-recognition of the unions had led to the absence of an effective channel of communication between management and the workforce. As one management representative stated, 'The workforce was saying that there was no vehicle for communication' (Management representative B). Significantly, however, the question of union recognition was not raised during the dispute, as a management representative pointed out, 'When the first dispute happened in December the men made it very clear that they didn't want the unions involved because it wasn't related to recognition' (Management representative B). This view was echoed by a workforce representative who stated, 'The strike was not about union recognition; that particular issue was never raised' (Workforce representative B).

Union representatives are not prevented from standing for election to the CC, as one management representative indicated, 'Everyone was eligible to stand for the Consultative Committee' (Management representative B). Members of the CC are, however, recognised only as workmen (Workforce representative). This is significant, since it indicates that management at Workham will not tolerate collective representation under any circumstances, and indeed currently, no member of the CC is a serving branch official with any union, although a number of committee members have held posts at branch level within the UDM in the past (Management representatives, workforce representatives and trade union representative).

Although the workforce themselves rejected a UDM branch official who stood for election to the CC (Management representatives and workforce representatives), it can nevertheless be argued that management at Workham have sought to utilise the CC as a conduit for communication with the workforce, whilst maintaining de-collectivised industrial relations at the colliery. Indeed, as one trade union representative observed, 'Management are seeking to utilise the skills of the individuals without the baggage of the organisation [the union]' (Trade union representative A).

Management at Workham have granted rights of consultation to the CC, but not bargaining rights, as a management representative pointed out, 'The Consultative Committee was for consultation not negotiation' (Management representative A). The commitment of the Workham management to meaningful consultation is however, open to question, since the CC has been side-stepped by management on a number of occasions. As one workforce representative remarked, 'It is bypassed sometimes. Sometimes things are introduced that weren't discussed at the Consultative Committee meeting the previous day. Management will say that they thought of it in the afternoon, after the meeting' (Workforce representative C). Furthermore, there is some suggestion that management regard consultation as a one-way process, and consequently see the CC as a medium for conveying the position of the company, and for gaining workforce acceptance of managerial decisions. As one workforce representative observed, 'Management's idea of consultation is different to the idea of consultation that the men had. They would tell us what to tell the men' (Workforce representative A), whilst another commented, 'We're like a government leak. Management let us let the men know a little bit. Let them smoulder before it comes in. Let them get used to it' (Workforce representative B).

Although there is little evidence of workforce resistance to the de-recognition of the trade unions, workforce discontent relating to the CC's lack of bargaining rights has been widespread, as a management representative acknowledged, 'The men thought that they could use the Consultative Committee to negotiate over heat money, water money etc, and they couldn't' (Management representative A). Another management representative moreover conceded that the perception of the workforce was that the CC did not provide a forum for genuine consultation, 'The men had no confidence in the Consultative Committee, they called it the insultative committee' (Management representative C). By contrast, a trade union representative suggested that members of the workforce also believed that the workforce representatives on the committee were too willing to concede to managerial demands: 'The men were saying that the Consultative Committee would agree to owt. They were saying they might as well be in the offices with them' (Trade union representative A).

Managerial efforts to marginalise the Consultative Committee nevertheless lay behind a second dispute which occurred at the colliery in May 1997. As one management representative observed, 'If you asked people, they would say that the dispute was caused by the fact that nothing had changed, and that the Consultative Committee wasn't working' (Management representative A). Such sentiments were echoed by a workforce representative who remarked 'Management were using the Committee for their own ends, but this led to another strike' (Workforce representative A).

It can thus be seen that management at Workham have sought to de-collectivise industrial relations at the colliery, by de-recognising the trade unions that operate in the industry, and by undermining their ability to organise effectively at the colliery. However, having de-recognised the unions, management have sought to maintain de-collectivised industrial relations by marginalising the Consultative Committee.

Because the trade unions have been refused recognition by EM, they have no input in relation to strategic decision making at corporate level, nor do they have any influence in relation to the everyday running of

Workham (Management representatives, workforce representatives and trade union representatives). It is not surprising therefore, that 80 per cent of respondents stated that management imposed their decisions without consulting the unions (Table 7.1).

Table 7.1 Which of the following best describes how decisions are made about the day to day running of your pit?

	%
Management impose their decisions without consulting the unions	80
Management consult the unions but still have the final say	10
Management and the unions come to joint decisions	1
No response	8

Source: workforce survey (n = 86).

A high priority is accorded to the maintenance of managerial prerogatives at Workham, and indeed strategic planning in relation to the long term future of the colliery is wholly a managerial concern, with decisions in relation to strategic matters being taken at corporate rather than colliery level (Management representatives).   The CC is informed of strategic decisions made by management, however this body has no role within the decision-making process itself.   As one management representative stated, 'The Consultative Committee are not involved in the decision-making process, but are informed and given an explanation' (Management representative B).

Decisions relating to everyday operational matters are similarly considered to be the prerogative of management, although management does consult with CC representatives in relation to these issues, and suggestions made   by   the   Committee   are   sometimes   adopted   (Management representatives and workforce representatives). One management representative, however, suggested that management had sought to consult directly with members of the workforce rather than with the CC in relation to operational matters, 'These decisions are made by management, but when it necessitates, the management meet the men. Where it's really major they meet the Consultative Committee' (Management representative C), whilst a second management representative made a similar point when he revealed that, 'There is some input into these decisions from the men that such decisions actually concern' (Management representative B). Management have, moreover, periodically sanctioned workforce ballots in relation to proposed changes to the terms and conditions of work at the colliery (Management representatives and workforce representatives). These developments are significant, since they are an indication that management has also sought to undermine collective representation by communicating directly with members of the workforce rather than with their elected representatives.

Industrial relations strategies at Workham are primarily determined at corporate, rather than colliery level. Indeed, the decision to refuse recognition to the unions was taken at corporate level, and there is some suggestion that this decision was prompted by a belief that the animosity between the NUM and the UDM would undermine effective relations between management and the trade unions at company level. As a management representative explained, 'Recognition is problematic. Workham is a UDM pit, but the other mine owned by the company is NUM. One union therefore couldn't represent the workforce. There are some advantages to having a body you can talk to, but when it's two bodies that don't talk to each other it's difficult' (Management representative B). There is some evidence to suggest that other members of management view this explanation with scepticism, however. Indeed one management representative suggested that EM had simply adopted the industrial relations policies implemented by their forerunner EC: 'English Coal didn't recognise the trade unions so I think they [EM] thought that was a good idea' (Management representative A), whilst another management representative intimated that the factor of personality was of greater importance than any practical considerations in relation to the decision not to recognise the unions, 'I've not bottomed it. I think the head of human resources has just got a bee in his bonnet about trade unions' (Management representative C).

The decision to appoint the current manager at Workham was also taken at corporate level, three months after EM acquired the colliery, and there is some suggestion that the objective of this appointment was to assert managerial prerogatives at the colliery more firmly. Indeed, one workforce representative stated, 'The manager was told by the Directors to beat us with a big stick' (Workforce representative B). A management representative however, suggested that the appointment of the current manager was designed to affect change in relation to the industrial relations culture at Workham, 'He was set on to alter the regime. Them at head office didn't like the way the previous manager was running the pit' (Management representative C), whilst a second management representative suggested that the previous manager, who had managed the colliery under both British Coal and English Coal ownership, had been replaced because he had adopted a more conciliatory approach towards the trade unions than the company approved of, 'There was a certain amount of collusion between the previous manager and the UDM. He was ignoring some aspects of company policy' (Management representative A).

There is some suggestion that the change in managerial style precipitated by the appointment of the present manager has been resented by the Workham workforce, because it has differed significantly from that which has traditionally prevailed within the Nottinghamshire coalfield. As one management representative commented, 'The manager doesn't know the men. He doesn't realise that he's not in Yorkshire now. Notts men don't like being shouted at' (Management representative C), and indeed one workforce representative suggested that the change in managerial style was a contributory factor in the disputes of both December 1996, and May 1997, 'We've always said 'look at them Yorkshire lads, they're always out on strike', but now we've had a manager from Yorkshire we say 'no bloody wonder!' He's had us out on strike twice in six months when Arthur [Scargill]couldn't get us out in a year' (Workforce representative C). The perceptions of the Workham workforce confirm the presence of an uncompromising managerial style at the colliery, since 52 per cent of respondents suggested that the regime was dictatorial, whilst a further 23 per cent of respondents described the regime as hard line (Table 7.2).

Table 7.2 Which of the following best describes the overall attitude of management at your pit?

	%
Dictatorial	52
Hard line	23
Firm but fair	23
Relaxed	0
Easy going	0
No response	1

Source: workforce survey (n = 86).

Privatisation has exerted a major influence on the style of management at Workham then, because this has resulted in the emergence of a new form of ownership at the colliery. This has in turn resulted in the establishment of a new managerial regime, which has introduced a more conflictual approach to labour relations issues than has traditionally been adopted within the Nottinghamshire coalfield. The new managerial regime, moreover, has also chosen to adopt, and extend, those managerial strategies developed by British Coal during the period 1984 to 1994, rather than those which were operative during the period 1947 to 1984.

The structure of the company which acquired Workham has also significantly influenced the development of management industrial relations strategies at the colliery, however, because the company owns more than one colliery, and industrial relations strategies are determined at corporate rather than colliery level. Indeed there is some suggestion that management at colliery level are constrained by the industrial relations policies developed at company level, since a trade union representative expressed the view that some members of the management team at Workham would welcome change in corporate policy in relation to the unions, 'There are some members of management who would like the union to be recognised, but it's not company policy' (Trade union representative A).

7.3 The Role of the Unions

EM does not recognise BACM, NACODS, the NUM or the UDM for collective bargaining at any level (Management representatives, workforce representatives and trade union representatives). This is significant since it indicates that the company has not sought to favour those unions which may have been prepared to support managerial objectives at the colliery. The perceptions of the Workham workforce confirm that management at the colliery does behave in the same manner towards all the unions which operate in the industry, since 55 per cent of respondents believed management treated the unions on an equal basis (Table 7.3). Furthermore, there was no significant difference between the perceptions of NUM and UDM members in relation to this issue.

Table 7.3 Are all the trade unions at your pit treated equally by management?

	%
Yes	55
No	5
No response	41

Source: workforce survey (n = 86).

It is particularly significant that recognition has been refused to the UDM, since this body entered into a consortium with EC, EM's forerunner, in order to bid for collieries offered to the private sector during privatisation (*Financial Times*, 13 October 1994). Moreover, the UDM was founded on a platform of political moderation and has, since its foundation, demonstrated its support for managerial objectives and its willingness to adopt a role commonly associated with company unions. EM's position in relation to the UDM would be inconsistent if the objective of the company was to promote company unionism at Workham, but if the objective of the company has been to de-collectivise industrial relations at the colliery, the de-recognition of the UDM can be regarded as a rational development.

Although none of the trade unions are recognised for collective bargaining, management and workforce representatives have stated that Workham employees are nevertheless free to join trade unions if they choose, and indeed one management representative stated that EM has not sought to promote non-unionism at Workham, 'The company's viewpoint is that you can join any union you wish. We don't actively discourage people from joining the unions. It's up to the individual' (Management representative B). The perceptions of the Workham workforce however, do not support the assertions that the creation of a non-union workforce is not a management objective. Although 56 per cent of respondents suggested that management are ambivalent in relation to this matter, a sizeable minority of respondents stated that management discourage trade union membership, despite this being illegal under the terms of existing employment legislation. Moreover, just 1 per cent of respondents stated that union membership was encouraged at the colliery (Table 7.4).

Table 7.4 What is the attitude of management at your pit to trade union membership?

	%
Workers are encouraged to join the union of their choice	1
Workers are encouraged to join a particular union	0
Workers are neither encouraged nor discouraged from joining a union	56
Workers are discouraged from joining a union	42
No response	1

Source: workforce survey (n = 86).

It is acknowledged by management representatives, workforce representatives and trade union representatives that a significant proportion of the Workham workforce does not belong to any of the trade unions which operate in the industry. Indeed one workforce representative suggested that the majority of Workham workers were not union members, 'The biggest sector at Workham is non-unionism. There are about 160 UDM, and a handful of NUM' (Workforce representative A). The responses of Workham employees to the question relating to trade union membership confirm that a large proportion of the workforce is not unionised, since 41 per cent of respondents stated that they were not union members (Table 7.5).

Table 7.5 Which union do you belong to?

	%
NUM	16
UDM	34
NACODS	2
BACM	2
None	41
Other	2
No response	2

Source: workforce survey (n = 86).

It is not clear whether the relatively high level of non unionism at Workham can be ascribed to management attempts to promote non unionism at the colliery, or to the fact that Nottinghamshire miners have traditionally had a weaker attachment to solidaristic behaviour than their counterparts in other coalfields. However, trade union de-recognition provides the pre-conditions for non unionism, as Winterton and Winterton (1993b: 24), have pointed out. Furthermore, a management representative suggested that trade union recruitment at Workham had been undermined by EM's refusal to grant check-off facilities to the unions, 'They'd all join tomorrow if they were on call off' (Management representative C).

Because EM has de-recognised the trade unions, there has been a complete cessation of collective bargaining, and indeed bargaining no longer takes place at any level. As one management representative observed: 'There isn't any discussion with the unions, that's a change in itself' (Management representative B). De-recognition has also resulted in a significant reduction in the range of bargaining issues falling within the jurisdiction of the local trade union branches, since management does not negotiate with the unions over any issue (Management representatives, workforce representatives and trade union representatives), although local and area UDM safety representatives are consulted over matters of health and safety, since this is a legal requirement (Management representatives, workforce representatives and trade union representative).

One workforce representative expressed the view that the trade unions are able to exert an indirect influence over the terms and conditions of their members, as a result of the existence of the CC: 'In a way management have given the unions a bit of collective bargaining back, unofficially like' (Workforce representative A). However, given that the trade unions are not represented on the CC, and that this body has been denied negotiating rights, and given also that management at Workham have endeavoured to marginalise the CC, such unofficial bargaining is clearly circumscribed by managerial prerogative.

The trade union branches at Workham then, have considerably less influence over the terms and conditions of their members than was the case when the colliery was owned by British Coal, and according to management representatives the unions are now unable to exert any influence at all in relation to such matters. Indeed one management representative stated: 'They [the unions] have no influence now' (Management representative B), whilst a second declared: 'They [the unions] have no influence at all' (Management representative A). The Workham workforce appears to recognise that the influence of the unions has declined since privatisation, since 72 per cent of respondents stated that trade union influence had decreased under the current ownership (Table 7.6).

Although the unions are not recognised, and have been denied collective bargaining rights, informal contact between corporate level management and Workham UDM branch officials has nevertheless taken place. Such contact has however occurred only in relation to the industrial disputes which have occurred at the colliery, and has been necessitated by management's need to secure a return to work. As a trade union representative pointed out, 'When the strike happened a few months ago XX [the head of human resources] came to ask the UDM reps what was going on' (Trade union representative A), and indeed, one management representative candidly suggested that corporate level management has been prepared to temporarily abandon company policy in relation to the unions when this has been seen to be expedient: 'The disputes focus minds at head office. This brings XX [the head of human resources] galloping down and then they [management and the unions] start talking' (Management representative C). However, as the informal contact between management and branch officials has been on an ad hoc basis and at management's behest, this cannot be said to have increased the influence of the trade union branches at Workham.

Table 7.6 Do you think the unions at your pit have more or less influence now than they did when the colliery was owned by British Coal?

	%
More influence now	1
About the same level of influence now	1
Less influence now	72
No response	26

Source: workforce survey (n = 86).

Informal contact has also taken place between members of management and UDM area officials as one management representative acknowledged, 'XX [a senior UDM official] has never been turned away from the pit. He's allowed to go underground even though the UDM is not recognised' (Management representative B). Indeed, one workforce representative suggested that the UDM Nottinghamshire Area officials were currently more influential than the Workham UDM branch officials, because the area representatives have been able to intervene in relation to matters of Health and safety, 'Area level is the most influential now, but this is because of safety issues, not collective bargaining ...When you have the route cut off to collective bargaining, you take up health and safety issues. That's what the area officials are doing. The Inspector has been called in on several occasions after anonymous "phonecalls"' (Workforce representative A).

It is however, somewhat questionable whether the area officials of the UDM are more influential than their local counterparts, since area representatives have, like the Workham branch officials, been unable to secure either recognition or collective bargaining rights. Indeed one management representative intimated that the UDM area representatives had no coherent strategy to gain recognition, other than to await changes in labour legislation proposed by the incoming Labour government, 'I think they've given up [trying to secure recognition]. They're hoping that Tony Blair is going to do it for them' (Management representative A). The perception of the Workham workforce moreover suggests that the unions are equally ineffective at all levels since 47 per cent of respondents stated that this was the case (Table 7.7).

Table 7.7 At which level do you think the unions have most influence?

	%
National level	9
Company level	0
Area level	2
Pit level	9
Influential at all levels	1
Ineffective at all levels	47
No response	31

Source: workforce survey (n = 86).

144

7.4 Institutions of Collective Bargaining

When Workham ceased production in April 1994, the entire workforce was made redundant. The subsequent acquisition of the colliery by EC was not, therefore, affected by the Transfer of Undertakings (Protection of Employment) legislation (TUPE), since EC's purchase of the colliery did not represent a transfer of undertakings. The institutional structures developed to support collective bargaining during the nationalised era, and the collective agreements which had been negotiated by the NCB / British Coal and the mining unions then, were no longer in force at the mine when it was re-opened by EC in April 1995.

When EM acquired Workham in June 1996 however, the workforce which had been employed by EC was retained, and their existing contracts were extended. As a workforce representative explained, 'They [EM] tippexed out English Coal and put English Mining instead. That was the only change to the contract' (Workforce representative C). A transfer of undertakings therefore did take place when EM acquired the colliery, and the TUPE regulations consequently applied. (Management representatives and workforce representatives). However, EC did not recognise any of the mining unions, and did not negotiate any collective agreements with those bodies (Management representatives, workforce representatives and trade union representatives), and consequently EM did not inherit any jointly negotiated procedural or substantive agreements under the provisions of TUPE. Because EM have also de-recognised the unions, few institutional structures have emerged at the colliery to replace those mechanisms which facilitated collective bargaining during the nationalised era.

There is no conciliation scheme in operation at Workham, and the grievance procedure outlined in the EM contract of employment applies only to individual grievances, rather than to both individual and collective disputes (English Mining Limited. Contract of Employment: 5). There is then, no formal mechanism for the resolution of disputes, and indeed the disputes which occurred at the colliery in December 1996 and May 1997 were both resolved on an ad hoc basis (Management representatives, workforce representatives and trade union representatives). One workforce representative suggested that the CC now provides a forum for the solution of disputes, 'We [the CC] try to stop problems being blown out of proportion' (Workforce representative B), however the absence of formal conciliation procedures indicate that any future disputes are also likely to be resolved by way of informal ad hoc arrangements. As one management representative observed, 'Now there aren't the back up structures, disputes are solved by sitting down and talking about it. You get a whole host of issues being brought up, and you have to sort the wheat from the chaff' (Management representative B).

In contrast to the disciplinary and grievance procedures which were operational in the industry between 1947 and 1984, the procedures currently in operation at Workham do not provide employees with the right to appeal against managerial decisions in relation to disciplinary matters. These procedures were inherited from EC under the provisions of TUPE (Management representatives and workforce representatives), and were drawn up by the Directors of EC, without trade union involvement. The disciplinary and grievance procedures then, do not constitute collective agreements.

The pay structure currently in operation at Workham is loosely based on the pay structure formerly operated by British Coal, and as in the nationalised era the pay received by each worker is related to his or her occupational grade, and is supplemented by a production bonus (Management representatives, workforce representatives and trade union representatives). This structure, like the disciplinary and grievance procedure was inherited from EC under the provisions of TUPE. The structure was, moreover, developed by the Directors of EC without union involvement, and therefore does not constitute a collective agreement.

The pay structure, and the disciplinary and grievance procedures currently in operation at Workham then, arguably owe more to the procedures developed unilaterally by British Coal following the end of the 1984-85 strike, than to the collective agreements negotiated by the NCB and the mining unions during the period 1947 to 1984. It could be argued, however, that whilst the structures imposed by British Coal in the final decade of public ownership were developed in order to institutionalise dual unionism in the industry, those structures currently in operation at Workham reflects management's objective to de-collectivise industrial relations at the colliery.

The pay structure and disciplinary and grievance procedures operated by EM at Workham apply only to those members of the workforce who are directly employed by the company. The contracting companies which

146

operate at the colliery have their own arrangements (Management representatives), although the structures employed by these companies are influenced by the relationship that the companies have with EM. One management representative commented, 'The wage paid by Coalcon varies according to the host colliery; at Workham the wages are in line with those paid by EM' (Management representative D). Another management representative observed, 'Minecon has to adopt some of the disciplinary policies that English Mining has adopted, but it's up to the site manager how to implement these' (Management representative E). The arrangements adopted by the contracting companies, moreover, were formulated without the involvement of the trade unions, and were imposed upon the workforce.

Informal bargaining between junior members of management and the workforce which did not involve the trade unions was an important feature of industrial relations at Workham throughout the nationalised era, and informal financial agreements were also commonplace (Management representatives). The current management team at the colliery have, however, sought to limit both the number and scope of informal agreements, although ad hoc financial contracts are nevertheless utilised for specific tasks, particularly if the completion of such tasks is a matter of urgency. As a management representative pointed out, 'We use ad hoc contracts for specific jobs, where these need doing quickly, but they are quite rare' (Management representative C).

Senior managers at Workham discourage 'Job and finish' agreements, where members of the workforce are allowed to cease work prior to the official end of their shift on completion of particular tasks, largely because operational strategies at the colliery have centred on maximising production. As a management representative commented, 'There is no job and finish now. We need the coal' (Management representative C). Informal agreements between members of junior management and the workforce in relation to deployment and shift times are, however, widespread at Workham, and indeed one management representative suggested that such agreements had compromised safety at the colliery, 'There's a lot of funny shifts here. It's all on the nod, and nobody knows where anybody is. They [members of junior management and the workforce] do it to suit themselves, and it's not safe. I don't know where people are' (Management representative A). The continued importance of informal agreements at the colliery is reflected in the perceptions of the Workham workforce, since only 6 per cent of respondents stated that reference was made to formal agreements when changes were made to working arrangements at the colliery (Table 7.8).

Table 7.8 How are changes to terms and conditions of work usually made at your pit?

	%
By reference to long standing formal agreements	6
By informal talks between management and the unions representing the workers concerned	13
By informal talks between management and the workers themselves	66
No response	15

Source: workforce survey (n = 86).

According to 66 per cent of respondents, changes in working arrangements are made by informal talks between members of management and the workforce without trade union involvement. This is not surprising given that the unions are not recognised at the colliery, but it nevertheless indicates that management have sought to communicate directly with members of the workforce rather than with their elected representatives in relation to working arrangements.

Informal bargaining which does not involve trade union representatives is also a feature of the contracting firms' operations at Workham. A management representative suggested that the policy of Coalcon was to restrict the number of informal agreements, 'I can't say they don't happen, but we try to avoid them if possible' (Management representative D). Ad hoc financial deals for weekend work, and job and finish agreements have nevertheless involved Coalcon employees at Workham, although the management representative emphasised that such agreements were, 'Very unofficial' (Management representative D).

148

7.5 The Labour Process

Productive operations under the current regime at Workham have been influenced by EM's need to repay the creditors of the company, and operational strategies at the colliery are consequently geared to maximising output, and increasing productivity. As one management representative stated, 'The priority is to churn out the coal so that we can pay the banks' (Management representative C).

Management have not sought to introduce new technology in order to increase output and improve productivity at Workham. The colliery was fully automated during the years of public ownership (Management representatives, workforce representatives and trade union representatives), and the scope for technological improvement has therefore been minimal. Those improvements which have taken place then, have focused on increasing the efficiency of existing machinery, and reducing downtime. MINOS has consequently been extended to new faces and parts of the mine currently under development (Management representatives), and all underground conveyors have been fitted with automatic start-up mechanisms, which has served to increase conveyor running times from 70 to 90 per cent (Management representatives).

Because the scope for technological improvement has been limited, management at Workham have sought to improve both output and productivity with the adoption of flexible working practices. Such developments have however largely focused on functional and temporal flexibility.

Functional flexibility and co-operation between workers has traditionally been associated with the mining industry. As a management representative commented, 'Mining is a co-operative type industry anyway. You'd always have fitters and electricians helping out, because miners work in teams' (Management representative B). Management at Workham have nevertheless sought to further reduce job demarcations, and one management representative alluded to the widespread adoption of multi-skilling at the colliery, 'Everyone is doing other jobs now. Only the winders are not multi-skilled, and that's because they can't do anything else' (Management representative C). Such sentiments were echoed by a trade union representative who observed, 'There is multi-skilling in a lot of senses now, because people are expected to do a lot more than what their normal job is. All workers are affected. If we see something that's wrong, or needs doing to help the job on, we're expected to do it' (Trade union representative A). The perceptions of the Workham workforce confirm the increased significance of functional flexibility at the colliery, since 83 per cent of respondents stated that they carried out a wider range of tasks in their current posts than was the case when they were employed by British Coal (Table 7.9).

Table 7.9 Do you perform a wider or narrower range of tasks in your current job than when you were employed by British Coal?

	%
Wider range of tasks	83
About the same range of tasks	14
Narrower range of tasks	3
No response	0

Source: workforce survey (n = 86).

Functional flexibility at Workham has contributed to the intensification of work at the colliery, because multi-tasking has facilitated reductions in staffing levels. A management representative stated that, 'The rationale behind multi-skilling is that we don't need so many men' (Management representative C), and indeed a workforce representative gave one example of how multi-tasking had affected two particular groups of workers at the colliery, 'The deputies now have to complete belt patrol work, and the belt patrol men have been got rid of' (Workforce representative C). Functional flexibility has also contributed to the intensification of work because it has reduced the porosity of the mineworkers' working day. As one management representative candidly revealed, 'I wouldn't call it multi-skilling, it's just giving the guy more to do because the time wasn't taken up' (Management representative A). The perceptions of the Workham workforce confirm that work intensification has been a feature of operations at Workham since privatisation, since 63 per cent of respondents stated that the pace of work at the colliery had increased a great deal following privatisation, whilst a further 29 per cent suggested this had increased a little (Table 7.10).

Table 7.10 Do you think the pace of work has increased or decreased since privatisation?

	%
Increased a great deal	63
Increased a little	29
Neither increased nor decreased	7
Decreased a little	1
Decreased a great deal	0
No response	0

Source: workforce survey (n = 86).

Temporal flexibility is a major feature of EM's operations at Workham, and indeed the contract of employment given to Workham employees states that, 'Employees will be required to work any shift pattern or roster so devised by the Company to meet operational or safety requirements' (English Mining, Contract of Employment: 2). EM has recently introduced coaling on four shifts at the colliery in order to increase machine availability time, and weekend coaling is also a routine occurrence (Management representatives, workforce representative and trade union representatives). Temporal flexibility at the colliery is, however, primarily manifest in overtime working, and one management representative indicated that many Workham employees were working considerably more than the standard 40 hour week described in the EM Contract of Employment, 'Many work 50, 60, 70 hours' (Management representative C), whilst another estimated that overtime working accounted for 30 per cent of all shifts worked at the colliery in any given week (Management representative A). The Workham workforce confirm that overtime working is a major feature of operations at the colliery, since fewer than 7 per cent of respondents stated that they normally worked 40 hours or less (Table 7.11).

Table 7.11 How many hours do you normally work each week, including overtime?

	%
40 hours or less	7
41 to 50 hours	30
51 to 60 hours	30
Over 60 hours	29
No response	3

Source: workforce survey (n = 86).

Workham employees are contractually obliged to work, 'a reasonable amount of overtime at such times and in such a manner as the Company shall, in its sole discretion determine, to meet the operational and safety requirements of the Company' (English Mining, Contract of Employment: 2). One workforce representative indicated that Workham employees had sometimes been pressurised by management to work overtime, 'Letters have been sent insisting that men work overtime, and men have been seen in the office and accused of holding the pit to ransom and jeopardising peoples' jobs' (Workforce representative C), whilst a trade union representative revealed that management had used the threat of dismissal to ensure that Workham employees worked overtime when required, 'They [management] tell them [the workforce] "You've got to work overtime or you're no good to us"' (Trade union representative A). A management representative similarly intimated that Workham employees had experienced a degree of coercion in relation to overtime working, 'Because we've been going through a bad patch, pressure is applied both directly and indirectly. The company is young. We need to pay the banks, and people know what they have to do' (Management representative C).

The Workham workforce do not perceive themselves to be under pressure to work overtime, as 87 per cent of respondents stated that overtime working was voluntary (Table 7.12). There is some suggestion, however, that many Workham employees have volunteered to work excessive hours because of low pay at the colliery. As a workforce representative declared, 'You have to work a decent amount [of overtime] to get a decent wage, especially when the bonus is down' (Workforce representative A). Members of the underground production teams at Workham are paid a basic hourly rate of £5.25, whilst the basic hourly rate for underground support workers is just £4.67 (English Mining, Contract of Employment: 1). There may then, be some validity in such claims.

Table 7.12 Is overtime working at your pit voluntary or compulsory?

	%
Voluntary	87
Compulsory	13
No response	0

Source: workforce survey (n = 86).

Numerical flexibility has also been adopted at Workham, if to a limited extent, since some 20 per cent of the workforce is employed by one of the three sub contracting companies which operate at the colliery. Coalcon, the largest sub contracting company on site was engaged by EM to carry out development work, whilst Minecon is employed to operate the Workham washery, and a smaller company provides underground workers for a small number of designated tasks (Management representatives and workforce representatives). All three companies then, perform limited functions at the colliery, and indeed management have no plans to extend sub contracting at Workham (Management representatives).

Management at Workham do not appear to acknowledge the negative health and safety implications of work intensification, and there is some suggestion that the intensification of work has indeed compromised safety standards at the colliery. A management representative acknowledged that a reduction in the time available for routine maintenance was an inevitable consequence of increasing machine availability time, 'You can't do maintenance without downtime' (Management representative C), and indeed a workforce representative made the point that reducing downtime had led to a reduction in coal clearance operations, and that this had increased the risk of underground fires, particularly around belts and transfer points, 'If you're not getting maintenance it doesn't help. Conveyor fires are a potential problem. We've had a couple of those already' (Workforce representative C).

There is also some suggestion that health and safety standards no longer receive the priority they were accorded when British Coal owned the mine, because commercial considerations have determined that the prime concern of the current management is to increase both production and productivity. One workforce representative remarked, 'Safety standards have deteriorated to an alarming extent. Productivity and production come before safety...The current climate is that they've [the workforce] got to meet production targets or they [management] will let men go. You put that in mens' minds and safety takes a back seat' (Workforce representative A). A trade union representative similarly observed; 'Standards have declined. There's that much pressure on people now, and if there's no one watching them they take shortcuts. The manager says he wants a safe pit, but the underlying message is get the job done. He's not bothered how the job is done and if there isn't an accident, that's o.k. and nothing changes' (Trade union representative A). Indeed, another workforce representative unreservedly declared: 'This is the most unsafe pit I've ever worked at' (Workforce representative B).

The Workham workforce appear to recognise that safety standards at the colliery have declined following privatisation, since 65 per cent of respondents stated that health and safety standards had deteriorated under private ownership (Table 7.13).

Management representatives at Workham concede that the accident rate at the colliery is higher than it was when the mine was publicly owned, but attribute this to changes in the way in which accidents are recorded (Management representatives). There is however, some suggestion that management at Workham have attempted to manipulate the accident figures for the colliery. One workforce representative intimated that management had discouraged employees from reporting accidents: 'There's a lot of accidents not being reported. There's a lot of men frightened to report accidents' (Workforce representative C). A second workforce representative, moreover, indicated that management had allocated injured workers light jobs above ground in order to avoid registering major accidents: 'The accident figures are a farce. There aren't no three day accidents because they [management] bring them [injured workers] in, and give them a job on the pit top' (Workforce representative A). Another workforce representative similarly remarked, 'Injured men are brought back to work and put on the pit top; There's one in the offices now who cut the guiders [tendons] in his hand' (Workforce representative C).

**Table 7.13 Do you think that safety standards at your pit
have improved or worsened since privatisation?**

	%
Improved	5
No change	29
Worsened	65
No response	1

Source: workforce survey (n = 86).

7.6 Conclusions

The developing pattern of industrial relations at Workham exhibits much continuity with those patterns which emerged nationally during the final decade of public ownership, since the unitary approach adopted by British Coal has been favoured by the present owners of the colliery, and relationships between management and the unions are characterised by conflict rather than co-operation. The apparent continuity with national developments between 1984 and 1994, however, disguises significant discontinuity with the style of industrial relations which has traditionally characterised the Nottinghamshire coalfield, and labour relations at the colliery are now considerably more adversarial than has previously been the case.

EM's acquisition of Workham has precipitated a marked change in the style of management at the colliery. This has been manifest in the abandonment of the conciliatory style of management which was formerley evident, and the adoption of a more confrontational approach to labour relations issues. Managerial industrial relations strategies at the colliery have reflected the labour relations policies adopted nationally by British Coal following the 1984-85 strike, rather than those which were operational between 1947 and 1984, as the maintenance of managerial prerogatives receives considerable emphasis at the mine, and management have employed policies which appear to have the objective of fostering workforce division. Change is also evident in relation to management industrial relations strategies at the colliery however, for whilst the labour relations policies introduced by British Coal during the final decade of public ownership were designed to institutionalise dual unionism in the industry, the de-recognition of all the mining unions, and the policies adopted to undermine collective organisation at Workham suggest that the current owners of the colliery have sought to de-collectivise industrial relations at the mine. There is then, no evidence at Workham to support the argument forwarded by Ferner and Colling (1991), that privatisation would engender changes in the environment in which contact between management and trade union representatives takes place, and that a more conciliatory managerial approach to labour relations would follow from this.

EM's decision to de-recognise the mining unions would similarly appear to refute the view of Fairbrother (1994), and Edwards and Heery (1989), that the increasing importance of de-centralised bargaining in the privatised industries would lead to the re-generation of local trade union branches. De-recognition, and the termination of collective bargaining rights, has brought about a profound change in the role that the trade unions play at Workham, resulting in a complete cessation of bargaining, and a consequent reduction in the range of issues dealt with by the local trade union branches. Indeed the unions at the colliery are unable to exert any influence in relation to the terms and conditions of their members, and branch organisation is itself wholly ineffective.

Because recognition has been refused to the mining unions, few institutional structures have emerged to facilitate collective bargaining at Workham. The pay structure and the disciplinary and grievance procedures which are operational at the colliery were inherited by the current owners of the colliery under the provisions of TUPE. They were nevertheless developed without union involvement, and were imposed upon the Workham workforce, and therefore bear a closer resemblance to those procedures introduced unilaterally by British Coal during the period 1984 to 1994, than to those collective agreements negotiated by the NCB and the mining unions between 1947 and 1984.

There has been no significant change in the labour process at Workham following privatisation, other than initiatives to increase productivity at the colliery through the intensification of work, and through reducing the porosity of the mineworkers' working day. The commercial pressures engendered by privatisation have, however, determined that management at the colliery have accorded a greater priority to production targets and productivity improvements than was the case under public ownership, and this has compromised safety standards at the colliery.

Since the emergent pattern of industrial relations at Workham exhibits both continuity with, and an extension of, the patterns established nationally during the period 1984 to 1994, rather than a return to the labour relations traditions which characterised the industry between 1947 and 1984, and because these patterns also represent a significant break with the established style of labour relations within the Nottinghamshire coalfield, it is possible to conclude that privatisation has had negative implications for organised labour at the colliery. The Workham workforce apparently recognise that privatisation has had adverse consequences for labour, since 72 per cent of respondents believed privatisation had been unfavourable for mineworkers (Table 7.14).

Moreover, more than one in three of those who stated that privatisation had been a detrimental development, suggested that this was because it had led to a more uncompromising style of management at the colliery. One Workham employee for example, remarked: 'I think it's a bad thing because the management have become more dictatorial in their attitude towards the employees, often quoting that if you don't like the job someone else will take your place' (Workham worker); whilst another commented: 'Privatisation has been a bad thing for the miners because the management totally impose their views and the workers have no say' (Workham worker).

Table 7.14 Do you think that privatisation has been a good thing or a bad thing for miners?

	%
Positive response	5
Negative response	72
Privatisation has had both negative and positive features	5
No response	19

Source: workforce survey (n = 86).

8 Coal UK

8.1 Introduction

In December 1994, the majority of the core collieries which were privatised by the Conservative government, were acquired by Coal UK (CUK). In addition, the company purchased a number of the mines which were offered for sale as 'stand alone' units in parallel with the main privatisation package. CUK had also purchased under the lease/licence arrangements, a number of those mines closed by British Coal following the 1992 coal crisis, and indeed, when the privatisation of the coal industry was completed, the company had secured ownership of over 60 per cent of the deep mines in the UK.

CUK acquired a number of mines in the Yorkshire coalfield, including Donborough colliery, which was purchased by the company as part of the main privatisation package, and Dearnley colliery, which was acquired under lease/licence following the 1992 coal crisis. Industrial relations in the Yorkshire coalfield have been characterised by bitter conflict in recent decades, and the workforce at both Donborough and Dearnley, as at the other mines in Yorkshire, has traditionally been represented by the NUM.

CUK also purchased several mines in the Nottinghamshire coalfield. These included Nottston colliery, which, like Donborough, was acquired as part of the main privatisation package, and Mansthorpe colliery, which, like Dearnley, was purchased by the company following the coal crisis of 1992, under the provisions of the lease/licence arrangements. The Nottinghamshire coalfield has not experienced the confrontational industrial relations characteristic of Yorkshire, traditionally enjoying labour relations based on co-operation. As at the other collieries in Nottinghamshire, the workforce at both Nottston and Mansthorpe has been represented by the UDM since its foundation in 1985, although a small number of workers continued to be members of the NUM at each of these mines.

Because CUK operated for some years in the private opencast sector before diversifying into deep mining, the company already had its own established industrial relations practices, and therefore did not simply adopt the labour relations practices which developed within the deep mine sector during the years of public ownership. Given this culture and the commercial pressures currently facing the company, coupled with the customary militancy of the NUM and the recent history of the Yorkshire coalfield, it might be expected that industrial relations at CUK collieries located within the Yorkshire coalfield would come to be characterised by confrontation rather than conciliation. However, given that privatisation removed the influence of government from the industry, the possibility cannot be discounted that labour relations at CUK's Yorkshire collieries might become less conflictual than has been the case in the recent past.

In the Nottinghamshire coalfield, by contrast, the removal of the influence of government and the customary moderation of the UDM might have been expected to result in the development of patterns of industrial relations based on co-operation rather than conflict. However given CUK's origins as a private sector company, and the commercial pressures facing companies operating in the deep mine sector, it was also possible that industrial relations at CUK's Nottinghamshire collieries would come to be somewhat more confrontational than has hitherto been the case.

It was also possible that the nature of privatisation would itself have implications for the development of industrial relations at individual collieries owned by CUK, since those mines such as Donborough and Nottston, which were purchased as part of the main privatisation package represented a transfer of undertakings, and were consequently subject to the provisions of the Transfer of Undertakings (Protection of Employment) Regulations 1981, (TUPE). The acquisition of mines such as Dearnley and Mansthorpe which were purchased under the provisions of the lease/license arrangements following their closure by British Coal, did not represent a transfer of undertakings, so the provisions of TUPE did not apply at these particular collieries.

8.2 Donborough Colliery

Management Strategies

The style of management which has emerged at Donborough following privatisation is strikingly similar to that which prevailed during the final decade of public ownership. Moreover, the industrial relations strategies which have been adopted by management at Donborough continue to reflect the unitary approach to labour relations developed by British Coal following the 1984-85 strike, and there has consequently been no return to pluralism at the colliery.

Within CUK industrial relations strategies are determined at corporate, rather than colliery level (Management representatives and trade union representatives). CUK has refused recognition to all the mining unions at national level, but has recognised the unions at colliery level. In respect of the NUM and the UDM, however, the company has granted sole recognition to the union with the largest membership at each colliery (Management representatives and trade union representatives), so that the NUM is the recognised union at Donborough.

Although the NUM is recognised at Donborough, it is significant that collective bargaining has not been fully restored at the colliery, since management will not discuss wage levels with the unions (Management representatives). Indeed an NUM representative intimated that bargaining rights at the colliery are delimited by management, when he expressed the view that: 'We have collective bargaining, to an extent' (NUM branch official A).

Management at Donborough provide office, stationery and telephone facilities for NUM branch officials, and officials are allowed time off work for union duties. Moreover an NUM representative pointed out that management at the colliery recognised that the work of the branch had increased as a result of the restructuring programme which preceded privatisation, and was also willing to sanction time off in relation to this: 'The outstanding compensation claims from all the pits that have closed came to this branch, because we're the only pit left in the area. We also deal with all the pensioners from the closed pits. There's a recognition [from management] that my workload is heavy, and they're flexible in this respect' (NUM branch official A). There is evidence that management is willing to facilitate union organisation at Donborough because this eases the task of managing the colliery. As an NUM representative observed: 'They're [management] not flexible for nothing. They get something out of this because it smoothes the running of things' (NUM branch official A).

CUK's unitary approach to industrial relations at Donborough is also evident because the maintenance of managerial prerogatives receives the same emphasis as was the case during the final decade of public ownership.

Strategic decisions in relation to the long term future of the colliery are entirely a managerial concern (Management representatives), but because Donborough is subject to the provisions of TUPE, the formal consultative meetings between management and the unions that occurred at colliery level throughout the nationalised era continue to take place, and questions of strategy are consequently discussed with the unions at the colliery (NUM representative). As strategic decisions are taken at corporate rather than colliery level however, (Management representatives), trade union branch officials are excluded from the decision making process itself, and as a consequence have little meaningful influence in relation to such matters.

Decisions relating to everyday operational matters at Donborough are similarly a managerial prerogative. However, branch officials have unlimited access to senior managers at the colliery, and requests for information are usually granted. As an NUM representative stated: 'I can just walk into the manager's office and ask for information' (NUM branch official A). Furthermore, the unions are able to exert some influence in relation to operational matters, because of the continued existence of formal consultative meetings (NUM representative).

In common with CUK employees at other collieries, each Donborough miner receives a copy of the company newsletter, but this is a corporate initiative, and colliery level strategies for communication with the workforce, have not been designed to undermine the position of the unions. Since privatisation management at Donborough have withdrawn the colliery newsletter (NUM representative), and an NUM representative pointed out that all communication between management and the workforce at the colliery is directed through collective channels: 'No, the union is not bypassed. All communication is directed through the union' (NUM branch official A). There is however, some suggestion that management at the colliery see communication as a one way process, and regard the unions as vehicles both for promoting, and gaining workforce support for managerial objectives. As an NUM representative commented: 'If I'm being cynical, I'd say we'd be used in a way to appease people, to let them [the workforce] know they'd [management] made the right decisions' (NUM branch official A).

The Role of the Unions

CUK has de-recognised all the mining unions at national and area levels. Selective recognition has been granted to the unions on a local basis however, and in accordance with corporate policy, management at Donborough has recognised the NUM, since this organisation represents the majority of the workforce at the colliery. It would appear that CUK has not sought to offer preferential treatment to the union most prepared to assent to managerial objectives at the colliery, since the UDM, which was founded on a platform of political moderation, has not been granted recognition at Donborough, and management at the colliery have not sought to promote the union. The decision not to recognise the UDM at Donborough, however, arguably reflects a pragmatic recognition that management would have little to gain from recognising this organisation because the UDM has never had significant support in the Yorkshire coalfield, and, moreover, has 'not one member' at Donborough colliery itself (NUM branch official A).

Management at Donborough have similarly not sought to promote non-unionism at the colliery (NUM representative), and indeed amongst the workforce directly employed by CUK, union density remains high (NUM representative). Some 40 per cent of the total workforce at the colliery however, is employed by a number of sub contracting companies, and an NUM representative conceded that some of these workers were not union members: 'Non-unionism is a problem amongst the contractors' (NUM branch official A).

It is not clear whether management within the sub contracting companies discourage trade union membership, although one management representative revealed that the sub contracting companies employed by CUK were under no obligation to adopt CUK's policy in relation to trade union affiliation: 'They [the sub contracting companies] have their own policies in relation to the unions' (Corporate management representative A). Nevertheless, some observers have suggested that sub contracting was

163

initially introduced in the mining industry in order to undermine trade union organisation (Prowse and Turner, 1996: 154), and given also that sub contract employment has become increasingly casualised, it is not surprising that union density is somewhat lower amongst the sub contract workers at Donborough than amongst the core employees.

Although collective bargaining has been re-established at Donborough, the scope of this is severely proscribed by managerial prerogative, because corporate policy dictates that wage levels are not subject to negotiation. As a management representative stated: 'There is no collective bargaining for pay' (Corporate management representative A). The restoration of collective bargaining at Donborough then, has not served to increase the influence of the trade unions in relation to the terms and conditions of their members at the colliery.

Changes in the locus of bargaining are evident at Donborough, because CUK has de-recognised all the mining unions at national and area levels, thereby increasing the importance of local bargaining. Moreover, national NUM officials are prohibited from entering colliery premises at Donborough, in common with all other collieries owned by CUK. As an NUM representative pointed out: 'They [CUK] won't allow me and Arthur [Scargill] within a mile of a pit' (NUM national official). During most of the years of public ownership the majority of contact between management representatives and union officials occurred at colliery level, but bargaining is now wholly a local preserve. An NUM representative however, suggested that the national union was able to influence local bargaining at Donborough in spite of their de-recognition, because local NUM branches were instructed by national NUM policies: 'National level has influence because they steer local branches. Local branches implement national policy' (NUM branch official A).

The increasing importance of local bargaining at Donborough has not, however, been accompanied by an increase in the influence of the local trade union branch. Indeed, a national NUM representative, whilst acknowledging the change in the locus of bargaining expressed considerable scepticism about the influence of local NUM branches at collieries such as Donborough: 'Local is the only level they [CUK] talk to anyway. Whether the branches have any influence is another question, of course. I don't think they have. I've never heard any reports that CUK has changed policy because of the influence of local branches' (NUM national official). Similarly, the increasing significance of local bargaining has not led to a wider range of issues being the subject of negotiation. Indeed an NUM representative stated that bargaining remained focused around the same issues as was the case when the colliery was publicly owned: 'It's more or less exactly the same. If you'd been in a coma for six years you wouldn't notice any difference' (NUM branch official A). There is then, little evidence of local trade union rejuvenation at Donborough, and the NUM branch at the colliery is largely ineffective.

Institutions of Collective Bargaining

Because Donborough was never closed by British Coal, and remained in production throughout the privatisation process, CUK's purchase of the colliery in December 1994 represented at transfer of undertakings and the provisions of TUPE consequently applied at the mine. Under the terms of this legislation, CUK had a legal obligation to recognise all the existing agreements negotiated by British Coal and the mining unions prior to privatisation, and because of this, those agreements continued to apply at Donborough after the colliery was privatised. Although CUK has sought to undermine the agreements protected under the provisions of TUPE, the institutional framework which was developed to facilitate collective bargaining in the industry during the years of public ownership nevertheless remains largely intact.

The British Coal conciliation scheme which applied throughout the industry prior to privatisation, was inherited by CUK under the provisions of TUPE. In 1996, however, CUK withdrew the existing scheme and replaced it with a corporate level agreement (Management representative). The current CUK scheme was negotiated by senior CUK managers and UDM national officials (Management representatives and UDM representatives). The NUM was opposed to the scheme, but the union was not party to the negotiations, and the scheme was consequently imposed at Donborough, along with all other collieries organised by the NUM where the provisions of TUPE applied (NUM national official). Like its predecessor, the CUK conciliation scheme is based on the majority/minority principle, although the automatic right to independent arbitration has been removed, except when disputes are referred to an independent body, with the agreement of the Chief Executive and the UDM National President (UDM national official).

The disciplinary and grievance procedure currently in operation at Donborough was also inherited by CUK under the TUPE legislation, but this machinery has been modified, and, as with the conciliation scheme, the right to independent arbitration has been withdrawn (UDM national representative). The revised disciplinary and grievance procedure was negotiated by senior CUK managers and UDM national officials (UDM national official). The NUM, by contrast had no input in relation to the changes to the procedure, which was unilaterally imposed at Donborough, along with other collieries organised by the NUM (NUM national official).

The pay structure inherited from British Coal under the provisions of TUPE, has also been amended by CUK. Employees at Donborough, as at all other CUK collieries continue to receive a basic weekly wage and a production bonus, as was the case when the British Coal pay structure was in operation, but the grading structure has been simplified, and differentials have been reduced as a consequence. The changes to the pay structure were negotiated by senior CUK managers and UDM national officials (UDM national official). The NUM, however, was not included in the negotiations, and the modified pay structure was imposed at collieries subject to the provisions of TUPE where the NUM was the majority union. As an NUM representative remarked: 'They told us what they were doing, and our members had got it whether they liked it or not' (NUM national official). The Donborough NUM representative however, described the modifications as 'minor cosmetic changes' (NUM branch official A), and indicated that the Donborough branch of the NUM would not have challenged the changes made to the pay structure, since no employee at the colliery was financially worse off as a result of re-grading.

The provisions of TUPE then, have ensured that formal structures are in place to facilitate collective bargaining at Donborough, however as these structures were not negotiated with NUM representatives they do not constitute collective agreements. Moreover, the NUM branch at the colliery has been unable to negotiate any formal substantive agreements as yet (NUM representative). The existence of such structures is, moreover, relatively meaningless in relation to corporate level bargaining, because the mining unions have no official recognition at national or area level, and because any contact between senior managers and national union officials is on an informal basis. NUM members at Donborough and other collieries owned by CUK have, on a number of occasions, voted in favour of industrial action in support of collective bargaining rights at corporate level, and the negotiation of new institutional arrangements. This strategy has, however, failed to secure its objectives, because industrial action has, in each case, been ruled unlawful.

A BACM representative expressed the view that 'TUPE is something that has been understated by management and overstated by the unions' (BACM national official), and indeed there may be some validity in this viewpoint, since unlike the nationalisation statutes, the provisions of TUPE, whilst safeguarding existing procedures, have not required CUK to enter into collective agreements with the mining unions. The institutional bargaining arrangements currently in force at Donborough therefore, bear more resemblance to those procedures introduced unilaterally by British Coal during the final decade of public ownership, than to those pertaining up to 1984. The negotiated structures operating between 1947 and 1984, were significantly delimited by managerial prerogative after 1984, with the objective of consolidating the institutionalisation of dual unionism within the company.

The institutional structures described above apply to all members of the workforce who are directly employed by CUK, but not to the 40 per cent of Donborough employees who work for the sub contracting companies which have operations on site, and indeed these companies each have separate arrangements (NUM representative). This is significant since it points to the emergence of a two-tier pattern of industrial relations at the colliery.

Although formal structures are in place to facilitate collective bargaining at Donborough, informal bargaining between junior members of management and members of the workforce which have no union involvement, continues to be a feature of labour relations at the colliery. Unlike in the final decade of public ownership, however, ad hoc financial agreements do not take place. As an NUM representative observed: 'there is no ad hoc' (NUM branch official A). Informal agreements in relation to shift times and deployment, however, remain widespread at Donborough, and are condoned by the NUM at the colliery, providing operational requirements are not compromised. As an NUM representative commented 'men often swap shifts. There is a lot of co-operation. There is no opposition to this from the union, but this would never be done where the position of the pit would be jeopardised' (NUM branch official A).

167

The change in ownership which has occurred at Donborough has been accompanied by some changes in the labour process at the colliery, although, as in the final decade of public ownership, maximising productivity remains a central objective of operations at the colliery.

Although the same emphasis is placed on improving productivity as was the case in when the mine was publicly owned, the current management at Donborough have not sought to introduce new technology in order to improve productivity further at the colliery. This is because Donborough had been the subject of large scale technological investment whilst under public ownership, and there has therefore been little scope for technological improvement. As an NUM representative commented: 'Technology has moved on in leaps and bounds in the last ten years, but the majority of damage was done under British Coal' (NUM branch official A).

Because the scope for increasing productivity through technological developments has been limited at Donborough, management at the colliery have instead sought to improve productivity with the adoption of flexible working practices. British Coal paved the way for the introduction of flexible working at Donborough after privatisation, because shortly before this, NUM members at the colliery who intended to remain in the industry after its return to the private sector, were, like those at other mines, offered a £6,000 one-off payment in return for accepting flexible working (NUM representatives). An NUM representative conceded that the majority of NUM members had accepted this payment during their employment at British Coal, and consequently have contracts which incorporate a flexibility clause. Indeed forms of functional, numerical, and temporal flexibility are all in evidence at Donborough.

Functional flexibility has been widely adopted at Donborough, and job demarcations have been reduced in many areas as a consequence (NUM representative). However, because functional flexibility has been utilised in order to reduce labour requirements, it has also contributed to the intensification of work, through reducing the porosity of the mineworkers' working day. As an NUM representative observed: 'They've [management] reduced manpower, and are expecting the remaining men to do more' (NUM branch official A). The NUM representative, however, suggested that even though multi-skilling was an initiative that was originally introduced by management, the workforce apparently recognised that productivity improvements generated by functional flexibility would prolong the life of the colliery: 'There's certainly a lot more flexibility in terms of what people are prepared to do. In part this is because of management pressure, but there's also a willingness on the part of the men to keep the pit open' (NUM branch official A).

Numerical flexibility is also a feature of CUK's operations at Donborough, since some 40 per cent of the workforce is currently employed by one of several subcontracting firms that operate at the colliery (NUM representative). There is some suggestion however, that it is a corporate objective to reduce the number of subcontractors employed by the company (NUM representatives), and indeed in November 1997, 49 sub contract workers were laid off at Donborough (NUM representative).

Temporal flexibility has also been introduced at Donborough, if to a limited extent. CUK employees at Donborough are contracted to work 37 hours per week over 5 days (Management representative), in addition to which, an NUM representative estimated that each worker completed an average of sixteen overtime hours each week. There is some evidence that management periodically expect Donborough employees are to work overtime. As an NUM representative commented: 'Pressure is applied, especially if development work falls behind' (NUM branch official A). The representative also suggested that workers at Donborough were under indirect pressure to work overtime because of the insecurity facing the industry: 'Because of the redundancy scheme, the men have to earn £300 per week to qualify for the maximum payout, and a lot work overtime because of this' (NUM branch official A).

Although increasing productivity continues to be a corporate objective, management are nevertheless mindful of the negative health and safety implications of work intensification. An NUM representative suggested that CUK had restored the health and safety functions performed by pit deputies, which had been undermined during the final decade of public ownership, and indeed he also indicated that health and safety standards had improved at Donborough under the current ownership: 'The accident rate is certainly running lower than in the last few years of British Coal' (NUM branch official A). At the same time, there is evidence to suggest that management at the colliery have manipulated the accident statistics under the current ownership. An audit of accident reporting within the company, conducted by the Mines Inspectorate, revealed that management at Donborough had failed to report a number of serious accidents, and indeed the manager of Donborough was suspended in November 1997 pending the outcome of an internal inquiry into these matters.

8.3 Dearnley Colliery

Management Strategies

The style of management which has emerged at Dearnley following CUK's acquisition of the colliery, exhibits much continuity with that which predominated during the final decade of the nationalised era. Management at the colliery have continued to pursue the unitary approach to labour relations embraced by British Coal following the end of the 1984-85 strike, and as a result there has been no return to a pluralistic approach to industrial relation issues at the mine. Continuity with the period 1984-94 is also apparent since the maintenance of managerial prerogatives continues to receive significant emphasis. There is, however, some evidence to suggest that CUK has sought not only to consolidate the patterns of labour relations developed at Dearnley during the last decade of public ownership, but also to de-collectivise industrial relations at the colliery.

The strategies adopted by management at Dearnley in relation to the trade unions which operate in the industry reflect corporate industrial relations policies, which in turn mirror those strategies adopted by British Coal during the final years of public ownership. In respect of the NUM and the UDM, recognition is granted only to the NUM, since the workforce at Dearnley has traditionally been represented by this body, and no employees at the mine are UDM members (NUM representative). However, whilst the NUM has been granted rights of representation, the union has no bargaining rights at the colliery, and no formal meetings take place between management representatives and trade union branch officials, with the exception of safety meetings, which are required by statute (NUM representative).

NUM branch officials at Dearnley are permitted to take time off work to attend to union business 'as and when required' (NUM branch official

B), and management provide office and telephone facilities for NUM branch officials at the colliery. There is, however, some suggestion that this is an informal local arrangement which may not accord with company policy. As an NUM representative observed: 'Yes, they give us an office, telephone and stationery, but whether it's official or not I don't know' (NUM branch official B). This question is significant, since it may indicate some dissent at colliery level from corporate level policies towards the trade unions at Dearnley.

The unitary approach in relation to industrial relations adopted by management at Dearnley is also apparent because the maintenance of managerial prerogatives continues to receive high priority, as was the case during the final decade of public ownership.

Strategic decision making in relation to the long-term development of Dearnley is wholly a managerial concern. Dearnley is not covered by the provisions of TUPE, and as a consequence management at the colliery have unilaterally abandoned the formal consultative meetings with the trade unions which were a feature of industrial relations at the colliery when it was publicly owned (NUM representative). The unions then, are not consulted in relation to strategic matters affecting the colliery (NUM representative), and as strategic decisions are, in any event, made at corporate rather than colliery level (Management representatives), the unions are unable to exert any influence in relation to strategic issues concerning Dearnley.

Decisions in relation to operational matters at the colliery are similarly a managerial preserve, and such issues are not discussed with the unions at the colliery. An NUM representative explained that although branch officials had access to management representatives, such contact was informal, and the scope of such meetings was highly restricted: 'There's not a problem getting to see the manager, but officially it's only over things like disciplinary matters' (NUM branch official B). The unions then, have no opportunity to influence decision making in relation to operational issues, and indeed, an NUM representative declared that the union had 'no influence whatsoever' (NUM branch official B), in relation to such matters.

In addition to placing great emphasis on the maintenance of managerial prerogatives, management at Dearnley have also sought to communicate directly with Dearnley employees. In order to facilitate this, management hold meetings in the pit canteen with members of the workforce. Moreover, an NUM representative revealed that such meetings take place regularly, both on a formal and informal basis: 'These [meetings] are called four times a year, but they also take place as and when required if anything special pops up' (NUM branch official B). It is interesting to note that management at Dearnley have employed a communications technique formerly utilised by the NUM at Yorkshire collieries (NUM National official), all the more so since they have adopted strategies designed to bypass collective channels of communication, and further marginalise the unions at the colliery.

The Role of the Unions

Although all the mining unions have been de-recognised by CUK at national and area levels, it is company policy to grant recognition to the unions on a local basis. Management at Dearnley have therefore recognised the NUM, because this organisation has traditionally represented the workforce at the colliery, and indeed continues to command the support of the majority of Dearnley employees. The UDM, which has been associated with political moderation since its foundation in 1985, has not been granted recognition at Dearnley, and management have not sought to promote the union at the colliery (NUM representative). It would then, appear that CUK has not treated more favourably the union most prepared to support managerial objectives at Dearnley. However, as the UDM has never been strongly supported in the Yorkshire coalfield, and as there are no UDM members at Dearnley (NUM representative), management would clearly have little to gain from recognising the UDM at the colliery.

There is no evidence to suggest that the creation of a non-union workforce is a managerial objective at Dearnley, and indeed, the majority of the workforce recruited by CUK when the colliery was re-opened, were former Dearnley employees, most of whom were previously members of the NUM. As an NUM representative observed: 'In most cases they re-employed the people who were there in the past' (NUM branch official B). Although management have not sought to promote non-unionism at the colliery, however, an NUM representative conceded that union density at Dearnley was nevertheless relatively low, with around 35 per cent of the workforce having no trade union affiliation (NUM representative). Winterton and Winterton (1993b: 24) have pointed out that falling union density may be attributed in part to workforce perceptions of trade union weakness, and indeed, this viewpoint is shared by an NUM representative at Dearnley, who commented: 'Yes, the level of [union] influence has fallen. I think that's part of the problem. A lot of the men are not in the union because they think "Well, what can they do for us?"' (NUM branch official B).

Although the NUM is recognised at Dearnley for the purpose of individual representation, collective bargaining has not been re-established at the colliery. This is because the provisions of TUPE do not apply at the mine, and management have therefore been able to abandon the consultative arrangements which existed during the years of public ownership. There is no formal contact between management representatives and NUM branch officials, but informal contact does take place. However, as all the collective agreements negotiated by British Coal and the mining unions at Dearnley were no longer in force when CUK acquired the colliery, because it was not subject to the provisions of TUPE, there is consequently no framework for negotiations between management and union representatives. As a result, management are able to impose change both in relation to terms and conditions of employment at the colliery and to working practices. As an NUM representative explained: 'There's a tendency for them [management] to make the rules up as they go along. Without agreements it's chaotic' (NUM branch official B). The NUM at Dearnley then, has considerably less influence in relation to the terms and conditions of their members employed at the colliery than was the case when the mine was owned by British Coal.

With neither formal contact between management and union representatives, nor institutional structures to support bargaining at Dearnley, the importance of local bargaining has not increased at the colliery, despite recognition being granted to the local branch of the NUM rather than to the national and area levels of the union. For the same reasons there has also been a significant reduction in the range of issues coming within the jurisdiction of the local NUM branch. There is then, no evidence of union renewal at Dearnley colliery, and indeed branch organisation at the colliery is wholly ineffective.

Dearnley colliery was closed by British Coal following the coal crisis of 1992, and the entire workforce was made redundant. Because of this CUK's acquisition of the colliery did not represent a transfer of undertakings, so the provisions of TUPE did not apply at the mine. All the existing agreements negotiated by British Coal and the mining unions prior to privatisation, therefore, were no longer in force at Dearnley when the colliery was returned to production in March 1994, and few institutional structures have emerged at Dearnley to replace those mechanisms which facilitated collective bargaining during the years of public ownership.

There is no conciliation scheme at Dearnley colliery (NUM representative), and therefore no formal mechanism exists for the resolution of disputes. As yet, there have been no disputes at Dearnley under the current ownership. An NUM representative however, indicated that in the absence of a formal disputes procedure, any future disputes were likely to be resolved by way of informal ad hoc arrangements: 'Because we haven't any collective agreements or anything, it's a bit of an as it happens situation. We would take it up with the manager, but it would probably be a correspondence exercise' (NUM branch official B).

The disciplinary and grievance procedure currently in operation at Dearnley, is the same as that which exists at those CUK collieries which were subject to the provisions of TUPE (NUM representative). The British Coal disciplinary and grievance procedure was inherited by CUK under the TUPE legislation, but this structure was modified, and the right to independent arbitration was withdrawn (UDM national representative). The revised disciplinary and grievance procedure was negotiated by senior CUK managers and UDM national officials (UDM national official). The NUM, however, had no influence over the changes to the procedure, and once modified, the revised procedure was imposed at all collieries organised by the NUM, including Dearnley (NUM representative).

The pay structure in operation at Dearnley is loosely based on the British Coal pay structure, although it differs from the structure in place at those collieries subject to the provisions of TUPE. Wages at Dearnley are related to the occupational grade of individual employees and the wages received by each employee comprise a flat rate weekly wage combined with a production bonus. Unlike during the years of public ownership, however, the production bonus at Dearnley does not vary, and is equal to

30 per cent of the basic weekly rate. This is because the production strategy at the colliery is based on the same quantity of coal being mined each week (NUM representative). Moreover, employees at Dearnley receive no additional payments for working in water or heat (NUM representative). The pay structure at Dearnley was not negotiated with the local branch of the NUM, but was imposed upon the workforce at the colliery by management (NUM representative).

Those formal structures which exist to facilitate bargaining at Dearnley are not collective agreements, because they were not negotiated with NUM representatives, and were imposed upon the workforce at the colliery. Furthermore, little significance can be attached to the presence of such structures because formal bargaining is not permitted at the colliery. The institutional arrangements currently in force at Dearnley then, have been significantly influenced by managerial prerogative, and as such, bear considerably more resemblance to those procedures introduced unilaterally by British Coal during the final decade of public ownership, than to those negotiated structures which were operational between 1947 and 1984. NUM members at Dearnley, as at the other collieries owned by CUK have voted for industrial action in support of collective bargaining rights, and the establishment of new jointly negotiated procedural agreements on a number of occasions. This strategy has not been successful, however, and planned industrial action was cancelled, having been ruled unlawful.

Informal bargaining between junior members of management and members of the workforce which does not involve union officials, is not a significant feature of industrial relations at Dearnley colliery. Unlike in the final decade of public ownership, job and knock agreements, where members of the workforce were allowed to go home before the end of their shift on completion of a specific task or tasks, no longer occur at the colliery (NUM representative), and informal agreements relating to shift times and deployment occur only 'occasionally' (NUM branch official B).

The Labour Process

Productive operations at Dearnley are governed by a different strategy to that which was in operation when the colliery was publicly owned. This is because the colliery is not required to increase output, but is instead expected to produce the same quantity of coal each week. As an NUM representative remarked: 'The pit is on a fixed tonnage. All they've [management] asked us, is to be consistent' (NUM branch official B).

Although less emphasis is placed on increasing output than was the case under public ownership, management at Dearnley have nevertheless sought to improve productivity at the colliery. MINOS and it's associated sub systems were installed at Dearnley during the years of public ownership (NUM representative), and there has consequently been little scope for improving productivity with further automation. Management have however, sought to secure productivity improvements by investing in other mining equipment, and by better utilising the skills and experience of the workforce. As an NUM representative explained: 'They've [management] learned the lessons of the past and now provide the right equipment for the job, unlike BC, who would buy equipment and then say "Make it work". They respect the experience of the men. The men are involved in planning work now' (NUM branch official B). Productivity improvements have also been achieved because management have reduced the labour force at the colliery under the current ownership (NUM representative).

Although some flexible working practices have been adopted at Dearnley in order to improve performance, such developments have been extremely limited.

Functional flexibility is evident at the colliery because job demarcations particularly in relation to face and outbye tasks have been reduced (NUM representative). An NUM representative however, pointed out that although management had encouraged the adoption of functional flexibility to some degree, this had not been widely embraced, and employees at the colliery continued to perform a similar range of tasks as when the mine was publicly owned: 'Multi-skilling has been introduced to a point. Courses have been run to give people additional skills, but it's not changed a great deal here' (NUM branch official B).

Numerical flexibility is not a major feature of operations at Dearnley, and at present, all the underground workers at the colliery are directly employed by CUK (NUM representative). Some surface work is completed by contractors, and an NUM representative acknowledged that underground contractors were periodically employed for specific tasks: 'Contractors are brought in for specialised work. For example, an electrical company might come to install equipment' (NUM branch official B). The contractors at Dearnley however, perform strictly limited functions, and there is no evidence to suggest that management plans to extend the role of the sub contracting companies at the colliery.

Temporal flexibility has similarly not been adopted at Dearnley to any significant extent. Under the terms of their contracts, employees at the colliery are expected to work 40 hours per week, and are also obliged to work a reasonable amount of overtime when required, in relation to production needs (NUM representative). In practice however, overtime working at the colliery is extremely limited. In part this is because the operational strategy of the colliery does not necessitate overtime working, since the weekly output target can be produced within the standard working week (NUM representative). However, an NUM representative also pointed out that the budget allocated to the colliery manager by CUK would not allow for large amounts of overtime working: 'Overtime is limited by the pit budget' (NUM branch official B). Furthermore, as the pay structure in place at the colliery does not incorporate an incentive scheme which would reward workers for increasing output (NUM representative), there is no incentive for Dearnley employees to volunteer for overtime.

Although it is a managerial objective to maintain production levels at Dearnley, corporate level management have continued to accord the same priority to health and safety as was the case when the mine was publicly owned. As an NUM representative stated: 'We were very much in the spotlight when we were first privatised. There was a lot of people watching. It was made very, very clear that safety wouldn't be compromised and this has continued' (NUM branch official B). There was, however, some suggestion that labour reductions amongst the pit deputies at Dearnley had jeopardised health and safety standards at the colliery, because the remaining workers no longer had the time to properly carry out safety inspections (NUM representative).

8.4 Nottston Colliery

Management Strategies

Like their public sector predecessors, the current management at Nottston colliery have favoured a unitary approach to industrial relations issues. As a result, there has been no return to the co-operative relationships between management and the trade unions which characterised the period 1947-84, and as in the final decade of the nationalised era, significant emphasis is placed on the maintenance of managerial prerogatives at the colliery.

Managerial strategies at Nottston reflect corporate industrial relations policies, which, as in the final decade of public ownership, have centred upon the maintenance of dual unionism, and upon the promotion of the moderate UDM. In keeping with corporate policy, the UDM has been recognised at Nottston, since the majority of employees at the colliery are members of this organisation. A UDM representative described the bargaining rights accorded to the union at the colliery as: 'exactly the same as under British Coal' (UDM branch official A), however, as CUK will not negotiate with any of the trade unions in the industry over the question of pay, collective bargaining cannot be said to have been fully re-established at the mine. The NUM, in contrast to the UDM, is not recognised at Nottston, even though a UDM official at the colliery conceded that some 17 per cent of the Nottston workforce are NUM members (UDM representative).

Management at Nottston provide office and telephone facilities for UDM branch officials. Moreover, UDM officials at the colliery are engaged full time in relation to union business, and are given unlimited access to the mine, and to Nottston employees (UDM representative). The NUM officials at the colliery however, receive notably different treatment to that accorded to their UDM counterparts. As a UDM branch official candidly revealed: 'The NUM reps are not given the same privileges' (UDM branch official A). Management at Nottston do not provide any facilities for NUM officials at the colliery, do not permit NUM representatives to take time off work in order to attend to their union duties and do not allow the distribution of NUM recruitment material on colliery premises (NUM representative). Furthermore, NUM officials are only allowed to represent their members in disciplinary hearings in an unofficial capacity, as a UDM representative pointed out: 'NUM reps are only allowed to represent their members as a friend, because they are the minority union' (UDM branch official A).

The unitary approach in relation to industrial relations adopted by management at Nottston is, however, not only manifest in relation to the maintenance of dual unionism at the colliery, and the promotion of the UDM, as the maintenance of managerial prerogatives also continues to receive high priority, as was the case during the final decade of public ownership.

Strategic planning in relation to the long term development of Nottston is a managerial preserve. However, as the colliery is subject to the provisions of TUPE, formal consultative meetings continue to take place between management representatives and representatives of the recognised unions at the colliery, as was the case when British Coal owned the mine. Because the NUM is not recognised at Nottston, the union is not allowed to send representatives to the consultative committee (NUM representative). A UDM representative indicated that the NUM has indirect representation on the consultative committee, since the delegates selected by some groups of workers are NUM members: 'Some groups are represented by the NUM as their rep is in the NUM' (UDM branch official A). However, an NUM representative suggested that even though the NUM organised the majority of faceworkers at Nottston, as at CUK's other Nottinghamshire collieries, the union nevertheless had little opportunity to influence strategic planning at the mine: 'Most Notts facemen are NUM, but to be perfectly frank we've very little influence' (NUM area representative).

The UDM, by contrast, is directly represented on the consultative committee, and is consequently consulted about strategic matters. A UDM representative however, indicated that in some instances, management at Nottston were prevented from disclosing information in relation to strategic concerns to branch officials because of corporate policy: 'There are constraints on them [colliery managers]. There are limits on what they can actually tell us. Less information is made available to colliery managers from headquarters about the state of the industry, CUK has really clamped down. The manager rings me these days to ask if I've heard anything' (UDM branch official A). Furthermore, the UDM representative also suggested that the union was excluded from the decision making process itself: 'We are not directly involved. We are informed' (UDM branch official A).

The UDM at the colliery has been able to influence both strategic decision making, and corporate policy, however, through recourse to industrial action. When the reserves of a nearby colliery closed before privatisation were allocated to another nearby mine, instead of to Nottston, the future of Nottston was placed in jeopardy. A ban on weekend work, however, led to a corporate level management statement that no decision had been taken in relation to the reserves (UDM representative). This is significant, since it suggests that trade union militancy may, in some circumstances, be able to force concessions from management at both colliery and corporate level. It is, however, perhaps equally significant that the limited action that took place at Nottston, did not challenge the unitary approach to industrial relations adopted by management, but was instead directed towards wholly economistic objectives.

Decisions relating to operational questions at Nottston are also subject to managerial prerogative. Because the NUM is prevented from sending representatives to the consultative committee, the union is not formally consulted about such matters. An NUM representative, however, pointed out that the union was informally consulted about operational issues, because the union represents the majority of workers employed at the point of production: 'We haven't got the influence we had, but because we represent the faceworkers we're spoken to unofficially underground' (NUM area official). This is significant, since it indicates that managerial strategies in relation to the NUM at Nottston have been constrained by practical considerations.

The UDM is represented on the committee, it is therefore formally consulted in relation to operational matters, although a UDM representative indicated that management often sought to marginalise the union by withholding relevant information: 'They [management] hold back with information until they think it's absolutely necessary. I have to ask more questions now' (UDM branch official A).

Having de-recognised the NUM in accordance with corporate policy, management at Nottston have also sought to marginalise the recognised unions at the colliery by communicating directly with members of the workforce, rather than by directing communications through their elected representatives. As a UDM representative observed: 'Management seek to resolve problems with individuals or groups rather than through collective channels' (UDM branch official A). A BACM representative suggested that direct communication between management and the workforce at collieries such as Nottston, which are competing with neighbouring mines for reserves, was designed to reinforce colliery, rather than company, loyalty (BACM national official). A UDM representative acknowledged that management at Nottston frequently urged the workforce to outperform their rivals: 'We're always being told we've got to be better than them' (UDM branch official A). This official nevertheless suggested that direct communication was also designed to by-pass the unions at the colliery, thus making their position less tenable: 'I think it's designed to eradicate the role of the trade unions. The more information they [management] can give to the men, the less need they have to go to the trade unions. If they [management] can eradicate your involvement there's no position for the union' (UDM branch official A).

The Role of the Unions

At Nottston colliery, management have clearly sought to offer more favourable treatment to the union most likely to be supportive of managerial objectives at the mine, since recognition has been granted to the moderate UDM, but not to the NUM, which has traditionally subscribed to a more militant brand of trade unionism. As at CUK's other Nottinghamshire collieries, however, management at Nottston have not endeavoured to sign a single union agreement with the UDM, since this would not be in accordance with corporate policy. As a corporate level management representative stated: 'No, there is no single union agreement with the UDM, and this won't be considered' (Corporate level management representative A). It is significant, given the history and traditions of the UDM, that CUK has rejected the possibility of a single union agreement with this organisation. This would suggest that CUK was opposed to collective organisation, however moderate, and indeed a corporate level management representative alluded to this when he declared: 'I don't think there would be any advantage to be gained [from signing a single union agreement with the UDM], because the company doesn't see the unions as a vehicle for representation. We prefer to deal with the workforce' (Corporate level management representative A).

Management at Nottston have not directly sought to encourage employees at the colliery to join the UDM rather than the NUM (UDM representatives and NUM representative). However, a UDM representative indicated that NUM members at Nottston were under indirect pressure to change their affiliation, because if they approached management with a problem they were directed to the UDM branch officials: 'If NUM members have a problem management refer them to the UDM secretary' (UDM branch official A).

An NUM representative expressed the view that CUK regarded trade unions per se as an irrelevance, and as a consequence, did not consider the

181

trade union affiliation of individual employees to be an important issue: 'They [CUK] have not interfered with the men like British Coal did. They couldn't care less what union they're in. The unions are seen as an irrelevance, therefore CUK sees it as an irrelevance which union they're in' (NUM area official). Given that CUK has expressly sought to maintain dual unionism within the industry however, it could be argued that this is an over simplistic view, and that if individual trade union affiliation is regarded as unimportant this is only because the UDM's majority support is not threatened at collieries such as Nottston, since if it were, this would undermine the basis on which recognition is denied to the NUM.

Management at Nottston have not sought to promote non-unionism at the mine (UDM representative), and a UDM representative indicated that there were few Nottston employees who did not belong to a trade union: 'There is no significant problem with non-unionism' (UDM branch official A). Even so, a national UDM representative conceded that no colliery in Nottinghamshire was fully organised: 'There are between 40 and 50 non-union members at each pit' (UDM national official). Nevertheless, as some 600 men are employed at Nottston, union density is high at the colliery.

Collective bargaining has been re-established at Nottston, but the scope of negotiations is severely proscribed by managerial prerogative, because corporate policy states that wage levels are not negotiable (Management representative). The restoration of collective bargaining at Nottston then, has not served to increase the influence of the trade unions in relation to the terms and conditions of their members at the colliery.

Changes in the locus of bargaining are evident at Nottston, because CUK has de-recognised all the mining unions at national and area levels, which has increased the importance of local bargaining. As a UDM representative commented: 'They [management] don't want anything to do with the full time officials. They always tell me not to bring anyone in from a higher level. They always want to sort things out at the pit' (UDM branch official A). This view was echoed by a UDM national official who suggested that local bargaining was being encouraged by the company in order to undermine the principal of corporate level bargaining, despite existing corporate level agreements being protected by TUPE: 'They'd [CUK] sooner do away with national and area officials. CUK's intention is to de-centralise agreements' (UDM national official).

182

Although all the mining unions have been officially de-recognised at national level, a UDM representative indicated that unofficial bargaining does take place between senior CUK managers and UDM national officials: 'CUK officially will not agree to collective bargaining. The Chief Executive has got a hang up over the term collective bargaining. Collective bargaining does occur, it's just not called collective bargaining' (UDM national official). Another UDM representative, moreover, indicated that although the national union was unable to influence local bargaining at Nottston, they did have some influence at corporate level because of the informal contact between national officials and senior managers, and because of the commercial environment engendered by privatisation: 'Berry Hill [UDM national office] is most influential in terms of the company. CUK are very conscious of the fact that adverse statements made by national officials could have a negative effect on the share price, and I think this gives the UDM some bargaining power' (UDM branch official A).

The increasing importance of local bargaining at Nottston has not, however, resulted in a wider range of issues coming within the jurisdiction of the Nottston UDM branch. Indeed, a UDM representative indicated that the branch was involved with fewer issues than in the days when the colliery was publicly owned, because of the emphasis placed on the maintenance of managerial prerogatives: 'They've [management] tended to phase us out of planning and operational matters. They don't think the union has a right to have an influence' (UDM branch official A). There is then, little evidence of union renewal at Nottston. It would, however, be wrong to suggest that the Nottston UDM branch is ineffective, since the use of limited industrial action has forced concessions from management, albeit in relation to economistic goals. The Nottston NUM branch is, by contrast, wholly ineffective.

Institutions of Collective Bargaining

Nottston colliery was never closed by British Coal, and consequently remained in production throughout the privatisation process. CUK's purchase of the colliery in December 1994 therefore represented at transfer of undertakings, bringing the colliery within the scope of the provisions of TUPE. Under the terms of TUPE, CUK was obliged by statute to recognise all the existing agreements negotiated by British Coal and the mining unions prior to privatisation, and because of this, those agreements continued to apply at Nottston following privatisation. The institutional framework which was developed to facilitate collective bargaining in the industry during the years of public ownership remains largely intact, although CUK has sought to undermine the agreements safeguarded by the provisions of TUPE.

When CUK purchased Nottston in 1994, the colliery continued to be subject to the British Coal conciliation scheme, since this was inherited by CUK under the provisions of TUPE. In 1996, however, CUK withdrew the existing conciliation scheme and replaced it with a corporate level agreement (Management representative). This was negotiated by senior CUK managers and UDM national officials (Management representatives and UDM representatives), and like the British Coal scheme it replaced, is based on the majority/minority principle. The automatic right to independent arbitration has, however, been removed, although there is provision for disputes to be referred to an independent body, given the agreement of CUK's Chief Executive and the UDM National President (UDM national official).

The disciplinary and grievance procedure currently in operation at Nottston was also inherited by CUK under the TUPE legislation. This structure has, like the conciliation scheme been modified however, and the right to independent arbitration has been withdrawn (UDM national representative). The revised disciplinary and grievance procedure was similarly negotiated by senior CUK managers and UDM national officials (UDM national official).

The pay structure which is currently operative at Nottston was also inherited from British Coal under the provisions of TUPE, although this structure has also been amended by CUK. Nottston miners continue to receive a basic weekly wage and a production bonus, as was the case when the British Coal pay structure was in operation, and similarly continue to receive additional payments for working in heat and water. As an NUM representative revealed: 'All the bit bob payments are still in force at Nottston' (UDM branch official A). The grading structure has been modified however, leading to a reduction in differentials (UDM representative). The changes to the pay structure were, like the changes to the conciliation scheme, negotiated by senior CUK managers and UDM national officials (UDM representatives).

The provisions of TUPE have then, ensured that formal structures are in place to facilitate collective bargaining at Nottston, although the UDM branch at the colliery has not, to date negotiated any formal substantive agreements (UDM representative). As the amendments to the institutions of collective bargaining inherited under TUPE were jointly negotiated by CUK and the UDM, these structures represent a collective agreement between the company and the UDM. The NUM was not involved in these negotiations, however, and the new structures were been imposed on NUM members at the colliery.

The institutional bargaining arrangements currently in force at Nottston then, have been greatly influenced by managerial prerogative, and furthermore, have been designed to consolidate the institutionalisation of dual unionism within the company. Because of this, they bear little resemblance to those negotiated structures which were operational between 1947 and 1984, and have more in common with the procedures introduced unilaterally by British Coal during the final decade of public ownership.

A UDM representative pointed out that, unlike during the years of public ownership, the current management team at Nottston discourage informal agreements between junior management and members of the workforce which have no union involvement: 'They [management] are more reluctant to have an off the cuff agreement. They'd prefer it in writing, signed by the Branch Secretary and the colliery manager' (UDM branch official A). This is significant, since it indicates that informal bargaining without union involvement, is no longer a significant feature of industrial relations at Nottston. As a UDM representative observed: 'There isn't any [informal bargaining] really' (UDM branch official A).

The Labour Process

Maximising productivity remains a central objective of operations at Nottston, as was the case during the final decade of public ownership. Nevertheless, a number of changes have occurred in relation to the labour process at the colliery following privatisation.

Because Nottston was fully automated during the years of public ownership (UDM representative), there has been little scope for improving productivity with further automation. The current management at the colliery have, however, sought to generate productivity improvements with the introduction of new mining techniques. Roof bolting has been widely

185

adopted at Nottston, and has contributed to improvements in productivity because it is easier to install than conventional steel roof supports, and thus speeds up development work at the colliery. The use of roof bolting has moreover reduced the labour requirements of the colliery because it is a less labour-intensive technique (UDM representative).

Management at Nottston have also sought to improve productivity by introducing flexible working practices, and indeed, functional, numerical, and temporal flexibility are all evident at the colliery.

Functional flexibility has been widely adopted at Nottston following privatisation, and many employees have been given training by CUK in order to enable them to perform a wider range of duties. For example some underground production workers have been trained for FSV or engine driving, and are now able to work as part of the underground haulage team if required (UDM representative). Functional flexibility at Nottston has also facilitated a reduction in labour requirements of the colliery however (UDM representative), and has thus contributed to the intensification of work, since the remaining employees are expected to carry out the same amount of work as was formerly performed by a larger number of workers. One UDM representative alluded to this when he observed: 'There's plenty of men doubling up' (UDM branch official A), and indeed, another UDM representative expressed the view that functional flexibility had not enskilled members of the workforce, but had instead led to the intensification of work by reducing the porosity of the working day: 'It's multi-tasking not multi-skilling. Better utilisation of the workforce they [management] call it. It's not so much flexible working as one man doing three men's jobs now' (UDM national official).

Numerical flexibility has been adopted at Nottston, if to a limited extent, since some specialised tasks on the surface are outsourced (UDM representative). All the underground workers at Nottston are directly employed by CUK however (UDM representative), and indeed, there is some suggestion that the company is seeking to reduce the role played by outside contractors. As a UDM representative commented: 'They [CUK] seem to be outing all the contractors now' (UDM branch official A).

Temporal flexibility is also a feature of CUK's operations at Nottston, with this being primarily manifest in overtime working. A UDM representative acknowledged that many Nottston miners volunteered for overtime: 'We've never had a problem with overtime. it's only when they [management] reduce overtime that it's a problem' (UDM branch official

A), however he also pointed out that some groups of workers were occasionally pressurised by management into working overtime: 'There is pressure put on the men. When a face is being prepared, they know they'll have to work extra' (UDM branch official A). In addition, there was some suggestion that labour reductions at the colliery have necessitated overtime working, with the supervisory staff being particularly affected by these developments. As a UDM representative remarked: 'The officials are doing a large amount of overtime to cover for fewer men' (UDM branch official A).

Although operations at Nottston have focused on increasing productivity since privatisation, a UDM representative nevertheless suggested that corporate level management have endeavoured to give the same priority to health and safety as was the case when the industry was publicly owned: 'CUK are throwing a hell of a lot of money at safety. There is a big emphasis on re-training' (UDM branch official A). The management team at Nottston itself however, do not appear to recognise the negative health and safety implications of work intensification, and a UDM representative indicated that there was a widespread belief that safety standards at the colliery had been jeopardised by the excessive overtime worked by pit deputies: 'The men are of the opinion that overworked deputies are compromising safety. There is a question as to whether safety monitoring is as effective when deputies are tired' (UDM branch official B). This view was echoed by a NACODS representative who remarked: 'When you talk to senior CUK managers they don't want people working excessive hours, but the colliery managers do, and it's there where we have problems' (NACODS national official).

A UDM representative expressed the view that the insecurity in the industry since privatisation had also had negative implications for safety standards at Nottston: 'The men haven't got their minds on the job because they're whittling about what's going to happen. I'm sure it's the uncertainty that's resulting in the accidents' (UDM branch official A), and indeed this representative acknowledged that the number of minor accidents had increased at the colliery under the current regime: 'There are more minor accidents now than under BC' (UDM branch official A). Another UDM representative moreover, revealed that management at Nottston, as at other Nottinghamshire collieries had sought to manipulate the accident statistics by discouraging members of the workforce from reporting accidents: 'They used to have this scheme called points win

187

prizes. The men would win points for not reporting accidents, which could be cashed in for gifts, TVs, toasters, that sort of thing, but this was stopped by the Health and Safety Executive' (UDM national official).

8.5 Mansthorpe Colliery

Management Strategies

As with the other CUK collieries, the style of management which has emerged at Mansthorpe following the company's acquisition of the mine, bears a strong resemblance to that which was apparent during the final decade of the nationalised era. Management at the colliery have continued to pursue the unitary approach to labour relations embraced by British Coal during the final decade of public ownership, and as a result there has been no return to pluralism at the colliery. Continuity with the period 1984-94 is also evident since the maintenance of managerial prerogatives at the colliery continues to receive much emphasis. There is, however, some evidence to suggest that CUK has sought not only to introduce the patterns of labour relations developed nationally by British Coal during the last decade of public ownership, at Mansthorpe, but also to de-collectivise industrial relations at the colliery, although there is also some suggestion that this strategy is being resisted by management at colliery level.

Managerial strategies at Mansthorpe reflect industrial relations policies developed at corporate level, and as in the final decade of public ownership, corporate strategies have focused upon the maintenance of dual unionism, and upon the promotion of the moderate UDM. In accordance with corporate policy the UDM has been recognised at Mansthorpe, since the majority of employees at the colliery have been members of this organisation since its establishment in 1985. The UDM has no formal bargaining rights at Mansthorpe, but informal bargaining suggests that in practice, the bargaining rights currently enjoyed by the UDM at the colliery do not differ significantly from those granted to the union in the final decade of public ownership. The NUM, by contrast, is not recognised at the colliery and consequently has no bargaining rights, although some 9 per cent of Mansthorpe employees continue to belong to the NUM (UDM representative).

Management at Mansthorpe provide office and telephone facilities for UDM branch officials, who are engaged full time on union business (UDM representative). The NUM officials at the colliery, receive significantly different treatment from their UDM counterparts, since management at the colliery do not provide any facilities for NUM officials, do not permit NUM representatives to take time off work in order to attend to their union duties and do not allow the distribution of NUM recruitment material on colliery premises (NUM representative). Moreover, NUM officials at Mansthorpe, as at other CUK collieries in Nottinghamshire, are only allowed to represent their members in disciplinary hearings in an unofficial capacity. As an NUM representative stated: 'NUM reps representing NUM members on disciplinary hearings are only recognised as a friend' (NUM area official).

The unitary approach in relation to industrial relations adopted by management at Mansthorpe is apparent both in relation to the maintenance of dual unionism at the colliery, reflected in initiatives to promote the UDM, and in the maintenance of managerial prerogatives at the colliery.

Mansthorpe colliery is not covered by the provisions of TUPE, and management at the colliery have, in accordance with corporate policy, unilaterally abandoned the formal consultative meetings with the trade unions which used to take place on a regular basis when the mine was publicly owned (UDM representative). The unions then, are not formally consulted in relation to strategic matters affecting the long term future of the colliery. The UDM is nevertheless able to make informal representations to management in relation to strategic matters because relationships between management and the union at the colliery have customarily been conciliatory, and managerial continuity at Mansthorpe has been preserved despite the change of ownership. As a UDM representative remarked: 'We were lucky that we had the same lot [management] here as we had before privatisation. It would probably be different if they'd [CUK] set new management on' (UDM branch official B). This is significant, since it suggests that colliery level management at Mansthorpe have been flexible in their interpretation of corporate policy in relation to the unions. However, as contact between management and UDM branch officials is entirely unofficial, and as strategic decisions are made at corporate rather than colliery level (Management representatives), the UDM is unable to exert any significant influence in relation to strategic issues concerning Mansthorpe. As a UDM representative explained: 'I wouldn't say we have a say in it [strategic decision making]. They'll [management] make the decision yea or nay. All we can do is put our ideas forward' (UDM branch official B). The NUM, by contrast, has neither formal nor informal contact with management at Mansthorpe, and is consequently unable to exert any influence in relation to strategic planning.

Decisions relating to operational matters at Mansthorpe are also the prerogative of management, and because consultative meetings have been withdrawn, the unions at the colliery are not formally consulted in relation to such issues. UDM officials however, meet informally with management 'on a daily basis' (UDM branch official B), and the conciliatory relations between management and UDM representatives at Mansthorpe facilitate some union influence in relation to operational matters, despite this being contrary to corporate policy. As a UDM representative observed: 'We try to keep all our problems away from Berry Hill [UDM national office] and away from CUK headquarters. We try to sort it out ourselves, even if we do F and B at each other at times'(UDM branch official B). The NUM, by contrast, has no influence in relation to operational decisions at Mansthorpe, since NUM representatives have no contact with management at the colliery.

Management at Mansthorpe have sought to communicate directly with Mansthorpe employees, and members of the management team go underground on a daily basis in order to facilitate this (UDM representative). Moreover, management at the colliery operate an open door policy, and encourage representations from members of the workforce independent of the unions. As a UDM representative commented: 'The manager is accessible to everyone' (UDM branch official B).

The Role of the Unions

Management at Mansthorpe have, as at CUK's other Nottinghamshire collieries, offered more favourable treatment to the union most likely to acquiesce to managerial objectives at the colliery, having recognised the moderate UDM, but not the more militant NUM. In accordance with corporate policy, however, management at Mansthorpe have not sought to enter into a single union agreement with the UDM.

There is no evidence to suggest that management at Mansthorpe have sought to promote UDM membership amongst employees at the colliery, and indeed a UDM representative stated: 'Management aren't bothered what union they're in' (UDM branch official B). The UDM representative did however reveal that UDM national officials endeavoured to persuade CUK to recruit former UDM members rather than members of other unions when the colliery was re-opened by the company in January 1994: 'There was pressure from Berry Hill [UDM national office] to recruit UDM only' (UDM branch official B).

Non-unionism has similarly not been encouraged by management at Mansthorpe (UDM representative). Indeed, a UDM representative pointed out that the majority of the workforce recruited by CUK when the colliery was re-opened, had previously worked at Mansthorpe, and that many employees were therefore former UDM members: 'The vast majority of the first men recruited were ex-Mansthorpe men' (UDM branch official B). Union density at Mansthorpe is nevertheless relatively low, and a UDM representative acknowledged that some 27 per cent of the workforce were not members of any of the mining unions (UDM representative).

The relatively high level of non-unionism at Mansthorpe was attributed to workforce apathy by a UDM representative, who remarked: 'If I were truthful, I'd say the men didn't care about the union now' (UDM branch official B). The notion that workforce perceptions of trade union weakness may lead to falling union density, Winterton and Winterton (1993b: 24), is also supported by evidence from Mansthorpe, as a UDM representative stated that some Mansthorpe employees without trade union affiliation had applied for union membership when they believed the union was able to make effective representations on their behalf: 'The only time they come and join is when they've had an accident, or when they want something sorted' (UDM branch official B).

Formal collective bargaining has not been restored at Mansthorpe, because the provisions of TUPE do not apply at the colliery, and management have been able to abandon the consultative arrangements which existed during the years of public ownership. Informal contact does take place between management and UDM representatives however, and unofficial collective bargaining does occur at the colliery (UDM representative). The UDM at Mansthorpe is, therefore, able to exert some influence in relation to the terms and conditions of their members employed at the colliery. However, as bargaining at Mansthorpe is informal, and is not supported by an institutional framework, it is clearly proscribed by managerial prerogatives. Moreover, an NUM area representative pointed out that terms and conditions at collieries not subject to the provisions of TUPE, were 'very much inferior' (NUM area official), to those at mines where the legislation applied.

There have been no significant changes in the locus of bargaining in relation to Mansthorpe, despite CUK's de-recognition of all the mining unions at national and area levels, and the majority of contact between management representatives and union officials continues to occur at colliery level, as was the case during the years of public ownership (UDM representative). The UDM branch at Mansthorpe, moreover, has a tradition of independence, and has sought to avoid the involvement of national and area union officials in local matters. As a UDM representative explained: 'It's hard to describe Mansthorpe. Even under British Coal we wouldn't have much truck with the union. It's never been an us and them pit. It's a family pit, a bit of a one off' (UDM branch official B). The same UDM representative, however, also expressed the view that there was greater opportunity for local bargaining at Mansthorpe, because the colliery was not subject to the provisions of TUPE: 'The lease / licence provisions mean there is greater scope for local settlements' (UDM branch official B). Indeed, there is some suggestion that corporate level management within CUK regard the informal local bargaining established at lease / licence collieries such as Mansthorpe as something of a model for the other collieries owned by the company, and has sought to extend local bargaining in order to undermine the existing agreements safeguarded by TUPE. As a UDM national representative revealed: 'Colliery managers try to engage branch officials in negotiations over new terms and conditions' (UDM national official).

According to a UDM representative, the continued significance of local bargaining at Mansthorpe has been accompanied by an increase in the range of issues dealt with by the local union branch: 'There are more issues now. I think I'm told more now than I was before [privatisation]' (UDM branch official B). Although management may be making more information available to UDM branch officials, the union is taking up fewer issues on behalf of their members. As a UDM representative observed: 'It's got to be really serious now before you hear anything from the men. Before [privatisation], they were in the office all the time. Men would come in if they had a sore tooth' (UDM branch official B). This is significant since it suggests that the apathy of UDM members at Mansthorpe has, alongside corporate industrial relations strategies, served to weaken the position of the UDM at the colliery.

There is then, little evidence of genuine local union renewal at Mansthorpe, and the UDM branch at the colliery is largely ineffective despite being party to unofficial bargaining. The Mansthorpe NUM branch, which has no contact formal or otherwise with management representatives at the colliery is, by contrast, wholly ineffective.

Institutions of Collective Bargaining

Following the coal crisis of 1992, Mansthorpe colliery was closed by British Coal and the entire workforce was made redundant. CUK's acquisition of the colliery therefore did not represent a transfer of undertakings, and because of this, the provisions of TUPE did not apply at the colliery. All the existing agreements negotiated by British Coal and the mining unions prior to privatisation, were consequently no longer in force at Mansthorpe when the colliery was returned to production by the new owners. Some formal institutional structures have nevertheless emerged at Mansthorpe to replace the mechanisms which facilitated collective bargaining during the years of public ownership.

Although Mansthorpe is not subject to the provisions of TUPE, the conciliation scheme in operation at the colliery is the same as that which is currently operative at collieries where this legislation did apply (UDM representative). When CUK purchased the core collieries in 1994, these mines continued to be subject to the British Coal conciliation scheme. In 1996, however, CUK amended the scheme (Management representative), withdrawing the automatic right to independent arbitration, although under the current arrangements, disputes may be referred to an independent body if CUK's Chief Executive and the UDM National President agree to this (UDM national representative). The amended conciliation scheme which was introduced at Mansthorpe, is, like its predecessor, based on the majority/minority principle, and was similarly negotiated by senior CUK managers and UDM national officials (Management representatives and UDM representatives).

The disciplinary and grievance procedure currently in operation at the colliery is also the same as that which exists at those collieries acquired by CUK which were subject to the provisions of TUPE (UDM representative).

The British Coal disciplinary and grievance procedure was inherited by CUK under the TUPE legislation, but this structure was modified, and the right to independent arbitration was withdrawn (UDM national representative). The revised disciplinary and grievance procedure was, however, like the amended conciliation scheme, negotiated by senior CUK managers and UDM national officials (UDM national official).

The pay structure in operation at Mansthorpe is loosely based on the British Coal pay structure, although it differs significantly from the structure in place at those collieries subject to the provisions of TUPE. Wages at Mansthorpe are related to the occupational grade of individual employees and the wages received by each employee are comprised of a basic rate combined with a productivity bonus, and an attendance bonus (UDM representative). Employees at Mansthorpe however, receive no additional payments for working in water or heat (UDM representative). The pay structure at Mansthorpe, moreover, was not negotiated with the local branch of the UDM, but was imposed upon the workforce. As a UDM representative stated: 'We were told "This is the pay structure for Mansthorpe colliery. Do you want it, or do you not want it?"' (UDM branch official B).

Although Mansthorpe is not subject to the provisions of TUPE, formal structures to facilitate collective bargaining have emerged at the colliery, because the conciliation scheme and the disciplinary and grievance procedure in operation at collieries where this legislation applies have been introduced at Mansthorpe. As the amendments to the conciliation scheme, and the disciplinary and grievance procedure which have been introduced at Mansthorpe were jointly negotiated by CUK and the UDM, it might be argued that these structures represent collective agreements between the company and the UDM, which were then imposed on NUM members at the colliery. The pay structure in operation at Mansthorpe, by contrast, was not negotiated with any of the mining unions, and therefore cannot be classed as a collective agreement under any circumstances.

The institutional bargaining arrangements presently in force at Mansthorpe then, resemble those procedures introduced by British Coal during the final decade of public ownership, rather than the negotiated structures which were operational between 1947 and 1984. This is because they have been greatly influenced by managerial prerogative, and moreover, have the objective of consolidating the institutionalisation of dual unionism within the company, as was the case with the British Coal structures they replaced.

Informal bargaining between members of junior management and groups of workers which have no union involvement, are less significant now than was the case when the colliery was publicly owned. Corporate policy does not permit job and knock agreements, where miners are allowed to go home early once a specific task had been completed, and consequently such agreements are no longer made at the colliery. As a UDM representative explained: 'There is no job and knock. A plan was put forward, but the Director of Mining will not hear of job and knock' (UDM branch official B). Informal agreements in relation to deployment and shift times continue to occur at the colliery however (UDM representative).

The Labour Process

The change in ownership at Mansthorpe has not been accompanied by any marked changes in relation to the labour process, and as in the years when the colliery was publicly owned, the objective of maximising productivity continues to guide operations at the colliery.

Output is limited to some extent at Mansthorpe, since the coal seams being worked are small, and the faces at the colliery are, as a result, less than half the height than those at other collieries in the Nottinghamshire coalfield. As a UDM representative explained: 'Production is limited at Mansthorpe due to the height of the faces. At Mansthorpe they are metre faces, rather than twelve foot as in the rest of Notts' (UDM branch official B). The colliery was nevertheless fully automated during the years of public ownership, and because of this the current management team has not sought further technological improvements in order to facilitate productivity improvements. As a UDM representative observed: 'There has been no real change between BC and CUK in terms of technology' (UDM branch official B).

CUK has sought to improve productivity at Mansthorpe by reducing labour requirements, and indeed in November 1997, the company announced some 80 redundancies at the colliery (UDM representative). Management have also introduced limited flexible working practices at Mansthorpe with a view to improving productivity, through functional and temporal flexibility.

Functional flexibility is a significant feature of operations at Mansthorpe, and workers at the colliery are currently expected to perform a wider range of tasks than was the case when the mine was publicly owned (UDM representative). A UDM representative suggested that the pace of work had increased at the colliery, and that members of the workforce were currently working to the limits of their physical capabilities: 'They [management] can't make them [the workforce] go any harder than they're doing at the moment' (UDM branch official B). Although functional flexibility has contributed to the intensification of work at Mansthorpe, through reducing the porosity of the working day, there is no evidence of workforce resistance to these developments. Indeed, a UDM representative indicated that members of the workforce had embraced functional flexibility because they viewed this as a means of improving the survival prospects of the colliery, and of increasing their own employment prospects in the event of Mansthorpe's closure: 'There is a willingness to be more flexible to keep the pit going. The men are asking to be trained for more jobs. They think they'll have a better chance of finding work if Mansthorpe closes if they're multi-skilled' (UDM branch official B).

Temporal flexibility has also been adopted at Mansthorpe, to a limited extent. According to the terms of their contracts, Mansthorpe employees are required to work 40 hours a week (UDM representative), but the majority of workers at the colliery work overtime on a regular basis: 'Most workers do a 48 hour week' (UDM branch official B). There is however, no suggestion that Mansthorpe employees are under any pressure to work overtime, and indeed a UDM representative indicated that many workers volunteered to work additional hours: 'Most of them want the overtime anyway. It's keeping them out that's the hard part' (UDM branch official B).

Numerical flexibility is not a major feature of operations at Mansthorpe, although a UDM representative acknowledged that some work had been outsourced in the past (UDM representative). At present however, no contracting companies are employed at the colliery.

Although management at Mansthorpe have continued to seek productivity improvements, there is no suggestion that this has had negative implications for health and safety at the colliery. A UDM representative suggested that this was because management were aware that falling safety standards would be likely to meet with employee resistance, and had therefore not imposed changes that would compromise safety at the colliery: 'They've never tried to push anything on us. We have the same men, and they wouldn't have accepted change' (UDM branch official B).

8.6 Conclusions

The pattern of industrial relations which has begun to emerge within CUK in the three years since privatisation, exhibits much continuity with those patterns that developed nationally during the final decade of public ownership. This is because the unitary approach to labour relations issues which was unilaterally introduced by British Coal has been embraced by CUK, and the relationships between corporate level management and the mining unions consequently continue to be characterised by conflict, rather than co-operation. A unitary approach to industrial relations is also evident at colliery level, as evidence from Donborough, Dearnley, Nottston and Mansthorpe collieries demonstrates. Significantly, however, the unitary approach is most apparent at Dearnley and Mansthorpe, where labour relations have been de-collectivised. By contrast, management at Donborough and Nottston have adopted a less robust approach in relation to the trade unions.

Corporate policy in relation to the unions at national and area level at first appears to be consistent, since all the mining unions have been de-recognised at these levels. In practice, however, corporate policy has been primarily designed to exclude the NUM, because there is no contact with NUM national officials, whilst informal negotiations between senior CUK managers and the national officials of the UDM have taken place (Management representatives, UDM representatives, and NUM representatives). BACM and NACODS national officials similarly have informal dialogue with the company (BACM representative, and NACODS representative). CUK's policy of maintaining of dual unionism within its operations is also evident at colliery level, since at each colliery, recognition has only been granted to the union which represents the majority of employees. This development has led to the de-recognition of the NUM at Nottston and Mansthorpe. The UDM, however, has not been de-recognised at any of the collieries which were studied.

At all four collieries, the same emphasis is placed on the maintenance of managerial prerogatives as was the case during the last decade of public ownership. As a result, the NUM has been unable to exert any meaningful influence in relation to either strategic or operational decision making at Donborough or Dearnley, whilst the UDM has similarly been unable to influence decision making in relation to these matters at Mansthorpe. By contrast, the use of industrial action at Nottston has enabled the UDM to have some influence in relation strategic and operational decisions at the colliery.

Developments in management industrial relations strategies at both corporate and colliery level then, do not lend weight to the predictions of Ferner and Colling (1991), that the new environment engendered by privatisation would result in the development of a more conciliatory managerial approach to labour relations issues. Privatisation has nevertheless had a major influence in relation to the development of management industrial relations strategies within CUK. This is because this has led to the emergence of a new form of ownership, which has, in turn, given rise to a new managerial regime at corporate level. The new regime has sought to maintain, and indeed in some instances intensify, the unitary approach to labour relations adopted by British Coal during the final decade of public ownership, rather than to abandon this approach.

Privatisation has, however, had a more direct bearing on the development of management industrial relations strategies within CUK. CUK purchased collieries at various points during the privatisation process, and because of this, some mines, including Donborough and Nottston were subject to the provisions of TUPE, whilst others like Dearnley and Mansthorpe were not. It is significant that management has taken the most robust approach towards the trade unions at Dearnley and Mansthorpe, and indeed it could be argued that the provisions of TUPE have constrained managerial strategies in relation to the unions at Donborough and Nottston, where this legislation has applied.

The structure of CUK has also had a significant influence on the development of management strategies however. CUK acquired collieries in both Yorkshire and Nottinghamshire, and as a result, the company has been able to focus its industrial relations strategies on the maintenance of dual unionism within its operations. Furthermore, because CUK acquired twenty collieries during the privatisation process, industrial relations strategies are developed at corporate rather than colliery level.

198

Management at colliery level are therefore constrained by company labour relations policies, although there is evidence which points to opposition to corporate level policies at colliery level. This is most apparent at Dearnley and Mansthorpe collieries, which is particularly significant, since this is where the unitary approach developed at corporate level has been most vigorously applied.

The role of the mining unions which represent CUK employees has undergone some change since privatisation, since all the unions have been de-recognised at national and area levels. It could be argued that this development has, with respect of the NUM, merely formalised the de facto situation which existed during the final decade of public ownership. It is, however, particularly significant that official recognition has also been denied to BACM, NACODS and the UDM, which suggests that CUK is unwilling to countenance formal corporate level bargaining under any circumstances. Nevertheless, since the company has an unofficial dialogue with the national officials of all these organisations (UDM representatives, BACM representative and NACODS representative), it is evident that corporate policy has been overlooked when this has been deemed to be expedient.

Because formal bargaining is not permitted at corporate level, the significance of colliery level bargaining has increased at Donborough and Nottston, where formal bargaining is permitted. This has not, however, resulted in a greater range of issues coming within the jurisdiction of the recognised trade union branches at these collieries, since the extent of bargaining is proscribed by managerial prerogative. Branch organisation at both Donborough and Nottston therefore, remains largely ineffective. At Dearnley, by contrast, formal bargaining has not been sanctioned, and local bargaining has not therefore assumed a greater significance. As a consequence of these developments, there has been a significant reduction in the range of issues dealt with by the NUM branch at Dearnley, and indeed branch organisation at the colliery is wholly ineffective. Formal bargaining is similarly not permitted at Mansthorpe, but informal bargaining does take place at the colliery, and there is evidence to suggest that the UDM branch at the mine manage a wider range of issues now than was the case in the final decade of public ownership. As bargaining at Mansthorpe is informal however, it is severely proscribed by managerial prerogative, and the UDM branch at the colliery therefore remains essentially ineffective. Because local recognition has been denied to the

NUM at Nottston and Mansthorpe, the NUM branches at both collieries are completely ineffective.

The cases of Donborough, Dearnley, Nottston and Mansthorpe then, provide no evidence to support the view forwarded by Fairbrother (1994) and Edwards and Heery (1989), that the increased importance of de-centralised bargaining following privatisation would result in the rejuvenation of local trade union branches. The current weakness of the trade union branches at these collieries cannot be wholly attributed to privatisation however, because the position of capital was strengthened relative to that of labour during the final decade of public ownership, when industrial relations in the coal industry were extensively restructured. Privatisation has nevertheless facilitated the consolidation of these developments.

Continuity with the patterns of industrial relations developed during the period 1984-94 is also apparent, because those institutional structures which are currently in place to support bargaining at collieries owned by CUK, have more in common with those structures introduced unilaterally by British Coal following the 1984-85 strike, than to the mechanisms which were operative during the period 1947-84. This is because the new structures have served to consolidate the institutionalisation of dual unionism within the company. Furthermore, the development of these arrangements has been significantly influenced by managerial prerogative, and only the UDM was consulted in relation to modifications to the structures inherited under the provisions of TUPE, with the new procedures being imposed on the NUM. The existence of an institutional framework to support bargaining then, cannot be said to represent the development of a pattern of industrial relations based on consensus, and indeed the presence of such structures is virtually meaningless given that CUK have denied formal collective bargaining rights to the trade unions at corporate level, and at individual collieries including Dearnley and Mansthorpe.

There have been few changes in relation to the labour process at Donborough, Dearnley, Nottston or Mansthorpe, other than initiatives to improve productivity at the collieries through the intensification of work. Management at corporate level are mindful of the negative health and safety implications of work intensification, and have continued to accord the same priority to safety matters as their predecessors. There is evidence that management at colliery level have overlooked these issues, however, and there is some suggestion that management at Donborough and Nottston have manipulated the accident statistics, and have discouraged members of the workforce from reporting accidents.

The emergent patterns of industrial relations within CUK then, exhibit considerable continuity with those patterns established during the period 1984-94, and there has been no return to the pluralism which characterised labour relations in the industry between 1947 and 1984. It could be argued, moreover, that corporate level management have sought to take a more robust approach in relation to the trade unions than was adopted by their public sector predecessors, at collieries such as Dearnley and Mansthorpe, where the legal framework has restricted managerial objectives to a lesser degree. It is therefore, possible to conclude that privatisation has had negative implications for organised labour in general within CUK, and for the NUM in particular.

9 Explaining Continuity and Change

9.1 Management Strategies

At six of the seven collieries considered within this study, management has adopted a unitary approach to industrial relations, although significant variations in the vigour with which this approach has been applied are evident (Figure 9.1). Management has taken a particularly robust attitude towards organised labour at Workham colliery, where all the mining unions have been de-recognised, and where industrial relations have been de-collectivised. At Dearnley and Mansthorpe, the managerial stance in relation to the trade unions has been only marginally less rigorous, since de-recognition has taken place on a selective, rather than general basis, but management has nevertheless sought to de-collectivise labour relations at these collieries also. Management at Abergoed, Donborough and Nottston collieries, whilst continuing to operate within a unitary framework, have adopted a less hostile attitude towards organised labour. At these collieries the trade unions have again been de-recognised on a selective basis, and the unions have experienced varying degree of marginalisation, but management has not attempted to de-collectivise industrial relations.

In contrast to the industrial relations strategies adopted by management at Workham, Dearnley, Mansthorpe, Abergoed, Donborough and Nottston, management at Cwmpridd colliery have abandoned the unitary approach to industrial relations which held sway during the final decade of public ownership. Although selective de-recognition has taken place at Cwmpridd, this has not had the objective of weakening collective organisation at the colliery, unlike at the other mines which were studied. Moreover, management at Cwmpridd have not introduced policies designed to marginalise those unions which have been recognised, and as a consequence industrial relations at the colliery are now based on consensus rather than conflict.

Figure 9.1 Management industrial relations strategies in the privatised coal industry

Most robust   Least robust

Workham   Dearnley   Donborough   Cwmpridd
                 Mansthorpe   Nottston
                                             Abergoed

The difference between the industrial relations strategies adopted by management at Cwmpridd, and those policies introduced by management at the other six collieries within the study, can be accounted for by the form of ownership at the mines in question. Cwmpridd, unlike any of the other mines within the study, was purchased by an employee buyout team which was formed by a number of former NUM and NACODS branch officials, and those same individuals now hold many of the senior management posts at the colliery. Management at Cwmpridd then, unlike at the other collieries studied, have an ideological commitment to organised labour, and have consequently demonstrated their willingness both to seek an accommodation with the trade unions at the mine, and to develop a more democratic management style than has previously been evident. The emergence of a democratic management style has, moreover, received further impetus because some 80 per cent of the Cwmpridd workforce are equal shareholders in the company which was established by the employee buyout team. It is likely, therefore, that any managerial attempts to introduce a unitary approach to industrial relations, would have been resisted by the workforce at the colliery, since the worker-shareholders are also trade union members.

The variations in the vigour with which the unitary approach has been applied at Workham, Dearnley, Mansthorpe, Abergoed, Donborough and Nottston cannot be explained by differences in the form of ownership which has emerged at the six collieries, however. Dearnley, Mansthorpe, Donborough and Nottston are all owned by CUK, but the industrial relations strategies pursued by the company at colliery level have not been consistent, and a more robust attitude in relation to the trade unions has emerged at Dearnley and Mansthorpe, than at Donborough and Nottston. Similarly, Workham and Abergoed collieries were both acquired by management buyout teams, yet managerial attitudes towards collective representation at Workham are considerably less compromising than those adopted by management at Abergoed.

Collieries organised by both the NUM and the UDM are represented amongst those where managerial strategies in relation to the unions have been most uncompromising, and similarly, both NUM and UDM collieries are amongst those where management has adopted a more accommodative attitude towards organised labour. This is significant, since it indicates that the differences between the industrial relations strategies pursued by management at Workham, Dearnley, Mansthorpe, Abergoed, Donborough and Nottston cannot be explained in terms of a managerial response towards the varying nature of trade union representation at these collieries.

An explanation for the differences identified in management industrial relations strategies at Workham, Dearnley, Mansthorpe, Abergoed, Donborough and Nottston becomes apparent when the legislative framework surrounding privatisation is considered.

Four of these collieries, Donborough, Nottston, Dearnley and Mansthorpe were acquired by CUK. However of these, only Donborough and Nottston were subject to the TUPE regulations. All the agreements which had been negotiated between British Coal and the mining unions were therefore still in force at Donborough and Nottston after privatisation, unlike at Dearnley and Mansthorpe, where the provisions of TUPE did not apply, and where those agreements consequently had no legal status. Legislative requirements then, have served to constrain managerial industrial relations strategies at Donborough and Nottston, and as a result, managerial attitudes towards organised labour have been less antagonistic at these mines than at Dearnley and Mansthorpe, where management were not subject to the same regulatory restrictions. The evidence therefore suggests that corporate level management within CUK have adopted a contingency approach to industrial relations, and that this accounts for the differing strategies pursued by management at individual collieries.

Like Dearnley and Mansthorpe, Workham and Abergoed collieries were not subject to the TUPE regulations, and management labour relations strategies at these mines have similarly not been constrained by statutory requirements. Although management at Workham and Abergoed have adopted differing attitudes towards the trade unions within a unitary framework, it can nevertheless be argued that management at both mines have also embraced a contingency approach to industrial relations. That different outcomes have followed from this is largely due to different personalities within the senior management teams of the companies that acquired these collieries. Senior management within EM, the company which acquired Workham, are openly hostile to the principle of organised labour, and have consequently fully exploited the opportunities presented by the fact that the colliery was not covered by the provisions of TUPE. Senior managers within AC by contrast, have taken a more pragmatic view in relation to organised labour at Abergoed. Unlike their counterparts at

Workham, they appear to recognise that management can derive some organisational benefits as a result of accommodating collective representation, and as a consequence they have not sought to take full advantage of the absence of legal restrictions influencing their relations with the trade unions at the colliery.

Because a unitary approach towards industrial relations has been adopted by management at Workham, Dearnley, Mansthorpe, Abergoed, Donborough and Nottston, a high priority is accorded to the maintenance of managerial prerogatives at each of these collieries. Some differences are nevertheless visible in the vigour with managerial prerogatives have been administered. At Abergoed, Donborough, Nottston and Mansthorpe, the local trade union branches are consulted in relation to both strategic and operational matters, but have been excluded from the decision making process itself. The trade unions at Workham and Dearnley, by contrast, have no input into either strategic or operational decision making.

The legal framework surrounding privatisation has to be given further consideration if the variations with which managerial prerogatives have been enforced at the collieries owned by CUK are to be accounted for. The TUPE regulations have protected the local consultative arrangements which existed during the nationalised era, and because of this, the company has been unable to withdraw formal consultative meetings at Donborough and Nottston. The unions at these collieries then, continue to have an opportunity to express their views in relation to strategic and operational matters. Because TUPE did not apply at Dearnley and Mansthorpe, formal consultative meetings have been withdrawn by the company, and as a result, the unions at these collieries have no such formal opportunity to express opinions. Within this context, Mansthorpe colliery can be seen as something of an anomaly however. Although formal consultative meeting have been abolished by CUK, the trade unions are consulted on an informal basis in relation to both strategic and operational issues by colliery level management. This is because the culture of the mine has resulted in particularly close relations between management and the unions, and as a result of this, management at the colliery have been prepared to disregard corporate industrial relations policies to some extent. The unions at Mansthorpe are nevertheless unable to exert any meaningful influence in relation to either strategic or operational decisions, because such consultations are unofficial.

It might be argued that the TUPE regulations have served to restrict managerial prerogatives at Donborough and Nottston, because CUK continues to have a legal obligation to consult with the trade unions. The existence of consultation, however, does not give the unions at these collieries access to the decision making process itself, and as a consequence managerial prerogatives remain intact throughout the company. The apparent variations in the vigour with which CUK have enforced managerial prerogatives at Dearnley, Mansthorpe, Donborough and Nottston, are therefore revealed to be somewhat superficial, since similar outcomes have resulted at each of these collieries.

Similar outcomes with respect to the maintenance of managerial prerogatives are also evident at Workham and Abergoed, even though management at Workham have placed more emphasis on such matters than their counterparts at Abergoed. Neither colliery was subject to the provisions of TUPE, and therefore there was no legal requirement for management to maintain the consultative meetings which were established under public ownership at either mine. Formal consultative meetings were therefore withdrawn by management at both collieries. As a consequence, the trade unions at Workham have no opportunity to influence either strategic or operational decisions. At Abergoed, by contrast, although formal consultations have been abandoned, management have continued to consult the unions on a regular, if informal, basis in relation to strategic and operational issues. The unions at Abergoed have nevertheless had no meaningful opportunity to influence managerial decisions, firstly, because such consultations occur after, rather than before, such decisions have been taken, and secondly, because the commercial environment faced by the company has limited the degree to which managerial prerogatives can be relaxed.

In keeping with the democratic management style which has emerged at Cwmpridd following privatisation, considerably less importance is attached to managerial prerogatives than was the case during the final years of public ownership. As a result, the trade unions at the colliery are consulted by management in relation to both strategic development and operational issues, and indeed, the unions are also able to influence decision making in these areas.

At Workham, Dearnley, Mansthorpe and Nottston, the unitary approach to industrial relations adopted by management has been accompanied by the introduction of communications strategies designed to undermine collective organisation at colliery level. Furthermore, at Workham, management have also implemented various policies with the objective of fostering division amongst the workforce. At Donborough, and Abergoed, by contrast, there is no evidence to suggest that such strategies have been employed, despite a unitary approach to labour relations having been adopted by management at these mines also.

The most robust management approach towards the trade unions is apparent at Mansthorpe, Dearnley and Workham, where strategies designed to weaken collective organisation are evident. It is however, arguably more significant that three of the four collieries where such strategies have been implemented are located within the Nottinghamshire coalfield, and are organised by the UDM rather than by the NUM.

Following the end of the 1984-85 strike, the industrial relations strategies developed by British Coal management centred upon the promotion of the UDM, and the maintenance of dual unionism within the industry. As a consequence of this, the UDM branches in Nottinghamshire were not subject to the same sustained assault that was experienced by NUM branches. Moreover, because the majority of the Nottinghamshire workforce did not take part in the 1984-85 strike, they did not suffer the same demoralising defeat as that endured by the workforce in other coalfields, and as a result, their commitment to solidaristic behaviour remained largely intact. Indeed, whilst none of the Yorkshire or Welsh collieries considered within this study has been affected by industrial action since privatisation, stoppages of work have taken place at both Workham and Nottston. Management at Workham, Mansthorpe and Nottston may therefore have embraced policies designed to undermine collective organisation, because the position of organised labour at these collieries remained relatively strong. By the same token, because organised labour had already been significantly weakened at Donborough and Abergoed as a result of the defeat of the 1984-85 strike and the post-strike restructuring of industrial relations, management may not have considered it necessary to adopt policies designed to erode collective organisation at these collieries.

Management at Cwmpridd, as at Donborough and Abergoed, have not sought to undermine collective organisation at the colliery, nor have they instigated measures designed to foster division within the workforce. At this colliery however, the absence of such policies can be attributed to a sympathetic managerial attitude towards the trade unions, rather than to the fact that organised labour had been weakened in the aftermath of the 1984-85 dispute.

9.2 The Role of the Unions

There is considerable variation in the nature of recognition granted to the unions operating at the collieries which have been examined within this study, and significant differences are apparent in terms of the locus of recognition, as well as in terms of which unions have been recognised. Indeed, the nature of the recognition accorded to the unions has had a major influence on the role of these organisations at each of the collieries which has been considered.

Three of the companies owning collieries which were examined within this study have introduced major changes in relation to the locus of trade union recognition. CUK and AC have recognised the mining unions on a local basis only, and have de-recognised the unions at national and area levels, whilst EM has withdrawn recognition at national, area and local levels (Table 9.2). The de-recognition of the unions at national and area levels by CUK, AC and EM can be partially explained by the fragmentation of the industry which accompanied privatisation, since this gave rise to single employer bargaining, which undermined national level negotiations. There is, however, some evidence to suggest that CUK has granted recognition at branch, rather than national level in order to prevent the establishment of corporate level bargaining, although the company does have an unofficial dialogue with some national union officials. The decision of EM to de-recognise the unions at local level in addition to national and area levels can, by contrast, be explained by the priority accorded to managerial prerogatives by the company, and by the overt hostility to organised labour amongst senior management, who are unwilling to tolerate collective representation at any level.

The change in the locus of recognition which has been introduced by CUK, AC and EM has had significant implications both for the locus of bargaining within these companies, and for the role of the unions at the collieries which have been considered within this study.

Table 9.1 The locus of trade union recognition

Company	Level of recognition		
	National level	Area level	Branch level
Welsh Anthracite	Yes	Yes	Yes
Anthracite Cymru	No	No	Yes
Coal UK	No	No	Yes
English Mining	No	No	No

Within CUK and AC local recognition has increased the potential significance of local bargaining, and indeed the national and area levels of the unions now have no influence over industrial relations developments at Abergoed, Donborough, Dearnley, Nottston and Mansthorpe. In practice however, whilst local bargaining has assumed a greater importance at Abergoed, Donborough and Nottston, at Dearnley and Mansthorpe the significance of local bargaining has not increased. This is because of the variations in the collective bargaining rights granted to the unions at these collieries which are analysed below. By contrast, because EM has withdrawn recognition from the trade unions at all levels, bargaining no longer takes place at any level within the company. At Workham colliery then, the local union branches are, like the national and area levels of the unions, unable to influence the emergent pattern of industrial relations.

211

Unlike CUK, AC and EM, WA has not introduced changes to the locus of trade union recognition, because management within the company have a sympathetic attitude towards organised labour. The mining unions then, continue to be recognised at all levels by the company, but in practice, the national and area levels of the unions have little influence over industrial relations at Cwmpridd. This is partly because the fragmentation of the industry which accompanied privatisation undermined national level bargaining, but is also a reflection that the substantive and procedural agreements negotiated by the Cwmpridd unions and WA are superior to those which exist in other parts of the industry.

Within this framework, differences are also apparent in terms of which unions have been recognised by the companies which own the collieries examined within this study, and indeed this factor has also had a significant influence on the role performed by the unions at several of the mines which were considered.

Corporate level industrial relations strategies within CUK, have focused on the maintenance of dual unionism within the company, and upon the promotion of the moderate UDM. At colliery level this strategy has been manifest in recognition being granted only to the union representing the majority of the workforce, and as a consequence, the NUM has been recognised at Donborough and Dearnley, whilst the UDM has been granted recognition at Nottston and Mansthorpe (Table 9.3).

This pattern of recognition has had few implications for the role played by unions at Donborough and Dearnley, since the NUM is the only union which represents mineworker grades at these mines. At Nottston and Mansthorpe, however, both the NUM and UDM have members, and CUK's policy in relation to trade union recognition has therefore had serious implications for the NUM. Because the NUM is not recognised at these collieries, the union is unable to make representations on behalf of its members. Moreover because CUK has refused to provide office or telephone facilities for the NUM at Nottston and Mansthorpe, and has also refused to allow NUM branch officials to take time off in order to attend to trade union business, the organisational ability of the union has been undermined at these collieries also. Management strategies at Nottston and Mansthorpe have therefore prevented the NUM from providing an adequate service for those it seeks to represent, and because of this there is arguably little incentive for mineworkers at these collieries to be members of this organisation.

Table 9.2 Trade union recognition at colliery level

Colliery	Union recognised	
	NUM	UDM
Cwmpridd	Yes	—
Abergoed	Yes	—
Donborough	Yes	—
Dearnley	Yes	—
Nottston	No	Yes
Mansthorpe	No	Yes
Workham	No	No

CUK has not sought to create a non-union workforce at any of the collieries which were included in the study, and indeed, union density has remained high at Donborough and Nottston, although it is somewhat lower at Dearnley and Mansthorpe. Leaving aside legal considerations, it is not surprising that CUK has failed to promote non-unionism at the collieries it owns, since the company's industrial relations strategy is based upon the continuation of dual unionism, and the endorsement of the moderate UDM. It is however also possible that management within CUK have not considered it necessary to encourage non-unionism since the position of organised labour within the company remains weak because the unions continue to be divided, and because the strength of the NUM was undermined in the aftermath of the 1984-85 dispute.

EM's policy in relation to trade union recognition is somewhat different from that adopted by CUK, since this company has sought to de-collectivise industrial relations, rather than to support dual unionism. Because of this, neither the NUM nor the UDM has been recognised at Workham colliery. Furthermore, neither union has been granted office nor telephone facilities, and neither NUM nor UDM branch officials are allowed to take time off work for union duties. The role played by both the NUM and UDM branches at Workham has been significantly influenced by their de-recognition, so that neither body is able to represent effectively the interests of its members.

There is some evidence that EM has sought to create a non-union workforce at Workham, even though this is illegal under the terms of existing employment legislation. This is unsurprising given that the company has endeavoured to de-collectivise industrial relations at the colliery, and has de-recognised all the mining unions to this end. Given these circumstances, it is hardly surprising that union density at Workham, is lower than at any other colliery examined within this study.

WA and AC have each granted recognition to the NUM, rather than to the more moderate UDM, although the rationale behind this pattern of recognition is different in the case of each company. Several members of the WA senior management team formerly held positions within the Cwmpridd lodge of the NUM, and these individuals consequently have both a personal and ideological commitment to the NUM, rather than to its rival organisation. Management within AC, by contrast have elected to recognise the NUM because the NUM is the only body to organise amongst mineworker grades at Abergoed, and there would be little to gain from granting recognition to the UDM at the colliery. Because the NUM is the only union to represent mineworker grades at Abergoed and Cwmpridd, the pattern of recognition adopted by WA and AC has had few implications for the role played by the trade unions at these collieries.

Neither WA nor AC have sought to discourage trade union membership at their respective collieries, and indeed union density is approaching 100 per cent at both Cwmpridd and Abergoed.

In addition to the differences which are evident in relation to the nature of trade union recognition, considerable variations are also apparent with respect to the bargaining rights which have been granted to the trade unions at colliery level. This factor, moreover, has also had significant implications for the trade union branches which operate at the collieries which were examined.

At the collieries owned by CUK, a complex pattern of bargaining rights is evident (Figure 9.4). This reflects both the company's policy relating to trade union recognition, and the differing impact of the provisions of TUPE at colliery level.

Both Donborough and Nottston collieries were subject to the TUPE regulations, and because of this, CUK has been legally required to maintain the existing bargaining arrangements at these mines. The NUM at Donborough and the UDM at Nottston, have consequently been accorded some collective bargaining rights by the company, in addition to rights of representation. However, since the bargaining rights granted to the unions have been restricted by managerial prerogative, and do not extend to the issue of pay, neither the NUM nor the UDM has increased its influence in relation to terms and conditions at Donborough and Nottston respectively, following privatisation (Figure 9.5), despite the increased significance of local bargaining at these collieries. The restoration of some bargaining rights at Donborough and Nottston, similarly has not led to an increase in the range of bargaining issues at either colliery. Indeed at Nottston, there has been a reduction in the number of bargaining issues, because management have sought to exclude UDM branch officials from discussions relating to strategic planning.

At Dearnley and Mansthorpe collieries, by contrast, CUK was not under any statutory obligation to maintain the existing bargaining arrangements, as the provisions of TUPE did not apply at these collieries. Collective bargaining rights have therefore been denied to the NUM at Dearnley and to the UDM at Mansthorpe, and as a result there has been no increase in the significance of local bargaining. Both the NUM and the UDM, however, have been granted rights of representation at Dearnley and Mansthorpe respectively. As a consequence of these developments, the NUM now has somewhat less influence in relation to the terms and conditions of those it represents at Dearnley than was the case during the final decade of the nationalised era. The denial of bargaining rights has, in

Figure 9.2 Bargaining rights at colliery level

No bargaining rights	Representation only	Partial collective bargaining	Full collective bargaining
Workham NUM	Dearnley NUM	Donborough NUM	Cwmpridd NUM
Workham UDM	Mansthorpe UDM	Nottston UDM	Abergoed NUM
Nottston NUM			
Mansthorpe NUM			

Figure 9.3 Changes in the level of trade union influence at colliery level since privatisation

Less influence since privatisation	No change since privatisation	More influence since privatisation
Dearnley NUM	Donborough NUM	Cwmpridd NUM
Mansthorpe UDM	Nottston UDM	
Workham UDM	Nottston NUM	
	Mansthorpe NUM	
	Workham NUM	
	Abergoed NUM	

addition, also served to reduce the number of bargaining issues at Dearnley.

The position of the UDM at Mansthorpe at first appears to be somewhat different, because informal bargaining takes place between branch officials and colliery level management. The UDM branch is able to express opinions in relation to the terms and conditions of its members, therefore, but as such bargaining is both unofficial and proscribed by managerial prerogative, it is questionable whether the UDM is able to exert any meaningful influence over the terms and conditions of Mansthorpe employees. Furthermore, although informal bargaining has led to an increase in the range of bargaining issues at the colliery, such negotiations are not sanctioned by corporate level management, and are therefore completely meaningless. The UDM branch at Mansthorpe, like its NUM counterpart at Dearnley then, has less influence in relation to the developing pattern of labour relations than was the case when the mine was publicly owned.

Because CUK has de-recognised the NUM at colliery level throughout Nottinghamshire, both bargaining rights, and rights of representation have been denied to the NUM branches at Nottston and Mansthorpe. These branches then, have no influence over the terms and conditions of their members, and are unable to negotiate with management over any issue. Such developments, however, represent continuity rather than change, since collective bargaining rights were also denied to the NUM branches at Nottston and Mansthorpe during the final decade of public ownership.

The bargaining arrangements at Workham colliery are considerably less complex than those at the collieries owned by CUK which were considered within this study, since the NUM and UDM branches have been denied both collective bargaining rights, and rights of representation by EM, reflecting the decision of the company to refuse recognition to all the trade unions. Because they are not able to negotiate on behalf of their members, neither the UDM nor the NUM branches have been able to exert any influence in relation to terms and conditions at Workham since privatisation. Moreover, because collective bargaining rights have been denied, there has been a marked reduction in the range of bargaining issues coming within the jurisdiction of the UDM branch at the colliery.

Parry, Waddington and Critcher have argued that trade union marginalisation is 'most visible' within RJB Mining (Parry Waddington and Critcher, 1997: 192). This study however, has demonstrated that the greatest degree of marginalisation has been experienced by the trade union branches at Workham colliery, which is not owned by this company. The research conducted by Parry, Waddington and Critcher was, like this research, comprised of a series of case studies. Workham was not one the collieries chosen for study by Parry, Waddington and Critcher, however, and it is therefore unsurprising that their findings differ from those of this research.

For the UDM, the developments in relation to bargaining rights at Workham represent a significant change, and indeed the UDM branch at the colliery has significantly less influence than was the case during the final decade of public ownership. Because the NUM branch at the colliery had been denied collective bargaining rights throughout the final decade of the nationalised era, however, the position of the NUM has not changed at Workham, and the branch continues to have no influence with respect of industrial relations developments at the colliery.

AC and WA, unlike CUK and EM, have both granted full collective bargaining rights and rights of representation to all the trade unions which have been recognised at Abergoed and Cwmpridd respectively, but different outcomes have followed from this at each colliery.

At Cwmpridd, the restoration of collective bargaining has resulted in the NUM branch having considerably more influence in relation to the terms and conditions of those it represents than was the case during the final years of public ownership. Furthermore, a wider range of bargaining issues has come within the jurisdiction of the branch, because management now consult branch officials in relation to strategic planning, commercial issues and investment. The NUM branch at Abergoed meanwhile, has not experienced any increase in its ability to influence terms and conditions at the colliery despite the restoration of collective bargaining. There has moreover, been no significant increase in the range of issues discussed by management and NUM branch officials at Abergoed, although management does now inform the branch of commercial developments affecting the colliery.

The different outcomes which have followed the re-establishment of collective bargaining at Cwmpridd and Abergoed can be largely explained by the differing emphasis placed upon the maintenance of managerial prerogatives by WA and AC respectively, since management within AC have accorded greater priority to this than their counterparts within WA, and have consequently been less willing to concede to trade union demands. The commercial situation faced by each company has also had implications for the bargaining power of the unions, however, and AC management have been prevented from making any significant concessions to the unions because the company is operating closer to the margins of profitability than WA.

It can thus be seen that there is a strong relationship between the effectiveness of the trade union branches at the collieries which were considered within this study, and the industrial relations strategies which were adopted by management at those collieries (Figure 9.6).

At Workham colliery, where managerial attitudes towards organised labour have been most hostile, and where neither trade union has been granted recognition, rights of representation, or collective bargaining rights, the UDM and NUM are both wholly ineffective, being unable to represent their members on either a collective or individual basis. The NUM is equally ineffective at Nottston and Mansthorpe, where management labour relations strategies have similarly been manifest in the denial of recognition, rights of representation and bargaining rights.

At Dearnley and Mansthorpe, where managerial attitudes towards the trade unions are only marginally less robust than at Workham, the NUM and UDM respectively, are only slightly more effective, for whilst they have been recognised and accorded rights of representation, and are thus able to represent their members on an individual basis, the denial of bargaining rights has prevented these branches from representing the collective interests of employees at these collieries.

The NUM branches at Abergoed and Donborough, and the UDM branch at Nottston, are somewhat more effective than those branches considered above, since management at these collieries have adopted a less rigorous approach to the trade unions. As a consequence, in addition to being recognised and having been granted rights of representation, the unions have also been accorded bargaining rights, and are consequently

Figure 9.4 Management industrial relations strategies and trade union effectiveness

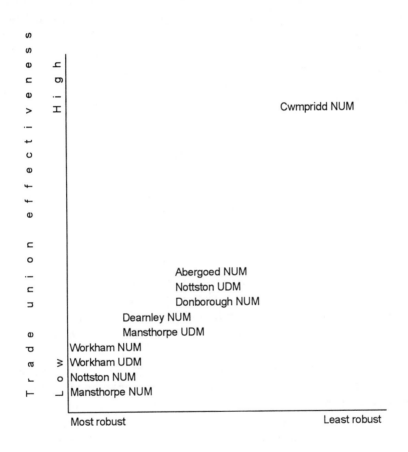

Trade union effectiveness

High

Cwmpridd NUM

Abergoed NUM
Nottston UDM
Donborough NUM
Dearnley NUM
Mansthorpe UDM
Workham NUM
Workham UDM
Nottston NUM
Mansthorpe NUM

Low

Most robust   Least robust

Management industrial relations strategies

able to represent both the individual and collective interests of their members.

The NUM branch at Cwmpridd, where management have adopted a sympathetic approach to organised labour, was the most effective of all the branches which were considered within this study. Having been recognised, and granted rights of representation and bargaining rights, this branch has, like its counterparts at Abergoed, Donborough and Nottston, been able to represent both the individual and collective interests of Cwmpridd employees. Unlike the recognised trade union branches at Abergoed, Donborough, and Nottston, however, the NUM branch at Cwmpridd has more influence in relation to the terms and conditions at the colliery than was the case during the final decade of public ownership.

9.3 Institutions of Collective Bargaining

Following privatisation, new institutions of collective bargaining have been established at each of the seven collieries which were considered within this study. Variations are nevertheless evident, both in terms of the extent of the institutional framework which has emerged at each mine, and in terms of the nature of those structures which have been established.

Formal pay structures are in operation at each of the seven collieries. There is, however, significant variation in the character of the structures which have emerged, reflecting both the operational strategies adopted at the different collieries, and the differing application of the provisions of TUPE.

CUK does not operate a single, company wide pay structure, and because of this, significant differences are visible in the remunerative packages at the four collieries owned by the company which were considered by this research. The pay structure in operation at both Donborough and Nottston provides workers at those collieries with a basic wage plus a productivity bonus. Donborough and Nottston employees however, also continue to receive all those additional payments which were negotiated locally by British Coal and the mining unions prior to privatisation. Workers at Mansthorpe similarly receive a basic wage and productivity bonus, but employees no longer receive any locally agreed additional payments. Employees at Dearnley colliery, like those at

Donborough, Nottston and Mansthorpe, receive a basic wage, and a productivity bonus. However, the productivity bonus does not vary at the colliery, and wage levels at Dearnley consequently do not fluctuate from week to week as is the case at Donborough, Nottston and Mansthorpe. Dearnley employees moreover, like their counterparts at Mansthorpe, receive no locally agreed supplementary payments.

Differences in the pay structures in operation at the collieries owned by CUK can be partially explained with reference to the provisions of TUPE. Donborough and Nottston collieries, unlike Dearnley and Mansthorpe, were subject to this legislation, and as a result, CUK was under a legal obligation to retain the existing British Coal pay structure at these collieries, in addition to all local agreements relating to supplementary payments, which had been negotiated locally whilst these mines were publicly owned. Although some minor modifications have been made to the pay structure at Donborough and Nottston, fundamental change has not been introduced, and indeed such amendments have served only to simplify the grading system, and to reduce differentials. At Dearnley and Mansthorpe, by contrast, CUK was under no obligation to retain the British Coal pay structure. The company has therefore amended the pay structure at these collieries, and has also withdrawn all additional payments. Differences in the production strategies which have been adopted at the four collieries have to be considered however, if differences relating to bonus payments are to be accounted for. CUK's operations at Donborough, Nottston and Mansthorpe have centred on maximising output, and as a consequence, bonus payments at these mines are linked to production levels. Dearnley colliery, by contrast, is required to produce the same quantity of coal each week, and employees at this colliery therefore receive a non-variable production bonus.

New pay structures have been established at Workham, Abergoed and Cwmpridd following privatisation, since none of these mines were subject to the provisions of TUPE, and EM, AC and WA respectively were therefore under no statutory obligation to maintain the arrangements which were established during the years of public ownership.

The pay structure which was instituted at Workham colliery, following its acquisition by EM is nonetheless loosely based on the British Coal arrangements. Employees at the colliery continue to receive a basic wage and a productivity bonus, as was the case when the mine was

223

publicly owned, however, all additional allowances which were paid during the years of public ownership have been withdrawn. The pay structure currently in operation at Abergoed, by contrast, differs considerably from the arrangements which were in place under public ownership. The wages paid to Abergoed workers are influenced by the operation of the pool system, and consequently do not fluctuate on a weekly basis, although Abergoed employees do receive a monthly productivity bonus if output targets are consistently exceeded. The pay structure at Cwmpridd similarly differs somewhat from the British Coal arrangements, since the bonus system which was in operation during the years of public ownership has been abandoned, and Cwmpridd employees are now paid a flat weekly wage.

An explanation for the new pay structures at Abergoed and Cwmpridd being different from the preceding British Coal arrangements, whilst the structure at Workham remains broadly the same, can arguably be found when the operational strategies of the three collieries are considered. Both AC and WA have abandoned the objective of maximising output, and as a result Abergoed is required to produce the same quantity of coal each week, whilst Cwmpridd operates on a just in time basis, and is therefore expected to produce sufficient coal to meet existing sales requirements only. It may therefore be the case that payment systems which do not include an incentive scheme, or where incentive payments make up only a small proportion of the total wage were considered to be more appropriate given such production strategies. At Workham, by contrast, it is possible that incentive payments have been retained, because, as in the nationalised era, the operational strategy of this colliery has centred on increasing output.

Disciplinary and grievance procedures have also been established at each of the   seven collieries which were considered within this study, however, variations in the character of the structures which have emerged are again evident.

Donborough, Dearnley, Nottston and Mansthorpe are subject to the same disciplinary and grievance procedure, since CUK has introduced a company wide structure which applies at all the mines owned by the company. The disciplinary and grievance procedure which is currently operative at CUK collieries is based on the British Coal arrangements which were inherited by the company under the provisions of TUPE.

Amendments have been made to this mechanism however, and the right to appeal against managerial decisions, which existed throughout the years of public ownership, has been withdrawn.

The disciplinary and grievance procedures which have emerged at Workham, Abergoed and Cwmpridd, are also based on the existing British Coal arrangements, although the owners of these mines were not required by law to retain the existing structures. The right to appeal against management decisions has, however, been withdrawn at Workham and Abergoed. At Cwmpridd, by contrast, the disciplinary and grievance procedure continues to incorporate such a facility.

The difference between the disciplinary and grievance procedure which has been established at Cwmpridd, and those arrangements which have been introduced at the other six collieries, arguably reflect the style of management which has emerged at the seven mines. A democratic management style has developed at Cwmpridd following privatisation, and because of this the disciplinary and grievance procedure at the colliery provides for employees to appeal against managerial decisions in relation to these matters. At the other collieries considered within this study, however, such procedures do not permit workforce challenges to management judgements, this being consistent with the unitary management style which has emerged at these mines.

Whilst formal pay structures, and disciplinary and grievance procedures have been established at all seven collieries which were examined by this research, conciliation procedures have, to date, only been instituted at some of the mines which were studied.

CUK inherited the existing British Coal conciliation scheme under the provisions of TUPE. The company however, withdrew this scheme in 1996, and introduced new arrangements. The new conciliation scheme, is loosely based upon the British Coal conciliation scheme, but the current structure does not provide an automatic right to independent arbitration. There is, however, provision for disputes to be referred to an independent body, given the agreement of CUK's Chief Executive and the National President of the UDM. The new conciliation scheme is not a company wide procedure, for whilst Donborough, Nottston and Mansthorpe, are subject to the new scheme, this procedure has not been introduced at Dearnley, and therefore no formal mechanism exists at this mine for the resolution of disputes.

It could be argued that CUK has declined to extend the conciliation scheme to Dearnley, because collective bargaining rights have been denied to the trade unions at this colliery, but the company has introduced conciliation arrangements at Mansthorpe, where bargaining rights have also been refused. This apparent inconsistency reflects the contingency approach to industrial relations which has been adopted by CUK at corporate level, however, since the absence of a conciliation scheme at Dearnley further facilitates the marginalisation of the NUM at the colliery, whilst the existence of conciliation arrangements at Mansthorpe is virtually meaningless given that the unions have no bargaining rights at the mine.

A conciliation scheme has also been instituted at Cwmpridd colliery. This procedure, like the one adopted by CUK, is based on the existing British Coal arrangements, although unlike the CUK scheme, the WA procedure provides for automatic access to independent arbitration.

The differences between the conciliation scheme which has been established by WA at Cwmpridd, and that introduced at Donborough, Nottston and Mansthorpe by CUK can to some extent, be attributed to the style of management which has emerged at these collieries following privatisation. The conciliation scheme currently in operation at Cwmpridd provides for automatic independent arbitration in the event of unresolved disputes, arguably because a democratic management style has developed at this colliery. Access to independent arbitration is, by contrast, restricted at Donborough, Nottston and Mansthorpe, this being consistent with the unitary style of management which has been adopted at these collieries.

Conciliation schemes have not been established at Workham or Abergoed, but as the disciplinary and grievance procedure at Abergoed applies to both collective and individual disputes, a mechanism does exist for the resolution of disputes at this mine. At Workham, by contrast, no mechanism exists for the resolution of disputes. The absence of a conciliation scheme at Workham arguably reflects the fact that bargaining rights have not been granted to the trade unions at this colliery, and indeed, all disputes between management and employees are now resolved on an ad hoc basis.

It can thus be seen that the institutional framework to support collective bargaining is highly developed at Cwmpridd, Donborough, Nottston and Mansthorpe, with formal pay structures, disciplinary and grievance procedures and conciliation schemes having been established at each of these mines. The framework is less developed at Abergoed, Dearnley and Workham, however, because no conciliation scheme exists at any of these collieries, although pay structures and disciplinary procedures have been instituted. It would appear then, that the extent to which the institutional framework to support bargaining has developed at individual collieries, to some extent reflects the bargaining rights which have been accorded to the unions at those mines, since institutional structures are more highly developed at collieries where collective bargaining has been established, than at those where bargaining rights have been denied to the trade unions. Two exceptions to this emergent pattern are, however, provided by the cases of Abergoed and Mansthorpe.

In addition to the differences which are evident in relation to the institutional frameworks to support collective bargaining which have emerged at the collieries considered by this study, the level of trade union involvement in the development of those institutional structures has also varied significantly.

All the trade unions which organise at Cwmpridd were involved in the development of the new institutions of collective bargaining which were introduced at the colliery following privatisation, and the new structures which have emerged at this colliery consequently constitute collective agreements. The institutions which have emerged at Abergoed and Workham, were, by contrast, developed without any trade union involvement. None of the structures in place at these collieries constitute collective agreements therefore, and indeed all were imposed upon the workforce at these mines.

At the collieries owned by CUK, a more complex pattern of trade union involvement is apparent. The institutions of collective bargaining which are currently in force at the collieries owned by the company were, with the exception of the pay structures at Dearnley and Mansthorpe, jointly negotiated by senior CUK managers and national officials of the UDM. The NUM, however, was excluded from these negotiations, and consequently had no input into the development of the new institutional framework. The new institutions therefore represent collective agreements at Nottston and Mansthorpe, since these mines are organised by the UDM. At the NUM strongholds of Donborough and Dearnley, however, the new institutional structures cannot be regarded as collective agreements, and indeed these arrangements were imposed upon the workforce at these collieries.

The pay structures currently in operation at Dearnley and Mansthorpe were, unlike the other institutional arrangements which have been introduced at CUK collieries, developed by CUK management without trade union involvement, and were imposed on CUK employees at these collieries. The pay structures at these collieries do not therefore constitute collective agreements.

The involvement of the unions in the development of new institutions of collective bargaining has to some extent reflected management industrial relations strategies. Thus the trade unions have had more involvement in the development of institutional structures at those collieries where management have adopted an accommodative approach towards organised labour, than at those mines where managerial attitudes towards the trade unions have been more robust. The role of the unions in relation to the development of those structures which have been introduced at collieries owned by CUK has, moreover, reflected CUK's objective of maintaining dual unionism within the company.

The institutions of collective bargaining which have emerged at each of the seven collieries which were considered by this research, apply only to those members of the workforce that are directly employed. The employees of contracting companies, are, by contrast, not subject to the new arrangements at any mine, and indeed, all the contracting companies which were examined had separate procedural arrangements. This is significant, since it is indicative that a dual system of industrial relations has begun to emerge at every colliery within this study where contractors have been employed.

Informal bargaining between junior management and members of the workforce which has no trade union involvement continues to be a feature of industrial relations at Donborough, Mansthorpe, Workham, Abergoed and Cwmpridd. At Dearnley, by contrast, informal agreements are rare, whilst at Nottston, informal bargaining has been completely phased out. Whilst the significance of informal bargaining varies from colliery to colliery, management initiatives to restrict the extent of informal bargaining have nevertheless taken place at every mine considered within this study, and indeed, at all seven mines, informal agreements are less significant than was the case during the years of public ownership.

9.4 The Labour Process

There has been no significant change in the strategies governing productive operations at Donborough, Nottston, Mansthorpe and Workham following privatisation, and at each of these collieries, the same emphasis is placed on increasing production as was the case during the years of public ownership. At Abergoed, Cwmpridd and Dearnley, by contrast, privatisation has been accompanied by marked changes in operational policy. Maximising output is no longer an objective of productive operations at these collieries, and instead production levels are strictly limited. Different factors have lead to the adoption of operational strategies based on restricted output in the case of each colliery however.

At Cwmpridd, strategic planning since privatisation has focused upon the controlled depletion of reserves, and the protection of existing employment levels at the colliery. Because of this, marketing and production are closely integrated at the mine, which is expected to produce sufficient coal to meet existing sales requirements only. Output is restricted at Cwmpridd then, because the colliery currently operates on a just in time, rather than just in case basis, as it had during the years of public ownership. At Abergoed, however, production levels under the current regime have been limited as a consequence of the abandonment of machine got long wall mining techniques, and indeed operational policy at the colliery since privatisation has centred upon maintaining aggregate production at a stable level. At Dearnley, by contrast, output levels have been restricted as a result of budgetary constraints.

The adoption of innovative production strategies at some of the collieries considered by this study is significant, since it points to the emergence of flexible specialisation (discussed in Chapter Three) within the coal industry, especially since Cwmpridd and Abergoed collieries also produce coal for niche, rather than mass markets. The majority of the collieries examined by this research, however, continue to produce coal for the mass market represented by the electricity supply industry, this being indicative that Fordism remains the dominant model of production within the industry.

Although differences are evident in the operational strategies which have been adopted at the collieries which were considered within this study, initiatives to increase productivity have nevertheless been adopted at all seven mines. Significantly, less emphasis has been placed upon improving productivity at Cwmpridd, than at the other collieries which were examined. This difference can, however, be explained with reference to the form of ownership which has emerged at Cwmpridd. Management at the colliery, being former trade union officials, recognise the negative health and safety implications of raising productivity through work intensification. Management at Cwmpridd, moreover, unlike at the other mines, acknowledge that work intensification contributed to productivity improvements during the final years of public ownership, and that there was consequently limited scope for further productivity increases at the colliery.

Management at Donborough, Dearnley, Nottston, Mansthorpe, Workham and Cwmpridd have not sought to increase productivity with the introduction of advanced technology. This is because all six mines had been the subject of large scale technological investment when they were publicly owned, and therefore the potential for generating productivity improvements through further technological investment has been minimal. Management at Abergoed have similarly not endeavoured to secure productivity improvements with the application of new technology. Indeed, at this colliery, machine got long wall mining techniques have been replaced by hand got short wall methods. At all seven mines then, initiatives to improve productivity have centred on the introduction, or extension of, flexible working practices.

Functional flexibility has been adopted to some degree at all the collieries considered by this study. Co-operation between workers has been a feature of operations within the mining industry for many years, and at Cwmpridd, the introduction of multi-skilling has merely served to formalise this tradition. At the other six collieries however, job demarcations have been further reduced since privatisation, with significant implications for the labour process.

At Donborough, Nottston, and Workham, functional flexibility has been utilised by CUK and EM respectively in order to facilitate labour reductions. Productivity improvements have thus been secured through the intensification of work, since the remaining employees at these mines have been expected to carry out the same amount of work as was previously completed by a larger number of employees. The introduction of functional flexibility at Dearnley, Mansthorpe and Abergoed, has, by contrast, not resulted in reductions in staffing levels. It has nevertheless contributed to the intensification of work at these collieries, by facilitating reductions in the porosity of the mineworkers' working day.

Although the introduction of functional flexibility has had negative implications for the workforce at Donborough, Dearnley, Nottston, Mansthorpe, Abergoed and Workham, because it has contributed to the intensification of work, there is no evidence that multi-skilling has been resisted by employees at any of these collieries. Indeed, at Donborough and Mansthorpe, functional flexibility has been actively embraced by members of the workforce. This is because Donborough and Mansthorpe employees believe that the productivity improvements generated by flexible working will render the long term future of these mines less uncertain. Mineworkers at the two collieries have also arguably adopted functional flexibility as a strategic response to the uncertainty within the industry, since they regard the acquisition of additional skills as a means to improve their employment prospects in the event of future colliery closures.

Temporal flexibility is a significant feature of operations at Donborough, Nottston, Mansthorpe, and Workham, where it is primarily manifest in overtime working. At three of these mines, Donborough, Nottston and Workham, a relationship between the introduction of temporal flexibility and reductions in labour requirements is evident, since members of the workforce at these mines have been expected to work additional hours in order to compensate for staff shortages. At Workham, moreover, temporal flexibility has also been utilised in order to increase machine availability time. At Abergoed, by contrast, temporal flexibility in the form of extended shifts, is associated with the operation of the pool system, and has not been utilised in order to facilitate reductions in staffing levels.

Workers at all the collieries considered by this study are contractually obliged to work overtime on request, and on some occasions, employees at Donborough, Nottston, Workham and Abergoed have been coerced into working excessive hours. There is, however, no evidence to suggest that temporal flexibility has been resisted at any of the collieries where it has been introduced, and indeed many workers at these mines voluntarily work additional hours.

The apparent acceptance of temporal flexibility at Donborough, Nottston, Mansthorpe, Workham and Abergoed can be explained by a number of factors, although many of these are colliery specific. At Donborough and Nottston, where the existing redundancy arrangements have been protected under the TUPE regulations, overtime working is primarily motivated by the need to maximise earnings in order to qualify for the maximum redundancy payment, should these collieries close in the future. At Workham, by contrast, overtime working appears to be the consequence of low pay. Employees at every colliery where temporal flexibility has been introduced have, however, arguably also been influenced by the uncertainty which has continued to characterise the industry, and have thus opted to work additional hours in order to maximise their earnings in advance of any future downsizing.

Temporal flexibility has not been introduced at either Cwmpridd or Dearnley, because this has not been necessitated by operational requirements. Cwmpridd and Dearnley both operate on the basis of restricted output, and the production targets at both mines can be met within the normal working week. Productive operations at the two collieries are therefore not reliant on overtime working.

Numerical flexibility is an important feature of operations at Donborough, Workham and Cwmpridd, where between 20 and 40 per cent of the workforce are employed by one of a number of contracting companies. Numerical flexibility has also been adopted at Dearnley, Nottston and Abergoed to a lesser extent, but at Mansthorpe, all the workforce is directly employed. The functions of the contracting companies are strictly limited at every colliery where work has been outsourced, and there are no plans to extend the use of contractors at any of the collieries that were surveyed.

There is evidence to suggest that RJB Mining is seeking to reduce its dependence on outsourcing. This is not because the company has sought to incorporate contract workers within it's own contracting company, as Parry, Waddington and Cricher (1997: 185) have suggested, but rather, because it is considerably cheaper for the company to dispense with contract workers, as Wallis, Winterton and Winterton have found, since contract employees, unlike members of the directly employed workforce, are not protected by the provisions of TUPE, and are consequently not entitled to the relatively generous redundancy payments which continue to be available to their directly employed counterparts under the terms of this legislation (Wallis, Winterton and Winterton 1998: 44).

There have been few changes in the labour process at Donborough, Dearnley, Nottston, Mansthorpe, Workham or Cwmpridd then, other than the introduction of measures designed to improve productivity by way of the intensification of work.

Corporate level management within CUK, whilst endorsing the introduction of flexible working, have nevertheless endeavoured to place the same emphasis on health and safety as was the case during the years of public ownership. There is, however, evidence to suggest that management at colliery level have failed to acknowledge the health and safety implications of work intensification, and that this has had a negative effect with respect of safety standards at a number of the collieries owned by the company which were considered within this study. Management at Workham have similarly overlooked the health and safety issues associated with work intensification. Moreover, as management at the colliery have also accorded a greater priority to increasing productivity than to health and safety since privatisation, safety standards at Workham have been compromised to an even greater extent than at those collieries owned by CUK.

Only at Cwmpridd has the current managerial regime placed more emphasis on health and safety than was the case during the years of public ownership. As mentioned earlier, management at this colliery have also recognised the negative health and safety implications of work intensification, and indeed, largely because of these considerations, the adoption of flexible working practices has been limited. Safety standards have therefore not been compromised at Cwmpridd as a result of changes within the labour process.

The labour process at Abergoed, has, unlike that at the other six mines which were considered, undergone a radical transformation since privatisation, because the machine got long wall mining techniques which were employed throughout the years of public ownership, have been replaced by hand got short wall methods. Management at the colliery have nonetheless continued to accord the same priority to health and safety issues as was the case when the mine was publicly owned, and safety standards have largely been maintained. The adoption of unmechanised mining has however had a number of negative implications for the health and safety of personnel employed at the coalface.

Although atypical, the changes within the labour process at Abergoed are nevertheless more significant than those experienced by the other six collieries which were considered within this study, since they challenge existing assumptions about the direction of technological change within coal mining (Winterton, 1994).

10 Conclusions

By analysing management industrial relations strategies, and the role played by the trade unions, alongside the development of institutional bargaining structures, and changes within the labour process at a number of British collieries, this study has attempted to describe and account for the patterns of industrial relations which have developed within the coal industry following privatisation.

A consideration of industrial relations during the years of public ownership enabled two distinct phases to be identified. Between the years 1947 and 1984, industrial relations were both pluralistic and highly regulated. Although the industry was relatively strike prone during this period, relationships between management and the trade unions at national level were based upon co-operation rather than confrontation, and the trade unions operated from a relatively strong bargaining position. During the period 1984 to 94 however, industrial relations were comprehensively reconstructed in order to facilitate the restructuring of the industry which was necessitated both by pressures within the global product market, and the objective of privatisation. During these years management within the industry adopted a unitary approach to labour relations, and managerial prerogatives were vigorously reasserted. The NUM adopted a confrontational response to these developments, and labour relations within the industry were characterised by bitter conflict as a consequence. This study has therefore attempted to assess whether the patterns of labour relations which have emerged following the privatisation of the industry in 1994 have had more in common with those patterns established during the period 1947 to 1984, or with the patterns which were characteristic of the final decade of the nationalised era. In so doing, the research has also sought to ascertain whether industrial relations developments since privatisation have had positive or negative implications for organised labour within the industry.

The privatisation of the coal industry was part of a wider privatisation programme which was undertaken by successive Conservative governments during the 1980s and early 1990s in order to facilitate the restructuring of the UK economy. An examination of the other concerns which were privatised during these years, found that their transition from publicly owned corporations to private sector enterprises was marked by continuity and change within the sphere of labour relations. It was therefore anticipated that continuity and change would emerge as a major theme of industrial relations within the privatised coal industry also.

One of the major findings of this study is that privatisation has precipitated sweeping changes in the patterns of labour relations at industry level. Because privatisation has resulted in the fragmentation of the industry, it has led to the collapse of national bargaining. As a consequence of these developments considerable variation is now evident between the companies which which now operate within the industry in terms of the emergent patterns of labour relations. Furthermore, the legal framework surrounding privatisation has led to the development of intra company variations in patterns of industrial relations.

The model outlined towards the end of Chapter Three anticipated that industrial relations at colliery level would be influenced by two major variables; these being firstly, the labour relations strategies adopted by management, and secondly, the responses of the various mining unions to those strategies. The model also expected that continuity with the patterns of industrial relations established during the last decade of public ownership would be most likely to occur at collieries where management had continued to favour a unitary approach towards labour relations matters, and where the trade unions had adopted a confrontational response to such strategies. By contrast, the model anticipated that change would be manifest at collieries where management and the trade unions both adopted a conciliatory approach to labour relations issues, and that the emergent pattern of labour relations at such mines would be more reminiscent of the period 1947 to 1984, than of the final decade of public ownership.

The empirical findings of this study have, however, revealed that this model is inadequate as an heuristic device designed to illuminate the dynamics of industrial relations within the privatised coal industry. This is because the response of the trade unions to management industrial relations strategies did not emerge as a significant variable. Although the NUM and UDM have adopted differing responses to management industrial relations strategies at national level, this is not the case at colliery level, and there is little discernible difference in the responses of NUM and UDM branches to the labour relations policies introduced by management within the new coal enterprises. All the trade union branches considered in this study have sought to accommodate corporate objectives, and no branch has attempted significantly to challenge the industrial relations policies which have been adopted by management.

The industrial relations strategies adopted by management within the new coal companies then, have had a determining effect on the patterns of labour relations which have developed at the collieries which were studied. Continuity with the patterns of industrial relations which characterised the period 1984 to 1994 are thus apparent at Donborough, Nottston and Abergoed collieries, because at these mines, management has favoured the industrial relations strategies adopted by British Coal during the final decade of public ownership. Changes in the prevailing patterns of labour relations are, by contrast, evident at Workham, Dearnley, Mansthorpe and Cwmpridd. This is because different industrial relations strategies to those favoured by British Coal between 1984 and 1994 have been adopted by management at each of these collieries.

The industrial relations strategies which have been adopted by management within the new coal companies have themselves been influenced by the form of ownership to have emerged within those companies, by the legal framework within which those companies operate, and also by the personalities of key management actors (Figure 10.1). The relative importance of these factors has varied between the new coal enterprises however, and differing patterns of industrial relations have emerged at the collieries which were studied as a consequence. This variation is indicative of the view that management at each of the collieries which were considered has adopted a contingency approach to labour relations.

Although all the trade union branches considered in this study have been prepared to lend support to corporate objectives, the industrial relations policies introduced by management within the new coal enterprises have nevertheless had a significant influence upon the role of the trade unions at the seven collieries which were surveyed. This is because these strategies have had a profound effect upon the ability of the trade union branches to influence industrial relations developments at these mines.

237

Figure 10.1 An heuristic model of the dynamics of industrial relations in the privatised coal industry

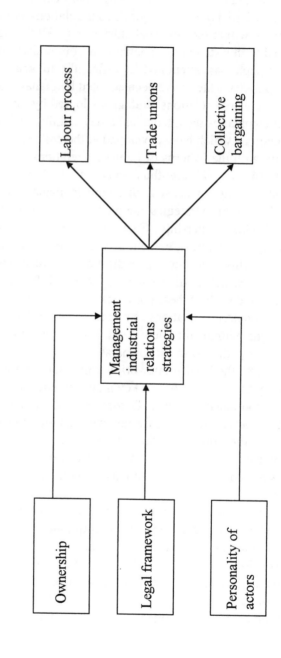

At six of the seven collieries considered by this research, the local trade union branches have been unable to exert any significant influence over the development of industrial relations following privatisation. In the case of the NUM branches at Workham, Nottston, Mansthorpe and Dearnley, and the UDM branches at Workham and Mansthorpe this is because management strategies have resulted in bargaining rights being denied to these organisations, and their ability to respond effectively to those strategies has therefore been constrained. At Donborough, Abergoed, and Nottston by contrast, the responses of the NUM and UDM branches, respectively, to management strategies, have not been limited by the denial of bargaining rights, but rather by the emphasis placed upon the maintenance of managerial prerogatives by management at these collieries.

At Cwmpridd colliery by contrast, the local trade union branches have had a significant influence over the development of industrial relations following privatisation. That this has been the case can nevertheless be attributed to the labour relations strategies adopted by management. Management at Cwmpridd have adopted an accommodative approach to the trade unions at the mine, have granted these organisations full bargaining rights, and have placed considerably less emphasis on the maintenance of managerial prerogatives than was the case during the final decade of public ownership. In adopting such strategies then, management at Cwmpridd have sought to facilitate, rather than constrain, the ability of the trade unions to influence labour relations developments at the colliery.

Because the industrial relations strategies adopted by management have had a such a profound effect on the ability of the trade unions to influence developments within the sphere of labour relations at the seven collieries that were studied, management has had significantly more influence than the trade unions over both the nature and extent of the institutions of collective bargaining that have emerged at all these but one of these mines. Similarly, management has had more influence than the trade unions with respect to developments within the labour process at six of the seven the collieries which were considered (Figure 10.1).

Parry, Waddington and Critcher (1997), have suggested that RJB Mining is more vulnerable to trade union sanctions than the smaller coal companies which emerged during the privatisation process. The empirical findings of this research do not support their argument however. The workforce within RJB continues to be fragmented as a result of the industrial relation strategies adopted by corporate level management, and whilst NUM national officials have continued to endorse the use of sanctions against RJB, such a strategy has, unsurprisingly, not been adopted by their UDM counterparts. A significant proportion of the RJB workforce, moreover, belongs to neither union, and as such would not be involved in any action taken by the mining unions. When it is also considered that a significant number of workers at RJB collieries are employed by one of a number of contracting companies rather than by RJB, it is clear that any trade union sanctions affecting the company would involve only a minority of the workforce, and would therefore be unlikely to be effective.

Of equal importance however, given that local bargaining has assumed a greater significance within RJB following privatisation, the use of trade union sanctions is simply not an issue at colliery level. This is partly because NUM and UDM branch officials alike are aware that such sanctions could seriously damage the company, and could thus jeopardise many hundreds of jobs. Branch officials from both unions are, however, also aware that disputes with the company would arise from local rather than national issues, and that localised industrial action could, given the continued uncertainty facing the industry, be used by corporate level management to justify the closure of the effected collieries.

Although trade union sanctions in the form of a short-lived ban on weekend work was endorsed by branch officials at one of the RJB collieries which was considered by this study, this was in pursuit of economistic objectives, and did not represent a challenge to management industrial relations strategies. Indeed, none of the trade union branches at the collieries owned by RJB which were examined in this study have initiated any challenge to the labour relations strategies adopted by management at those mines. Industrial action has taken place at Workham colliery in relation to such issues, but this was manifest in spontaneous unofficial strike action rather than in officially sanctioned disputes. The fact that such developments have taken place at Workham, however, suggests that it is the smaller companies, rather than RJB, that are likely to be the most vulnerable to trade union sanctions, since Workham is not owned by RJB.

The position of capital was strengthened relative to that of labour during the final decade of public ownership, and because of this, one of the hypotheses advanced towards the end of Chapter Three anticipated that continuity with the patterns of labour relations established during the period 1984 to 1994 would have negative implications for the trade unions that operate within the industry. This hypothesis has been largely supported by the research findings, since the local trade union branches continue to be marginalised at Donborough, Nottston and Abergoed collieries, where management have continued to favour the unitary approach to industrial relations adopted unilatrally by British Coal during the final decade of public ownership. Furthermore, dual unionism continues to be a significant feature of labour relations within CUK, the company whose corporate level industrial relations strategies exhibit the most continuity with those developed by British Coal between 1984 and 1994.

The alternative hypothesis outlined in Chapter Three, by contrast, suggested that change within the sphere of industrial relations at colliery level would bring benefits for the trade unions. This is because it was expected that change would result in the abandonment of the unitary approach to industrial relations adopted by British Coal between 1984 and 1994, and in the return of pluralism which was characteristic of the period 1947 to 1984. The empirical findings have not supported this hypothesis, however, and have instead revealed that changes in the patterns of industrial relations emerging since privatisation are more complex than was initially anticipated. Firstly, change has firstly been multi-directional rather than uni-directional (Figure 10.2). Secondly, the context of change has determined whether such developments have been beneficial or disadvantageous for the trade unions. Thus at Cwmpridd colliery, change has had favourable implications, because this has resulted in the emergence of co-determination and in an increase in trade union influence. At Dearnley, Mansthorpe and Workham collieries by contrast, change has had negative implications for the trade unions, this is because change has been manifest both in the de-collectivisation of industrial relations, and in a reduction of the influence of the trade unions which operate at these mines, compared with the final decade of public ownership.

Figure 10.2 Industrial relations in the privatised coal industry continuity and change

CHANGE De-collectivisation	CONTINUITY Trade Union Marginalisation	CHANGE Co-determination
Workham Dearnley Mansthorpe	Donborough Nottston Abergoed	Cwmpridd

It is, then, possible to conclude that privatisation has had negative implications for organised labour within the coal industry, except at Cwmpridd colliery, since the trade unions continue to be largely ineffective at colliery level, and, in the case of CUK and EM, at corporate level also. It must be remembered however, that the position of the trade unions was systematically weakened during the final decade of public ownership, and for this reason, the industrial relations strategies adopted by management within the new coal enterprises can, with the exception of those introduced by WA at Cwmpridd colliery, be said to be saprophytic upon the strategies implemented by British Coal between 1984 and 1994.

Like all research, this study has been the subject of a number of limitations, and it would be ambitious to regard this as the definitive study of industrial relations within the privatised coal industry. The twin constraints of time and resources necessitated that a relatively small number of collieries were selected for study. As a consequence, no collieries were chosen in order to facilitate literal replication, and collieries belonging to only 75 per cent of the coal companies currently operating within the UK were included in the study. A more complete study might therefore have included more collieries, and might have involved all the coal companies with operations in the UK. Indeed, given the small size of the privatised industry, and the greater availability of time and resources, future research into labour relations within the coal industry might involve a consideration of developments at every UK colliery. At the same time, the timing of the research in the early aftermath of privatisation, provided a unique window of opportunity to assess the changes taking place.

In addition to the shortcomings described above, it could also be argued that this study suffers from a methodological weakness. Problems relating to access necessitated the adoption of a methodological approach which was slightly unorthodox. This was manifest in the fact that three of the case studies contained within this research analysed industrial relations developments at individual collieries, whilst the fourth case study examined labour relations developments at an additional four collieries within the wider context of a corporate level analysis. Access problems also prevented identical research instruments being utilised at each of the collieries which were studied. It is likely that any research into industrial relations within the coal industry would encounter problems relating to access. A superior study might nevertheless have anticipated the access problems likely to be encountered by such research, and a methodological approach might have been developed which took such factors into consideration.

Appendix A

Interview Schedule: Management Representatives

Introduction/Labour Process

1. How many men does your company employ?
   (How many on this site?)

2. What sort of employment contracts do your employees have?
   (What proportion of the workforce are employed on each type of contract?)

3. What proportion of the men on short term contracts are usually re-employed?   (If not, on what basis are they not re-employed?)

4. What proportion of men are finished before their contracts have expired? (On what basis are contracts terminated?)

5. How many hours a week (excluding overtime) do your employees normally work? (And how many days per week?)

6. How much overtime does the average employee normally work each week?

7. Is overtime working a contractual obligation?

8. Has flexible working been introduced by your company?
   (e.g. combining production and maintenence/electrical and mechanical functions?)

9. What sort of job demarcations exist at this colliery? (Has your company sought to reduce job demarcations?)

245

10. Can you outline any steps that your company has taken to improve productivity?

11. What are the arrangements for the supervision of your employees?

12. Can you give me some details about your company's health and safety policies?

Management Strategies

13. Does your company recognise all the trade unions which operate in the industry?

IF ALL UNIONS RECOGNISED GO TO QUESTION 15 AND OMIT QUESTION 26

IF SELECTIVE DE-RECOGNITION HAS TAKEN PLACE GO TO QUESTION 14, AND OMIT QUESTIONS 18 AND 26

IF NONE OF THE UNIONS ARE RECOGNISED GO TO QUESTION 26.

14. Why did you recognise the NUM/UDM/NACODS, but not the NUM/UDM/NACODS?

15. Do you encourage your employees to join the union or unions that you have recognised? (Why/why not?)

16. Have you considered the possibility of/taken steps towards signing a single union agreement with the NUM/UDM/NACODS?
    (How far has this gone?)

17. What form does recognition take?
    (Bargaining rights, or rights of representation only?)

18. OMIT IF SELECTIVE DE-RECOGNITION IS EVIDENT, OR IF NO UNIONS ARE RECOGNISED
Does your company prefer to deal with any particular union?
(Which one, Why?)

19. Does your company provide any facilities for the trade unions e.g. offices?

20. Does your company allow trade union officials time off for union duties?

21. How are decisions made about the day today running of the pit?
(Are the unions involved in this?)

22. How are strategic decisions about the long term future of the pit made?
(Are the unions involved in this?)

23. Does your company communicate individually with members of the workforce, e.g. with letters sent to their homes/newsheets/teletext messages on the pit top etc?

24. Does your company prefer to recruit labour locally or from further afield?

25. What role would your company like the trade unions to play at this colliery?

26. OMIT IF ANY UNION RECOGNISED

What factors influenced your company's decision not to recognise the unions?

Union Responses/Role.

27. Now that the coal industry has been restructured, is there a greater emphasis on local agreements?

28. Has there been any change in the range of issues discussed with local trade union representatives since privatisation? (Examples of local agreements / changes)

29. How much influence would you say that local trade union branches have over managerial decisions compared with during the years of public ownership?

30. How often does your company meet with national/area union officials?

31. Does your company prefer to deal with local trade union representatives or national/area officials? (Why one or the other?)

32. Are there differences between the unions in the way in which they respond to managerial decisions/corporate strategy?

33. Do you, as colliery manager/site manager have the ultimate say on HRM policies at this pit or is there an overarching company policy on this issue?

34. Do you think that privatisation has affected the environment in which contact betweeen management and the unions takes place?

Institutions of collective bargaining

35. Can you tell me how the provisions of TUPE have applied at this pit?

36. Can you tell me about the pay structure your company operates at this pit?

37. How was this established?

38. Can you tell me about the disputes procedure your company operates at this pit?

39. How was this established?

40. Can you tell me about the disciplinary/grievance procedure your company operates at this pit?

41. How was this established?

    If no formal structures exist, how is pay determined, and how are disputes and disciplinary/grievance matters resolved?

42. Have any company wide/industry wide agreements been negotiated jointly by your company and the unions since privatisation?

43. How important are informal agreements between management and the men which have no union involvement?

44. Has your company introduced performance related pay? (If yes, in what form?)

45. Are any of your employees engaged on individual contracts?

Appendix B

Introduction/Labour Process

1. What sort of employment contracts do your members have?
   (What proportion of the workforce is on each type of contract?)

2. What proportion of the workforce on short term contracts is usually re-employed? (On what basis does management decide who to re-employ?)

3. What proportion of the workforce is finished before their contracts expire? (On what basis does management decide to finish men?)

4. Do the different companies on site offer standardised terms and conditions of work e.g. pay/hours?

5. How many hours a week (excluding overtime) do your members usually work? (How many days per week?)

6. How many hours overtime does the average worker normally complete each week?

7. Is overtime working a contractual obligation?

8. What job demarcations exist at this colliery? (Has there been any erosion in job demarcations since this colliery was privatised?)

9. What steps have management taken to improve productivity at the mine?

10. Do you think there has been any change in the pace of work at this pit since privatisation?

11. Has there been any change in the way that miners are supervised at this pit since privatisation? (Examples)

12. Do you think that there has been any change in health and safety standards at this pit since privatisation? (Examples)

Management Strategies

13. Do all the companies on site recognise the NUM/UDM/NACODS?

IF RECOGNITION GRANTED GO TO QUESTION 14, AND OMIT QUESTIONS 25 TO 29

IF RECOGNITION REFUSED OMIT QUESTION 14

14. OMIT IF RECOGNITION REFUSED
What form does recognition take?

15. How would you describe the general attitude of management to the NUM/UDM/NACODS?

16. Do any of the companies on site provide facilities for the union e.g. offices?

17. Are Branch Officials allowed time of for union work?

18. Is the NUM/UDM/NACODS consulted about the day to day running of the pit?

19. Is the NUM/UDM/NACODS involved in strategic decision making about the long term future of this pit?

20. Do any of the companies on site prefer to deal with another union other than the NUM/UDM/NACODS? (Which one/Why?)

21. Do any of the companies on site seek to recruit labour with a particular trade union background?

22. Does management at this pit communicate individually with the men, e.g. with letters sent to their homes/colliery/company newsheets etc?

23. Does the NUM/UDM/NACODS have check off facilities at this colliery?

24. How many members do you have at this colliery?

OMIT QUESTIONS 25 TO 29 IF RECOGNITION GRANTED

25. Do you still organise in companies where recognition has been refused?

26. How successful has this been?

27. Do any of the companies that have refused to recognise the NUM/UDM/NACODS recognise any other union (Which one, Why?)

28. Do the companies which have refused to recognise the NUM/UDM/NACODS prefer to employ men with a particular trade union background?

29. What attempts have been made by the NUM/UDM/NACODS to gain recognition from the companies which have so far refused to recognise them?

Union Responses/Role

30. At which level does contact between management representatives and trade union representatives most commonly take place?

31. Do you think that the companies operating at this pit prefer to deal with local trade union officials or with national/area officials?

32. Has there been any change in the range of issues dealt with by the NUM/UDM/NACODS at this pit since privatisation?

33. Has there been any change in the amount of influence that the NUM/UDM/NACODS has over managerial decisions at this pit since privatisation? (Or since 1984, or both?)

34. Which level of the union would you say is the most influential now?

35. Does the colliery manager/site managers of contracting firms have a free reign in dealing with the unions at this pit, or is industrial relations policy determined at a higher level?

36. Unlike BC, the company which owns your pit would not have state backing and government resources at its disposal in the event of a strike. Do you think this has made management more cautious in their dealings with the NUM/UDM/NACODS?

Institutions of collective bargaining.

37. Can you tell me how the provisions of TUPE have applied at this pit?

38. Can you tell me about the pay structure at this pit?

39. How was this established?

40. Can you tell me about the disputes procedure at this pit?

41. How was this established?

42. Can you tell me about the disciplinary/grievance procedure at this pit?

43. How was this established?

If no formal structures exist, how are disputes and disciplinary/grievance matters resolved ?

44. Are these structures/procedures standardised throughout the pit, or does each company have its own arrangements?

45. Is this pit covered by any company wide/industry wide agreements negotiated jointly by management and the unions?

46. At this pit, how important are informal agreements between management and the men which have no union involvement?

47. Has performance related pay been introduced at this pit? (If yes, in what form?)

48. Are any of the men at this pit employed on individual contracts?

Appendix C

This questionnaire is part of a larger research project which aims to assess how privatisation has affected industrial relations in the coal industry. Information will also be gathered from management and the trade unions, but this questionnaire seeks the views of the miners themselves. If you could spend 15 to 20 minutes filling in this questionnaire, this would be very helpful. All your answers will be treated in the strictest confidence.

Guidance for completing this questionnaire.

- Most of the questions will relate to your current job.
- Some questions will ask you to compare what it is like to work for a private company with what it was like to work for British Coal.
- Most of the questions should be answered by placing a tick in the relevant box.
- Unless otherwise stated please tick **one** box only.

1. Which colliery do you work at?

    ----

2. Who are you employed by?
    - ❑ The company which owns your pit e.g. RJB
    - ❑ A firm of sub contractors e.g. Thyssens.

3. Which of the following best describes your position at the pit?
   - ❑ Development / Face worker.
   - ❑ Outbye worker.
   - ❑ Surface worker.
   - ❑ Craftsman.
   - ❑ Deputy.
   - ❑ Overman.
   - ❑ Other.

   Please state -------------------------

4. Did you work for British Coal or the NCB before the industry was privatised?
   - ❑ Yes.
   - ❑ No.

5. Which union do you belong to?
   - ❑ NUM.
   - ❑ UDM.
   - ❑ NACODS.
   - ❑ None.
   - ❑ Other.

   Please state ------------------------

6. Are you more than one month in arrears with your union subscriptions?
   - ❑ Yes.
   - ❑ No.

7. What is the length of your contract?

☐ 0 to 12 months.

☐ 13 to 24 months.

☐ 25 to 36 months.

☐ Over 36 months.

8. How many hours do you normally work each week (including overtime)?

----

9. Is overtime working at your pit voluntary or compulsory?

☐ Voluntary.

☐ Compulsory.

10. Do you perform a wider or narrower range of tasks in your current job than when you were employed by British Coal?

☐ Wider variety of tasks.

☐ About the same variety of tasks.

☐ Narrower variety of tasks.

11. Do you think the pace of work has increased or decreased since privatisation?

☐ Increased a great deal.

☐ Increased a little.

☐ Neither increased nor decreased.

☐ Decreased a little.

☐ Decreased a great deal.

12. Do you think that safety standards at your pit have improved or worsened since privatisation?

- ❑ Improved.
- ❑ No change.
- ❑ Worsened.

13. What is the attitude of management at your pit to trade union membership?

- ❑ Workers are encouraged to join the union of their choice.
- ❑ Workers are encouraged to join a particular union.
- ❑ Workers are neither encouraged nor discouraged from joining a union.
- ❑ Workers are discouraged from joining a union.

14. Which of the following best describes the attitude of management to the unions themselves at your pit?

- ❑ No unions are recognised at this colliery.
- ❑ Management only recognise the unions they want.
- ❑ Unions only have rights of representation.
- ❑ Unions have full bargaining rights.

15. Which of the following best describes how decisions are made about the day to to day running of your pit?

- ❑ Management impose their decisions without consulting the unions.
- ❑ Management consult the unions but still have the final say.
- ❑ Management and the unions come to joint decisions.

16. Does management communicate with the workforce using any of the following methods?
    - ❏ Letters sent directly to workers homes.
    - ❏ Company/colliery newsheets sent directly to workers homes.
    - ❏ Videos/teletext messages on colliery premises.
    - ❏ Team briefings.

    Please tick all which apply at your pit.

17. Which of the following best describes the overall attitude of management at your pit?
    - ❏ Dictatorial.
    - ❏ Hard line.
    - ❏ Firm but fair.
    - ❏ Relaxed.
    - ❏ Easy going.

18. Are all trade unions at your pit treated equally by management?
    - ❏ Yes, management treats all the unions in the same way.
    - ❏ No, some unions are treated better than others.

19. If you ticked the second box in the last question could you say which union or unions are favoured by management, and why you think this is?

    ----

20. Which of the following best describes the range of issues trade unions have to deal with at **your pit** today?

   ❑   The unions deal with a wider range of issues now than when British Coal owned the pit.

   ❑   The unions deal with about the same number of issues as when British Coal owned the pit.

   ❑   The unions deal with fewer issues now than when British Coal owned the pit.

21. Do you think the unions at your pit have more or less influence now than they did when the colliery was owned by British Coal?

   ❑   More influence now.

   ❑   About the same level of influence now.

   ❑   Less influence now.

22. At which level do you think the unions have most influence?

   ❑   National level.

   ❑   Company level.

   ❑   Area level.

   ❑   Pit level.

   ❑   Influential at all levels.

   ❑   Ineffective at all levels.

23. Since privatisation, have any of the following been introduced at your pit?

   ❑   Formal pay structure.

   ❑   Formal disputes procedure.

   ❑   Formal disciplinary and grievance procedure.

Please tick all which apply.

24. How are changes to terms and conditions of work usually made at your pit?

- [ ] By reference to long standing formal agreements.
- [ ] By informal talks between management and the unions representing the workers concerned.
- [ ] By informal talks between management and the workers themselves.

25. To what extent are wages at your pit related to the performance of individual workers?

- [ ] Wages are totally dependent on performance related pay.
- [ ] Wages are partially dependent on performance related pay e.g. productivity bonuses.
- [ ] Wages are not related to performance at all.

26. Are you employed on an individual contract?

- [ ] Yes.
- [ ] No.

27. Finally, do you think that privatisation has been a good thing or a bad thing for miners? Why is this?

Thank you very much for your help in completing this questionnaire.

Bibliography

Adeney, M. and Lloyd, J. (1986) *The Miners' Strike 1984-5, Loss without Limit*, Routledge and Kegan Paul, London.

Advisory, Conciliation and Arbitration Service (1988) *Labour Flexibility in Britain*: The 1987 ACAS Survey, Occasional Paper 41, ACAS, London.

Aglietta, M. (1979) *A Theory of Capitalist Regulation*, NBL, London.

Allen, V. L. (1981) *The Militancy of British Miners*, The Moor Press, Shipley.

Andreff, W. (1984) 'The international centralisation of capital and the re-ordering of world capitalism', *Capital and Class*, vol. 22, pp. 58-80.

Ashworth, W. (1986) *The History of the British Coal Industry, Volume 5, 1946-1982 The Nationalized Industry*, Clarendon Press, Oxford.

Atkinson, J. (1984) *Flexibility, Uncertainty and Manpower Management*, IMS Report No. 89, Institute of Manpower Studies, Brighton.

--- and Gregory, D. (1986) 'A flexible future, Britain's dual labour force', *Marxism Today*, April, pp. 12-17.

Avis, R. (1990) 'British Steel: a case of the de-centralisation of collective bargaining', *Human Resource Management Journal*, vol. 1, no. 1, pp. 90-99.

Baldwin, G.B. (1955) *Beyond Nationalization, The Labour Problems of British Coal*, Harvard University Press, Cambridge.

Barnsley Women Against Pit Closures (1984) *Women Against Pit Closures*, BWAPC, Barnsley.

--- (1985) *Women Against Pit Closures, Volume 2*, BWAPC, Barnsley.

Beynon, H. (ed.) (1985) *Digging Deeper, Issues in the Miners' Strike*, Verso, London.

--- and McMylor, P. (1985) 'Decisive power: the new Tory state against the miners', in H. Beynon (ed.) *Digging Deeper, Issues in the Miners' Strike*, Verso, London, pp. 29-45.

--- Hudson, R. and Sadler, D. (1986) 'Nationalised industry policies and the destruction of communities: some evidence from North East England', *Capital and Class*, vol. 29, pp. 27-57.

Bickerstaffe, R. (1983) 'Foreward', in Hastings, S. and Levie, H. (eds), *Privatisation?*, Spokesman, Nottingham, pp. 7-8.

Bishop, M and Thompson, D (1993) 'Privatization in the UK, Deregulatory reform and public enterprise performance', in V.V. Ramanadham (ed.) *Privatization, a global perspective*, Routledge, London pp. 1-28.

Blyton, P. (1992) 'Steel: a classic case of industrial relations change in Britain', *Journal of Management Studies*, vol. 29, no. 5, pp. 635-650.

--- (1993) 'Steel', in A. Pendleton and J. Winterton (eds) *Public enterprise in transition, Industrial relations in state and privatized corporations*, Routledge, London, pp. 166-184.

--- and Morris, J. (eds) (1991) *A Flexible Future? Prospects for Employment and Organisation*, de Gruyter, Berlin.

Bradbury, J.H. (1985) 'Regional and industrial restructuring processes in the international division of labour', *Progress in Human Geography*, vol. 9, no. 1, pp. 38-63.

Braverman, H. (1974) *Labor and Monopoly Capital*, Monthly Review Press, New York.

Burns, A., *et al* (1983) 'The miners and new technology', *Industrial Relations Journal*, vol. 14, no. 4, pp. 7-20.

Burns, A., Newby, M. and Winterton, J. (1985) 'The restructuring of the British coal industry', *Cambridge Journal of Economics*, vol. 9, no. 1, pp. 93-110.

Clapham, M. (1990) *The 1984-85 Miners' Strike and British Industrial Relations*, M.Phil Thesis, University of Bradford.

--- (1991) 'The local and area bargaining unit in the UK coal mining industry', *Industrial Tutor*, vol. 5, no. 4, pp. 59-75.

Claydon, T. (1989) 'Union de-recognition in Britain in the 1980s', *British Journal of Industrial Relations*, vol. 27, no. 2, pp. 214-224.

Clegg, H. A. (1979) *The Changing System of Industrial Relations in Great Britain*, Blackwell, Oxford.

Colling, T. (1991) 'Privatisation and the management of IR in electricity distribution', *Industrial Relations Journal*, vol. 22, no. 2, pp. 117-129.

--- and Ferner, A. (1992) 'The limits of autonomy: devolution, line managers and industrial relations in privatized companies', *Journal of Management Studies*, vol. 29, no. 2, pp. 209-227.

Conservative Party (1979) *The Conservative Manifesto 1979*, Conservative Central Office, London.

Crick, M. (1985) *Scargill and the Miners*, Harmondsworth, Penguin.

Croney, P. (1996) 'Industrial relations in the coal industry after privatisation', British Universities Industrial Relations Association Conference, University of Bradford, 5-7 July.

De Vroey, M. (1984) 'A regulation approach interpretation of contemporary crisis', *Capital and Class*, vol. 23, pp. 45-66.

Department of Trade and Industry (1993) *The prospects for coal, Conclusions of the government's Coal Review*, Cm 2235, HMSO, London.

--- (1994) *Digest of United Kingdom Energy Statistics*, HMSO, London.

Disney, R., Gosling, A. and Machin, S. (1995) 'British unions in decline: determinants of the 1980s fall in union recognition', *Industrial and Labor Relations Review*, vol. 48, no. 3, pp. 403-419.

Dolby, N. (1987) *Norma Dolby's Diary: An Account of the Great Miners' Strike*, Verso, London.

Douglass, D. (1986) *A Year of Our Lives: A Colliery Community in the Great Coal Strike of 1984/85*, Hooligan Press, London.

Edwards, C. (1993) *Restructuring the European Community Coal Industry: A Study of the Social Consequences for the UK Mining Areas*, Kingston University, Kingston Business School, Occasional Paper Series.

--- and Heery, E. (1989) *Management Control and Union Power, A Study of Labour Relations in Coal Mining*, Clarendon, Oxford.

Edwards, P. *et al* (1992) 'Great Britain: Still Muddling Through', in A. Ferner and R. Hyman (eds) *Industrial Relations in the New Europe*, Blackwell, Oxford, pp. 1-68.

Eisenhardt, K.M. (1989) 'Building theories from case study research', *Academy of Management Review*, vol. 14, no. 4, pp. 532-550.

Elson, D. and Pearson, R. (1981) '"Nimble fingers make cheap workers": an analysis of womens' employment in third world export manufacturing', *Feminist Review*, vol. 7, pp. 87-107.

Fairbrother, P. (1994) 'Privatisation and local trade unionism', *Work, Employment and Society*, vol. 8, no. 3, pp. 339-356.

Ferner, A. and Colling, T. (1991) 'Privatization, regulation and industrial relations', *British Journal of Industrial Relations*, vol. 29, no. 3, pp. 391-409.

--- (1993) 'Electricity Supply', in A. Pendleton and J. Winterton (eds) *Public enterprise in transition, Industrial relations in state and privatized corporations*, Routledge, London, pp. 100-133.

Ferner, A. and Hyman, R. (eds) (1992) *Industrial Relations in the New Europe*, Blackwell, Oxford.

Fine, B. and Millar, R. (eds) (1985) *Policing the Miners' Strike*, Lawrence and Wishart, London.

Fothergill, S. and Guy, N. (1993) *The End of Coal? The Impact of the 'Dash for Gas' in UK Electricity Generation*, Coalfield Communities Campaign, Barnsley.

Foster, C.D. (1992) *Privatisation, public ownership and the regulation of natural monopoly*, Blackwell, Oxford.

Froebel, F., Heinrichs, J. and Kreye, O. (1980) *The new international division of labour*, CUP, Cambridge.

Gall, G. and McKay, S. (1994) 'Trade union de-recognition in Britain, 1988-1994', *British Journal of Industrial Relations*, vol. 32, no. 3, pp. 433-448.

Gibbon, P. and Bromley, S. (1990) '"From an institution to a business"? Changes in the British coal industry 1985-9', *Economy and Society*, vol. 9, pp. 151-160.

Gittens, J.A. (1986) *Striking Stuff*, "1 in 12" (Publications) Collective, Bradford.

Gladstone, B. and Dewhirst, D. (1988) *Electricity, Linked Industries and Privatisation*, Coalfield Communities Campaign Special Report No. 4, Coalfield Communities Campaign, Barnsley.

Goodman, J. (1984) *Employment Relations in Industrial Society*, Philip Allan Publishers Limited, Oxford.

Grahl, J. (1983) 'Restructuring in west European industry', *Capital and Class*, vol. 19, pp. 118-42.

Green, F. (ed.) (1989) *The Restructuring of the UK Economy*, Harvester Wheatsheaf, Hemel Hempstead.

Green, F. (1989) 'Evaluating structural economic change: Britain in the 1980s', in F. Green (ed.) *The Restructuring of the UK Economy*, Harvester Wheatsheaf, Hemel Hempstead, pp. 3-22.

Green, R. (1994) 'Electricity privatisation, coal and gas', *Economic Review*, vol. 11, no. 3, pp. 24-8.

Hakim, C. (1987a) 'Trends in the flexible workforce', *Employment Gazette*, November, pp. 549-560.

--- (1987b) *Research Design, Strategies and Choices in the Design of Social Research*, Allen and Unwin, London.

Harrison, R. (1978) *Independent collier: The coal miner as archetypal proletarian reconsidered*, Harvester, Hassocks.

Hastings, S. and Levie, H. (eds) (1983) *Privatisation?*, Spokesman, Nottingham.

Haynes, W.W. (1953) *Nationalization in Practice: The British Coal Industry*, Bailey Bros and Swinfen Ltd, London.

Heald, D. (1988) 'The United Kingdom: privatsation and its political context', *West European Politics*, vol. 11, no. 4, pp. 31-48.

Hirst, P. and Zeitlin, J. (1989) *Reversing Industrial Decline? Industrial Structure and Policy in Britain and her Competitors*, Berg, Oxford.

Hudson, R. (1988) 'Labour market changes and new forms of work in "old" industrial regions', in D. Massey and J. Allen (eds) *Uneven Re-Development, Cities and Regions in Transition*, Hodder and Stoughton, London, pp. 147-166.

Hughes, J. and Moore, R. (1972) *A Special Case ? Social Justice and the Miners*, Penguin Books Ltd, Harmondsworth.

Hyman, R. (1988) 'Flexible Specialisation: Miracle or Myth?', in R. Hyman and W. Streeck (eds) *New Technology and Industrial Relations*, Basil Blackwell, Oxford, pp. 48-60.

Hyman, R. and Streeck, W. (1988) *New Technology and Industrial Relations*, Basil Blackwell, Oxford.

Incomes Data Services (1984) *Craft Flexibility, IDS Study 322*, IDS Ltd, London.

--- (1986) *Flexibility at Work, IDS Study 360*, IDS Ltd, London.

--- (1994) *Multi Skilling, IDS Study 558*, IDS Ltd, London.

International Energy Agency (1995) *Coal Information 1994*, OECD / IEA, Paris.

268

International Labour Office (1994a) *Recent developments in the coalmining industry, Report I*, ILO, Geneva.

--- (1994b) *Productivity and its impact on employment and labour relations in the coalmining industry, Report II*, ILO, Geneva.

Industrial Relations Review and Report (1986a) *NCB proposes changed bargaining machinery*, Report No. 365, Eclipse Publications, London.

--- (1986b) *Using temporary and sub-contract labour, IRRR Survey*, Report No. 365, Eclipse Publications, London.

--- (1987) *1987: IRRR Annual Review*, Eclipse Publications, London.

--- (1989a) *Decentralised bargaining in perspective*, Employment Trends 451, Eclipse Publications, London.

--- (1989b) *Industrial relations after privatisation*, Employment Trends 439, Eclipse Publications, London.

Jenkins, R. (1984) 'Divisions over the international division of labour', *Capital and Class*, vol. 22, pp. 28-57.

Jones, C. and Novak, T. (1985) 'Welfare against the workers: benefits as a political weapon', in H. Beynon (ed.) *Digging Deeper, Issues in the Miners' Strike*, Verso, London, pp. 87-100.

Kay, J., Mayer, C.and Thompson, D. (1986) *Privatisation and Regulation, The UK Experience*, Clarendon, Oxford.

Lawrence, D.H. (1994) *Sons and Lovers*, Penguin, Harmondsworth.

Leman, S. and Winterton, J. (1991) 'New technology and the restructuring of pit level industrial relations in the British coal industry', *New Technology, Work and Employment*, vol. 6, no. 1, pp. 54-64.

Lipietz, A. (1982) 'Towards global Fordism?', *New Left Review*, vol. 132, pp. 33-47.

--- (1984) 'Imperialism or the beast of the apocalyse', *Capital and Class*, vol. 22, pp. 81-109.

Littek, W. and Charles, T. (1995) *The New Division of Labour, Emerging Forms of Work Organisation in International Perspective*, de Gruyter, Berlin.

Lynch, L. (1978) 'Research Note: Strike Frequency in British Coal Mining 1950-1974', *British Journal of Industrial Relations*, vol. 16, no. 1, pp. 95-98.

Marsh, D. (1991) 'Privatization under Mrs Thatcher: a review of the literature', *Public Administration*, vol. 69, pp. 459-480.

Martin, R. (1988) 'Industrial capitalism in transition: the contemporary reorganisation of the British space-economy', in D. Massey and J. Allen (eds) *Uneven Re-Development, Cities and Regions in Transition*, Hodder and Stoughton, London, pp. 202-231.

Massey, D. and Allen, J. (eds) (1988) *Uneven Re-Development, Cities and Regions in Transition*, Hodder and Stoughton, London.

McCarthy, W. (1988) 'Privatisation and the Employee', in V.V. Ramanadham (ed.) *Privatisation in the UK*, Routledge, London, pp. 73-84.

McCormick, B.J. (1979) *Industrial Relations in the Coal Industry*, Macmillan, London.

Macgregor, I. (with R. Taylor) (1986) *The Enemies Within: the story of the Miners' Strike 1984-5*, Collins, London.

Miller, J. (1986) *You can't Kill the Spirit: women in a Welsh mining village*, Womens' Press, London.

Millward, N. (1994) *The New Industrial Relations?*, Policy Studies Institute, London.

Mitchell, J. Clyde. (1983) 'Case and situation analysis', *Sociological Review*, vol. 31, no. 2, pp. 187-207.

Moore, J. (1983) *Why Privatise?*, Conservative Political Centre, London.

National Coal Board (1974) *Plan for Coal*, NCB, London.

National Union of Mineworkers (1987a) *National Executive Committee Annual Report 1986/7*, Macdermott and Chant Ltd, London.

--- (1987b) *Report of Annual Conference 1987*, Macdermott and Chant Ltd, London.

--- (1989a) *The attack on union organisation in the deep mined coal industry, A report on management strategy and the expansion of sub-contracting within the UK coal industry* (Industrial Relations Department, mimeo).

--- (1989b) *Report of Annual Conference 1989*, G. Askew and Son (Printers) Ltd, Doncaster.

--- (1991) *National Executive Committee Annual Report 1990/1*, G. Askew and Son (Printers) Ltd, Doncaster.

--- (1992) *Report of Annual Conference 1992*, G. Askew and Son (Printers) Ltd, Doncaster.

Newbery, D.M. (1993) 'The impact of EC environmental policy on British Coal', *Oxford Review of Economic Policy*, vol. 9, no. 4, pp. 66-95.

Nichols, T. and O' Connell Davidson, J. (1993) 'Privatisation and economism: an investigation amongst 'producers' in two privatised utilities in Britain', *Sociological Review*, vol. 41, no. 4, pp. 707-730.

O' Connell Davidson, J. (1990) 'The commercialisation of employment relations: the case of the water industry', *Work, Employment and Society*, vol. 4, no. 4, pp. 529-549.

--- (1991) 'Subcontracting, flexibility and changing employment relations in the water industry' in P. Blyton and J. Morris (eds,) *A Flexible Future? Prospects for Employment and Organisation*, de Gruyter, Berlin, pp. 241-48.

Ogden, S. (1993a) 'Decline and fall: national bargaining in British water', *Industrial Relations Journal*, vol. 24, no. 1, pp. 44-58.

--- (1993b) 'Water', in A. Pendleton and J. Winterton (eds) *Public enterprise in transition, Industrial relations in state and privatized corporations*, Routledge, London, pp. 134-165.

270

--- (1994) 'The reconstruction of industrial relations in the privatised water industry', *British Journal of Industrial Relations*, vol. 32, no. 1, pp. 67-84.

Ottey, R. (1985) *The Strike: An Insider's Story*, Sidgwick and Jackson, London.

Page Arnot, R. (1979) The Miners: One Union, One Industry. A History of the National Union of Mineworkers 1939-46, George Allen and Unwin, London.

Parry, D., Waddington, D. and Critcher, C. (1996) 'Industrial relations in the privatized mining industry', *British Journal of Industrial Relations*, vol. 32, no. 5, pp. 173-196.

Pattison, K. and Beynon, H. (1984) *Easington August '84*, Side, Newcastle.

Pendleton, A. and Winterton, J. (eds) (1993) *Public enterprise in transition, Industrial relations in state and privatized corporations*, Routledge, London.

People of Thurcroft (1986) *Thurcroft A village and the miners' strike*, Spokesman, Nottingham.

Piore, M.J. and Sabel, C.F. (1984) *The Second Industrial Divide*, Basic Books Inc, New York.

Pollert, A. (1988) 'Dismantling flexibility', *Capital and Class*, vol. 34, pp. 42-75.

Prowse, P. and Turner, R. (1996) 'Flexibility and coal: a research note on workplace relations', *Work, Employment and Society*, vol. 10, no. 1, pp. 151-160.

Pryke, R. (1981) *The Nationalised Industries: Policies and Performance since 1968*, Martin Robinson, Oxford.

Purcell, J. (1993) 'The end of institutional industrial relations', *Political Quarterly*, vol. 64, no. 1, pp. 6-23.

Ramanadham, V.V. (1988) *Privatization in the UK*, Routledge, London.

--- (1993) *Privatization, A Global Perspective*, Routledge, London.

Raynes, J.R. (1928) *Coal and its Conflicts : A Brief Record of the disputes between Capital and Labour in the Coal Mining Industry of Great Britain*, Benn, London.

Redwood, J. (1980) *Public Enterprise in Crisis: The Future of the Nationalised Industries*, Basil Blackwell, Oxford.

Richards, A.J. (1996) *Miners on Strike, class solidarity and division in Britain*, Berg, Oxford.

Richardson, R. and Wood, S. (1989) 'Productivity change in the coal industry and the new industrial relations', *British Journal of Industrial Relations*, vol. 27, no. 1, pp. 33-55.

Robinson, C. (1985) 'Coal policy in Britain', *Economic Review*, vol. 2, no. 4, pp. 2-6.

--- (1992) *Making a Market in Energy, Current Controversies No. 3*, Institute of Economic Affairs, London.

--- and Marshall, C. (1985) *Can Coal be Saved? Hobart Paper 105*, Institute of Economic Affairs, London.

--- and Sykes, A. (1987) *Privatise Coal. Policy Study No. 85*, Centre for Policy Studies, London.

Rose, J. (1985) 'Deliberate victimisation', *New Statesman*, 12 April, p. 14.

Rost, P. and Pargeter, M (1985) 'Pits, privatisation and politics', *Economic Affairs*, vol. 5, no. 4, pp. 39-41.

Rutledge, I. and Wright, P. (1985) 'Coal worldwide: the international context of the British miners' strike', *Cambridge Journal of Economics*, vol. 9, no. 4, pp. 303-326.

Sabel, C.F. (1989) 'Flexible specialisation and the re-emergence of regional economies', in P. Hirst and J. Zeitlin (eds) *Reversing Industrial Decline? Industrial Structure and Policy in Britain and her Competitors*, Berg, Oxford, pp. 17-70.

Samuel, H.L. (1925) *Report of the Royal Commission on the Coal Industry*, HMSO, London.

Saunders, P. and Harris, C. (1994) *Privatization and Popular Capitalism*, OUP, Buckingham.

Seddon, V. (ed.) (1986) *The Cutting Edge: Women and the pit strike*, Lawrence and Wishart, London.

Sheffield Women Against Pit Closures (1987) *We are women we are strong*, SWAPC, Sheffield.

Smith, N. (1997) *The 1984 Miners' Strike The Actual Account*, Oyster Press (Whitstable), Whitstable.

Smith, P. and Morton, G. (1993) 'Union exclusion and the decollectivisation of industrial relations in contemporary Britain', *British Journal of Industrial Relations*, vol. 31, no. 1, pp. 97-114.

--- (1994) 'Union exclusion - next steps', *Industrial Relations Journal*, vol. 25, no. 1, pp. 3-14.

Stead, J. (1987) *Never the same again: women and the miners' strike*, Womens' Press, London.

Stoecker, R. (1991) 'Evaluating and rethinking the case study', *Sociological Review*, vol. 39, no. 1, pp. 88-112.

Tailby, S. and Whitston, C. (1989) 'Industrial relations and restructuring', in S. Tailby and C. Whitston (eds) *Manufacturing Change, Industrial Relations and Restructuring*, Basil Blackwell, Oxford, pp. 1-22.

Tailby, S. and Whitston, C. (eds) (1989) *Manufacturing Change, Industrial Relations and Restructuring*, Basil Blackwell, Oxford.

Taylor, A.J. (1988) 'Consultation, conciliation and politics in the British coal industry', *Industrial Relations Journal*, vol. 19, no. 3, pp. 222-233.

Thomas, D. (1986) 'The union response to denationalisation' in J. Kay, C. Mayer and D. Thompson (eds) *Privatisation and Regulation, the UK experience*, Clarendon, Oxford, pp. 299-321.

Thrift, N. (1988) 'The geography of international economic disorder', in D. Massey and J. Allen (eds) *Uneven Re-Development, Cities and Regions in Transition*, Hodder and Stoughton, London, pp. 6-46.

Tomaney, J. (1990) 'The reality of workplace flexibility', *Capital and Class*, vol. 40, pp. 29-60.

--- (1991) *Technical Change and the Transformation of Work: The case of British Coalmining*, PhD Thesis, University of Newcastle.

--- and Winterton, J. (1995) 'Technological change and work relations in the British coal mining industry' in W. Littek and T. Charles (eds) *The New Division of Labour, Emerging Forms of Work Organisation in International Perspective*, de Gruyter, Berlin, pp. 473-489.

Turnbull, P. (1993) 'Docks', in A. Pendleton and J. Winterton (eds) *Public enterprise in transition, Industrial relations in state and privatized corporations*, Routledge, London, pp. 185-210.

Veljanovski, C. (1987) *Selling the State, Privatisation in Britain*, Weidenfeld and Nicholson, London.

Vickers, J. and Wright, V. (1988) 'The politics of industrial privatization in western Europe: an overview', *West European Politics*, vol. 11, no. 4, pp. 1-30.

Waddington, D. and Wykes, M. (1989) 'Voting with their feet', *New Statesman and Society*, 6 January, pp. 26-27.

Wade, E. (1985) *Coal Mining and Employment: A study of Blyth Valley*, Borough of Blyth Valley Council.

Wallis, E., Winterton, J. and Winterton, R. (1998) *Consequences of Subcontracting in the UK Coal Industry*, Employment Research Institute, Napier University, Edinburgh.

Whitfield, D. (1983) *Making it Public, Evidence and Action Against Privatisation*, Pluto Press, London.

Williams, K. *et al* (1987) 'The end of mass production', *Economy and Society*, vol. 16, no. 3, pp. 405-439.

Wilsher, P., Macintyre, D., and Jones, M. (1985) *Thatcher, Scargill and the Miners*, Coronet, London.

Winterton, J. (1981) 'The trend of strikes in British coal mining 1949-1979', *Industrial Relations Journal*, vol. 12, no. 6, pp. 10-19.

--- (1991) 'Flexibility, new technology and British Coal', in P. Blyton and J. Morris (eds) *A Flexible Future? Prospects for Employment and Organisation*, de Gruyter, Berlin, pp. 275-294.

--- (1994) 'Social and technological characteristics of coal face work: a temporal and spatial analysis', *Human Relations*, vol. 47, no. 1, pp. 89-118.

--- and Winterton, R. (1989) *Coal, Crisis and Conflict: The 1984-85 Miners' Strike in Yorkshire*, MUP, Manchester.

--- and Winterton, R. (1993a) 'Coal', in A. Pendleton, and J. Winterton (eds) *Public enterprise in transition, Industrial relations in state and privatized corporations*, Routledge, London, pp. 69-99.

--- and Winterton, R. (1993b) 'Undermining the union: the National Union of Mineworkers since 1985', Unions on the Brink: The Future of the Trade Union Movement, Cardiff Business School, University of Wales 28-30 September.

--- and Winterton, R. (1995) 'Industrial relations in a declining coal industry', *The Review of Policy Issues*, vol. 1, no. 3, pp. 61-74.

Worsborough Community Group (1985) *The Heart and Soul of it*, Bannerworks, Barnsley.

Wright, P. (1985) 'Coal communities and energy policy', Coalfield Communities Campaign, Working Paper No. 3, Vol. 1, CCC, Barnsley.

Yin, R.K. (1982) 'Studying phenomenon and context across sites', *American Behavioural Scientist*, vol. 26, no. 1, pp. 84-100.

--- (1994) *Case study Research, Design and Methods*, Sage, Thousand Oaks CA.

Young, S. (1986) 'The nature of privatisation in Britain, 1979-1985', *West European Politics*, vol. 9, no. 2, pp. 235-252.

Zola, E. (1954) *Germinal*, Penguin Books, London.

Index

health and safety at 196
informal bargaining at 189, 190, 192-93, 195
pay system at 194, 222-23
subcontracting at 196
trade union membership at 188-191
trade union recognition at 188, 189, 190, 211-13
Margam development 16, 19, 20
subcontracting at 186
trade union membership at 181-82
trade union recognition at 178-80, 211-13
Novak, T. 9
NPLA 7
nuclear power 22
NUM 5
Cokemens Section 29
COSA 29, 89
Derbyshire Area 19
Leicester Area 20
North Western Area 19
Nottinghamshire Area 15
policy on privatisation 28-29
policy on technology 11-12
relations with UDM 20
Scottish Area 17, 29
South Wales Area 16-17, 19, 20, 84, 92, 103
Yorkshire Area 8

O' Connell Davidson, J. 50
OECD coal production 39-40
Ogden, S. 49, 50, 51, 53
operational restructuring
Ottey, R. 1

Page Arnot, R. 5
Pargeter, M. 10
Parkinson, C. 20
Parry, D. 2, 219, 232

Pattison, K. 2
Pay systems 7-8, 222-24
at Abergoed colliery 117-18
at Cwmpridd colliery 94, 223-24
at Dearnley colliery 174-175, 222-23
at Donborough colliery 166, 222-23
at Mansthorpe colliery 194, 222-23
at Nottston colliery 184, 222-23
at Workham colliery 146, 223-24
Pearson, R. 33
People of Thurcroft, 2
Pendleton, A. 2, 42, 49, 50, 51, 52, 53, 54
pillar and stall working 120, 121
pilot study 73
Piore, M.J. 34
Plan for Coal 6, 7, 11
Pollert, A. 35
Privatisation
and industrial relations 42-54
forms of 42
of coal industry 20-29
rationale for 42
Prowse, P. 18, 164
Pryke, R. 42
punishment period 17
Purcell, J. 14

questionnaires 72-3, 74, 78, 80

Raynes, J.R. 1
Redwood, J. 42
Richards, A.J. 9, 18
Richardson, R. 18
Ridley, N. 9
Ridley Report 9-10, 42
RJB Mining 25, 26, 27, 45, 48, 57, 219, 232, 239-240
at Donborough colliery 168
at Mansthorpe colliery 195
at Nottston colliery 188

at Workham colliery 149

Robinson, C. 9, 10, 21, 23, 25
Rose, J. 17
Rost, P. 10
Rutledge, I. 6, 38, 39

Sabel, C.F. 34
Sadler, D. 2
Samuel, H.L. 1
Sankey, H. 19
Saunders, P. 53
Scargill, A. 8, 20, 92, 137, 164
Seddon, V. 1
Selby Complex 11
shortwall mining 233
  pillar and stall working 120, 121
Sheffield Women Against Pit Closures 2
single union agreements 14, 181, 190
Smith, N. 2
Smith, P. 14
Stead, J. 1
steel industry 49, 51, 52
Stoecker, R. 62, 63
strikes 7
  national strike, 1972 8
  national strike, 1974 6, 8
  national strike, 1984 1, 6, 10, 12
  unofficial strikes 8, 18
sub-contracting 18, 19, 28-29
  at Abergoed colliery 121-22
  at Cwmpridd colliery 97-8
  at Dearnley colliery 176-7
  at Donborough colliery 163, 167
  at Mansthorpe colliery 196
  at Nottston colliery 186
  at Workham colliery 131, 147, 153
Sykes, A. 21, 25

Tailby, S. 31, 41
Taylor, A.J. 16, 17, 18, 19, 20

Taylorism 34, 37
technology 6, 8, 10-12, 35, 36, 40, 47,
    49, 230, 234
  at Abergoed colliery 120
  at Cwmpridd colliery 99-100
  at Dearnley colliery 176
  at Workham colliery 130, 131, 132-33,
    134, 136-37, 139, 214
telecommunications industry 49, 52
Thatcher, M. 9, 41
third world coal production 37-39
Thomas, D. 43
Thompson, D. 50
Thrift, N. 32, 33
Thurcroft colliery 29
Tomaney, J. 35, 37, 40
Tower colliery 29
Turner, R. 18, 164
TUPE 67, 75, 76, 93, 116, 145, 146,
    160, 162, 165-67, 171, 173, 174,
    179, 183-85, 189, 191, 192, 193,
    194, 198-200, 206, 207, 208, 215,
    222, 223, 224, 225, 232
Turnbull, P. 52

UDM 15-16
  policy on privatisation 27-28
  relations with NUM 19, 20
union membership 14
  at Abergoed colliery 111-13
  at Cwmpridd colliery 87
  at Dearnley colliery 172-3
  at Donborough colliery 163
  at Mansthorpe colliery 188-91
  at Nottston colliery 181-82
  at Workham colliery 131-32, 140-41
union recognition 14, 53, 210-15
  at Abergoed colliery 106, 110-11, 211,
    214
  at Cwmpridd colliery 84, 89, 212, 214
  at Dearnley colliery 170, 172, 211-2